BRETHREN
IN TRANSITION

*20th Century Directions
& Dilemmas*

BRETHREN IN TRANSITION

20th Century Directions & Dilemmas

Edited by Emmert F. Bittinger

Forum for Religious Studies
Bridgewater College
Bridgewater, Virginia

PENOBSCOT PRESS
CAMDEN, MAINE 1992

Cover design and graphics by Carl F. Bowman

First printing June 1992

For information contact:
Forum for Religious Studies
Bridgewater College
Bridgewater, Virginia 22812

Manufactured in the United States of America
Printed on 60# acid-free paper

CONTENTS

The Contributors

F. W. Benedict, of Union City, Ohio, a member of the Old German Baptist Brethren, is printer and editor of <u>Old Order Notes</u> and President of the board of Brethren Encyclopedia, Inc.

Emmert Bittinger is a professor of sociology emeritus of Bridgewater College in Virginia.

Carl Bowman is a professor of sociology at Bridgewater College in Virginia.

Dale W. Brown is a professor of Christian theology and Brethren history at Bethany Theological Seminary, Oak Brook, Illinois.

Christina Bucher is a professor of religious studies at Elizabethtown College in Pennsylvania and Editor of <u>Brethren Life and Thought</u>.

Allen C. Deeter is Director of Brethren Colleges Abroad and a professor at Manchester College in Indiana.

Donald F. Durnbaugh, former professor of Church History at Bethany Theological Seminary, is currently the Carl W. Zeigler Professor of Religion and History and Fellow of the Young Center for the Study of Anabaptist and Pietist Groups at Elizabethtown College in Pennsylvania.

Hedwig T. Durnbaugh is a special collections librarian and archivist and Fellow of the Young Center for the Study of Anabaptist and Pietist Groups at Elizabethtown College in Pennsylvania.

Vernard Eller is a professor of religion at the University of La Verne in California and a Staley Distinguished Christian Scholar Lecturer.

Donald R. Fitzkee, a former editorial assistant for <u>Messenger</u>, is pursuing graduate studies at Eastern Baptist Seminary in Philadelphia.

Thomas D. Hamm, a member of the Society of Friends, is a professor of history at Earlham College in Indiana.

James C. Juhnke, a member of the Mennonite Church, is a professor of history at Bethel College in Kansas.

Warren Kissinger, of Hyattsville, Maryland, editor emeritus of <u>Brethren Life and Thought</u>, is a subject cataloguer for the Library of Congress.

Donald B. Kraybill is a professor of sociology and Director of the Young Center for the Study of Anabaptist and Pietist Groups at Elizabethtown College.

Stephen L. Longenecker is a professor of history at Bridgewater College in Virginia.

Melanie May is a visiting lecturer at Garrett-Evangelical Theological Seminary and at Bethany Theological Seminary in Illinois.

David G. Metzler is a professor of philosophy and religion at Bridgewater College in Virginia.

Donald E. Miller, a former professor of Christian education and ethics at Bethany Biblical Seminary, is currently General Secretary of the General Board, Church of the Brethren at Elgin, Illinois.

Dale R. Stoffer, pastor of the Smokey Row Brethren Church, is a professor of historical theology at Ashland Theological Seminary in Ohio.

The Pastors

Karen Carter of Daleville, Virginia, is pastor of the Monte Vista and Mount Bethel Churches of the Virlina District.

Earle W. Fike, Jr., of Huntingdon, Pennsylvania, is a retired pastor and former Moderator of the Church of the Brethren.

Terry Hatfield is District Executive of the Northern District of Indiana and editor of the Brethren periodical, Evangel 21.

Harold Martin, of York, Pennsylvania, is pastor of the Pleasant Hill Church of the Brethren in the Southern Pennsylvania District, and editor of BRF Witness.

Steven Mason, of Harrisonburg, Virginia, is pastor of the Pleasant Valley Church of the Brethren of the Shenandoah District of Virginia.

David Rittenhouse, of Dunmore, West Virginia, is pastor of the Kerr Chapel, Pine Grove, and New Hope churches in West Virginia which belong to the Shenandoah District.

Dawn Ottoni-Wilhelm has served as a hospital chaplain and soon will become a pastor of the Stone Church at Huntingdon, in the Middle District of Pennsylvania.

Preface

From the inception in 1990 of the plan for the Brethren in Transition Conference, held at Bridgewater College, October 3-5, 1992, the committee foresaw the need and desirability of publishing the papers to be presented. Having recently retired, I was asked to initiate the plans required for the preparation for the volume. January 1992 was set as a deadline for submission of final drafts of the manuscripts. The committee is grateful to each contributor for cooperation in following the editor's suggestions and for meeting the suggested due date. My task was greatly facilitated by the excellent quality of the submitted manuscripts. The writing of a general introduction and the brief opening paragraphs for each paper was both challenging and rewarding.

An extra measure of gratitude is due to the donors who provided funds to underwrite the costs of the conference and the publication of the papers. Their kindness and openness in response to the solicitation was encouraging. Without their generous support, the conference could not have been held. Thanks is expressed also to Dr. Wayne F. Geisert, President of Bridgewater College, for agreeing to host the conference and for his help in contacting some of the prospective donors.

Finally, I am especially grateful for the support, encouragement, and proof-reading assistance provided by the other members of the planning committee, Carl Bowman, Stephen Longenecker, David Metzler, and Robbie Miller. Their suggestions and guidance during the lengthy editorial work were always of the highest order. Much credit must go to Carl Bowman whose expertise in the final formatting of the document was crucial to the appearance of the volume. Also, the kindness and help of my wife, Esther, is gratefully acknowledged. Altered plans and lonely hours were endured with patience and a generous attitude. Each of these and others have made a significant contribution to this volume. The finished product is submitted in the hope that it will increase understanding and strengthen commitment to our beloved denomination. May it provide a measure of inspiration and source of direction as we pass through the final decade of the twentieth century.

Emmert F. Bittinger, editor
May, 1992

Introduction

The twilight of the twentieth century provides a timely occasion for the people called Brethren to come together and examine their common history and to ask: "To what state of commitment and faithfulness has the passage of three centuries brought us?" This question is appropriate because in sixteen years the Brethren will celebrate the beginning of their fourth century. The issue is no less urgent because of the uncertainty of the times and the nature of the situation in which the church presently finds itself.

The largest branch of the Brethren, the Church of the Brethren, has been in numeric decline for a quarter of a century. In this respect they are not unique, for many mainline Protestant denominations have been losing members since the 1960s. The Christian Church has lost thirty percent of its membership since 1965, and the United Methodists have lost nearly two million. These developments have stimulated much research, but no simple solutions have come forward. Some researchers examine why conservative, independent, and evangelical groups are growing. Others analyze the characteristics which contribute to a decrease in mainline commitment.

Contextual factors, over which a denomination may have little control, such as birth rates, population movement, changing cultural values, shifts in economic profiles, competition with other religious and secular groups, and increases in educational levels, certainly play a large role. Internal processes, such as denominational divisions, Annual Conference decisions, doctrinal controversies, the degree of professionalization of the ministry, membership requirements, and the nature and content of church doctrines or statements of mission, also have a substantial impact.

A recent study of the Disciples of Christ reveals that their pastors were unable to maintain high levels of commitment among the membership in part because of an educational and theological gap between ministers and their congregations.[1] Part of this had to do with differences in liberal and conservative outlooks, but it also involved a failure to articulate a theological foundation for belief. The scholars pointed to what they called "theological failure" within the educated ranks, an inability of the educated clergy "to identify a distinctively Christian standard for judging acceptable belief and moral action."[2] This failure eroded commitment and blurred the distinction between the church as the body of Christ and a mere social club.

Denominations within the so-called noncreedal tradition, including Brethren, Mennonites, and Baptists, may be especially subject to this problem of theological failure and drift. Lacking an explicit creedal statement of core belief to pass on to the young and to serve as anchor point, such denominations must work very hard to maintain strong commitment to those beliefs and practices perceived as essential. Without a strong and conscious effort at teaching, there is a continual danger that the core of denominational beliefs and practices will diminish, permitting the loss of major elements of a religious vision within a couple of generations. A denomination such as the Church of the Brethren with as complex a "creed" as the New Testament may face an even more difficult problem of retention and reformulation.

The Church of the Brethren currently faces additional critical problems. These include: 1) a serious shortage of pastors; 2) decline of smaller churches due to lack of adequate economic and membership bases; 3) decisions regarding the relocation of the seminary and the kinds and levels of pastoral training needed; 4) restrictions and changes of program because of financial shortages; 5) dangers to unity and denominational identity because of contrasting views regarding pressing social and doctrinal issues; 6) divergent images of the church and its mission; and, 7) failure to define, redefine, and make relevant to contemporary members the central core of historic Brethren faith and practice. Aware of these crises, the Church of the Brethren is responding to the urgent need to pause in its pilgrimage and study the directional signs.

Some of the most subtle yet far-reaching changes in the twentieth century have had to do with perceptions of the nature of the body of believers and with denominational identity. Prior to the beginning of the century, Brethren held a vision of the church as a unified body of believers having a common mission which they had gained through radical obedience to the New Testament, through a consistent pattern of church discipline, and through a pattern of separation from and non-conformity to the world.

At the end of the present century, a new vision has emerged, one that is more compatible with contemporary cultural and demographic settings. Today many call for the church to view itself as including a world community of believers. Such a church will be characterized by diversity rather than ethnic unity and by contrasting beliefs and life styles rather than uniformity in outward expressions. These pluralistic features, along with divergent understandings of mission, are to be celebrated as gifts of God and embraced in a spirit of openness and loving acceptance. This new vision treasures diversity of gifts, styles, and expressions.

Further reinforcing this major transition has been an increasing emphasis upon freedom and individual choice, relativism in belief systems, gradual release from formal church restraints, and increasing attention to other validating "authorities." Some of these new authorities which today underlie our beliefs and styles arise from values originating in the various established bodies of knowledge as taught in the great universities and seminaries. They arise also from patterns of trained, critical thinking growing out of increased awareness of the canons of logic holding sway within science and philosophy. Also formative to our thinking has been the pervasive optimism regarding the progress of humanity and civilization, which has its roots in the Enlightenment period, and from the guiding norms of the various professional and business spheres which carry increasing weight at every level of the denomination. These new validating authorities competed with and thereby weakened the allegiance formerly reserved in simpler times solely to Christ and the New Testament as a creed, a creed which was interpreted by the unified and gathered body of believers under the guidance of the Holy Spirit.

These changes came gradually and imperceptibly over the period of a century or more. They do not flow from any one process or group of leaders. They reflect transitions that were occurring simultaneously within the fabric of American society. They represent, on the one hand, an incomplete adaptation to the modern setting and, on the other, a departure from major aspects of our historic tradition. The church struggles to define adequately its relationship to the world. Yet, because change is continuous, the task is unfinished. Perhaps part of the continuing mission of the church today is for the body of believers to discover how the church in its current context can be faithful to the best within its ancient calling.

Not all members or groups are equally committed to this new vision which affirms God's presence in diversity of belief and life style. Indeed, the contemporary church is characterized by a multiplicity of competing and sometimes conflicting visions. Issues, such as war, drug use, child abuse, abortion, women's rights, gay rights, poverty, homelessness, unemployment and many others, divide the membership into an arena of clashing views. The lines of cleavage coincide remarkably with the familiar three-way conservative, moderate, and progressive stances which have marked American public opinion at large and have stalked the Brethren as far back as the 1880s and beyond.

What may be different today is the increased visibility and volatility of these clashing views as they center on the issues named above. The implications for diversity and the potential for division remain unassessed. The difficulties of reconciliation are magnified because the antagonists base their arguments on different moral authorities and are guided by different views of the church's mission. Bound by a literal interpretation of Biblical authority and an older view of the church, traditionalists cannot compromise without appearing to surrender. Progressives are freer to reinterpret the scriptures and to drop or modify what seem to be outmoded views and practices from the sectarian past.

Additional challenges to the old image of unity and consensus come forward. As with other denominations in the cultural mainstream, we are torn by the tensions of the times. Various kinds of diversities born of individualism, social movements, and special interests call us to expand our vision. Ethnic groups gradually come into greater participation in the life of the church. Numerous interest groups seek furtherance of their special goals. These developments are not new to America, but they have come rather lately to the Brethren, prompting them to pause, listen, and accommodate. The church's willingness to become inclusive arises not only from the love ethic of the New

Testament, but also from the culture, including the influence of the civil rights movement, awareness flowing from the communications media, and knowledge of the successes of litigation in the courts by numerous groups for harm suffered. Reinforced by the historic American social doctrines of individual freedom and equality of opportunity, special groups have been highly successful in achieving at least some of their aims in these and in other ways. Because of their commitment to the Sermon on the Mount, Brethren have been quick to respond to many of these human needs, and this has been a significant aspect of Brethren mission.

Having emerged from a sectarian background which strongly emphasized family values and uniformity in outward expressions, some Brethren find it difficult to embrace pluralism and diversity. Founded in Germany in 1708, its first eight members sought to find a pattern of organization that would be true to their image of the New Testament Church. From exposure to the Pietist movement, they sought a vital relationship with God through closeness to Christ and through the indwelling of the Holy Spirit. From this experience came "awakening" or new birth, and this expressed itself in love of neighbor and godly life style. Very much concerned about the "falling away" within the formal church religion of the times, the Pietists sought to maintain their individual spiritual renewal through Bible study, prayer, and Christian community. Seeing a purely *personal* awakening, however, as contrary to the New Testament church, the Brethren founders adopted the Anabaptist view of the church as a disciplined community seeking to be faithful to God's calling. Breaking with the individualist stance of the radical Pietists, they sought to discover the pattern of the "primitive" Apostolic church both in inward spirit and in outward form. The study of the scriptures revealed both the New Testament pattern for church life and the pattern for the daily life of the believers. Obedience to Christ and His teachings became a founding doctrine.

Due to persecution and difficult times, most Brethren left Germany and came to Pennsylvania between 1719 and 1735. The rural "Pennsylvania Dutch" background of the Brethren is well known, and today the areas of greatest density of Brethren population are the fertile valleys originally populated by German settlers and in areas where they migrated southward and westward, that is, in Pennsylvania, Maryland, Virginia, Ohio, Indiana, and Illinois. Gradually they relinquished the German heritage, and the English language was adopted. By 1908 the denomination was willing to change its name from German Baptist Brethren to Church of the Brethren.

Despite great changes in American society, eighteenth and nineteenth-century Brethren generally sustained the emphasis upon exacting obedience to what they believed were New Testament requirements. In their devotion to this principle, the Brethren pressed strongly for a high degree of uniformity in life style and church life. Believing this to be a mark of true Christianity, they imposed strict requirements regarding membership in outside organizations, oaths of allegiance, avoidance of force and violence, style of clothing, and numerous other behaviors. These were upheld through strong church discipline until around the beginning of the twentieth century.

So important was unity to the Brethren that the church required consensus in reaching decisions at Annual Meeting and in congregational councils. Before a decision could be reached, all votes had to be unanimous. If a vote was not required, the discussion continued until the bishop or elder gained the sense that the members "were of one mind."[3]

It is difficult to comprehend the magnitude of the shift in values implied in this change from required uniformity and unity in the mid-nineteenth century to the strong commitment to individualism and diversity which marks the end of the twentieth century. The high value placed upon individual worth and uniqueness is, of course, a strong element of American secular culture. The former arises in significant measure from the heritage of humanistic psychology. Also this value easily meshes with the Christian emphasis upon the worth of the individual so well noted in the teachings of Christ. Therefore, the Brethren easily accepted it. Unfortunately, the value of individualism when held in extreme may discount and belittle the value of the community and the contribution of the group.

Denominations, seeking to respond to the needs of persons in our radically individualistic and pluralistic society, tend to develop values that are compatible with social diversity rather than ethnic uniformity. The popular stance of openness and acceptance of diversity in belief and lifestyle is consistent with this situation. Is it not a remarkable twist of fate that a denomination which has only recently emerged from the relative uniformity of its own ethnic heritage is now challenged with the urgent need to be increasingly open to Hispanics, Asians, Africans, and a new set of Europeans fleeing their periodic crises?

An additional challenge arises internally from the diversity which is already commonplace within the church. How can we sustain the loyalty and commitment of a large number of special interest groups? Some of these groups represent limited and sometimes controversial concerns. Frequently they use promotional methods that have been effective in the secular society to gain our attention and commitment. Such groups are now suggesting that we need to be more "evangelical," more "charismatic," more "fundamental," or more "Brethren." Others suggest that we need to be more "active" or more "social" in our mission, or more "missionary" in establishing new churches, or more "ecumenical" in our outlook. Some feel that we are losing our "peace heritage" or other essentials of our faith.

The challenges arising within the church, as various groups articulate their special needs and interests, are not unique to the Brethren. Nearly all denominations have struggled with the issues of women's rights, ordination or acceptance of homosexuals, and the participation of a variety of older and newer ethnic groups which seek equality and acceptance within the church at every level.

We struggle in good Brethren fashion to accommodate all views by being tolerant and accepting. But an open attitude toward divergent and contradictory positions is itself problematic if we accept the stance that openness must be adequately grounded in theological and Biblical roots. Connection to a sound Biblical and theological rootage will not allow the surrender of basic truths in order to be all things to all people.

The forces at work pull us in different directions, and we wonder if we are losing our identity and our morale as a denomination. Are we losing the very reason for our existence? Or are we called to be faithful in just such a time as this? How do we "earnestly contend for the faith" in a modern setting of moral indifference and ambiguity?

The Brethren in Transition Conference was designed to stimulate thoughtful consideration of these kinds of questions. No easy solutions are anticipated. Rather, extended effort and perseverance are called for. Academic discussion, interchange, debate, and dialogue may provide insights and open up avenues. But the recovery of our equilibrium, our identity, and our mission cannot happen so easily. It can come only through study, prayer, denominational dialogue, divine guidance, and difficult decisions. May it happen.

* * * *

Held on the campus of Bridgewater College, October 3-5, 1991, the aim of the conference was to assess the changes and trends that have occurred during the past one hundred years in the Church of the Brethren. Timely because of the recent decline in church membership, the conference brought together important information relating to influences which may have contributed to that decline. Should this assessment be accurate, the papers published in this volume may become a significant reference point for the denomination. They herald a time of thoughtful evaluation and dialog which in turn may provide guidance and understanding for the church in these uncertain times.

The design of the conference was to invite scholars, preferably published, who have done research or demonstrated special interest in some aspect of Brethren or Protestant history or theology. For each group of presentations, a respondent critiqued the individual papers.

Believing that ministers and pastors might be able to share important insights which would enrich the background against which the scholarly papers would be presented, a preliminary session was arranged for the evening prior to the conference date. This session proved to be especially useful in illuminating the diverse perspectives and viewpoints present in the church. Passionate pleas for openness and involvement in the world contrasted with pleas for faithfulness to the New Testament and to Brethren tradition.

Stephen Longenecker introduced the academic sessions with a paper which focused on the Germantown and Philadelphia congregations. These two groups served as powerful examples of how Brethren congregations were influenced by urbanism even in the nineteenth century. Carl Bowman's ground-breaking analysis, a centerpiece of the conference, described the radical transformation which occurred in several major areas of Brethren thought and symbolism during the twentieth century. Allen Deeter and Vernard Eller, whose informative presentations completed an overview of Brethren change, followed this.

To compare changes in other faiths of similar tradition or origin, the committee invited Thomas Hamm of the Society of Friends, James Juhnke of the Mennonite Church, Dale Stoffer of the Brethren Church, and Fred Benedict of the Old German Baptist Brethren, to describe the patterns of transition in their own churches during the past century.

Thursday evening was devoted to the consideration of two special topics. These included Emmert Bittinger's analysis of the growth of organization in the West Marva District and its implications for denominational life, and Don Fitzkee's case study of change in the Lititz Church in Lancaster County, Pennsylvania.

Additional intriguing topics were presented on Saturday morning: Hedda Durnbaugh on Brethren hymnody and Dale Brown on the peace witness. These papers were in stark contrast, revealing both losses in heritage, of which Brethren have been almost totally unaware, and losses which have been highly publicized. In especially powerful language, Melanie May called for a rejection of a separatist stance and for an embracement of diversity as a gift of God. The conference concluded with Donald F. Durnbaugh's comments which provided integrative themes together with several hopes for the Brethren in the twenty-first century.

[1] D. Newell Williams, (A Case Study of Mainstream Protestantism (Grand Rapids: William B. Eerdmans Publishing Co., 1991), 11.

[2] Ibid., 21.

[3] This procedure tended to favor a strong conservative stance because a single vote against a proposal could prevent its adoption. Undoubtedly this voting procedure contributed to what has often been called the legalistic stance of the Brethren during most of the Nineteenth Century. It was retained at considerable cost to the church, for it surely contributed to the growth of a more radical liberal reaction, thereby contributing to the divisions in the church in the 1880s. Decision by consensus was abandoned in the 1880s.

PART I

PASTORAL TESTIMONIES:
THE STATE OF THE CHURCH

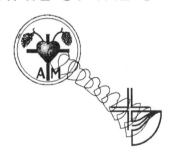

Pastors, due to their direct contacts with the membership, are in a unique position to evaluate the health and life of the church. Seven pastors were chosen to share their views on the state of the church. To some degree, these presentations will reflect special viewpoints, coming as they do from persons who stand in some specific vantage point. These witnesses differ in various ways, such as being seminary or non-seminary trained; male or female; professional or free ministry tradition; younger or older. Some differ because they are knowledgeable of, or influenced by, some trend which diverges from the main cultural stream of the denomination.

Movements or stances evident today within the denomination include members who identify themselves as evangelicals, charismatics, fundamentalists, peace activists, social activists, ecumenists, traditionalists, and supporters of civil rights (seen in special concerns such as feminism, acceptance of ethnic diversity, homosexual lifestyles, etc.). In addition, members have been influenced by modes of thought such as psychologism (as represented in expressions such as group dynamics and religion as self-fulfillment), theological modernism, and biblical criticism. The statements of the seven pastors reflect in complex ways several of the above currents. Not only are pastors diverse in views, but the stance and attitude of the membership of the denomination is shaped also in the ripples and cross currents generated by the interactive nature of the movements described above.

I

Harold S. Martin

I view the church from the perspective of having served in a plural team ministry as a non-salaried minister in the Pleasant Hill Congregation of the Southern Pennsylvania District. I have served in the same congregation for just a few months less than forty years. In addition, I view the condition of the church from the perspective of having been asked to deliver sermons in more than 250 congregations across the Brotherhood in all of its twenty-four districts. Many of these appointments were filled in relation to my serving on the staff of the Brethren Revival Fellowship. I share five major concerns that I have for the Church of the Brethren.

1) The tendency to practice a Sunday morning religion. In more and more congregations services other than Sunday morning are losing support. Sunday night, mid-week, the full love feast, revival series, and Bible conferences in many cases have been dropped altogether. Many of the church activities make the church seem to be merely a social club. The impacts of television and materialism are causing many to let spiritual nurture become a mere sideline concern.

2) An erosion of confidence in the entire New Testament as applicable for the church today. Many persons with significant responsibilities in the Church of the Brethren seem uncomfortable with affirming belief in the Bible as free from error. They are more and more using a cafeteria approach to interpreting and applying the New Testament. They prefer to select what is palatable to the human mind, rejecting the hard sayings, especially those from the writings of the Apostle Paul.

3) A proneness to regard sin and salvation as social rather than personal. The proclaiming of the crucified and risen Christ as our only Savior has been increasingly replaced by a message of social involvement. The teaching about personal sin and its forgiveness, about the assurance of salvation, and about a right relationship with God (in many settings) does not constitute the major message of the church.

4) A breakdown of strong convictions about Biblical moral standards. One-fourth of all Church of the Brethren members drink alcoholic beverages. Most of our churches look the other way when pre-marital or extra-marital sex is evident. Divorce and remarriage are rapidly increasing even among the clergy. It is difficult to maintain a consistent peace witness to a world of five

billion people when in our own Brethren families two individuals under the same roof cannot get along.

5) A movement away from the Biblical, Anabaptist position on peace. The kind of pacifism that is popularized through anti-war demonstrations and refusal to pay taxes is not the Biblical nonresistance taught by the mainline Anabaptists, nor is it the approach of the pietists who influenced Alexander Mack. The nonresistant Christian promotes and exemplifies peacemaking through peaceful living and non-participation in the military rather than through direct political action.

Having listed these five concerns, I am pleased to observe five positive developments.

1) There is an increased emphasis by some on prayer and spiritual life.

2) A new stress is being placed on the practice of evangelism especially as it relates to the Passing on the Promise program.

3) There is liberty in the local churches to map out their own programs and to determine the direction of their ministry and outreach.

4) Efforts are being made to work at leadership training below the seminary level.

5) The Church of the Brethren is continuing its excellent program for meeting human needs.

Along with these five observations, there is also a friendliness and warmth and family spirit among the Brethren which is not always found among other groups of church people.

In addition to the five negative concerns and the five points for joy, there are five areas of hope. The following statements constitute my "wish list" for the Church of the Brethren.

1) That we would become more clear and more intentional in sharing the simple message of eternal salvation found only in Jesus Christ.

2) That we would observe the distinctive ordinances and practices of the Brethren with greater enthusiasm and unity.

3) That the spiritual renewal called for in the 1990 and 1991 would be a growing fire warming all of us.

4) That we would be able to keep more of our marriages intact.

5) That we would accept the Annual Conference statement already in place which says that homosexual practices are unacceptable behavior.

These are the concerns, joys, and hopes which many of us in the Church of the Brethren have for the future of our brotherhood.

We read in I Corinthians 1:10 (JB), "All the same, I appeal to you brothers, for the sake of our Lord Jesus Christ, to make up the differences between you, and . . . to be united again in your belief and practice." That is my hope for the Church of the Brethren.

II

Steven Mason

I am having a difficult time working up a real, serious concern regarding the survival of the church. I just cannot believe that the church as a whole is in any real trouble. When Jesus instituted the church as recorded in the sixteenth chapter of Matthew, he said "and the gates of hell shall not prevail against it." I believe that. I believe that nothing shall ultimately prevail against the church of Jesus Christ.

However, I will deal with the question before us. The question is: what is the state of the Church of the Brethren, and how does it fit into God's scheme for the whole church?

I believe God established the Church of the Brethren for a specific task and purpose. Our purpose may grow and change, but to understand the fundamental nature of our corporate calling, we need to take a look at those specific circumstances in which our denomination was called into existence.

Frankly, I have difficulty believing that in 1708 God looked about, surveyed the situation, and declared, "I think what I need is another denomination!" Quite the contrary. There were specific forms of unfaithfulness in the church to which a tiny group of people were called to address as faithful witnesses. That witness grew into a denomination with a special calling.

So what is this calling? It could probably be stated many different ways, but I have identified three specific elements of this calling upon which we should be able to agree as being vital. They are so integrally tied together that they are actually one unified calling, but we will look at them separately.

First, the separation of church and state. Our denomination was born at a time when the church and the state were essentially one, and the resulting compromises of Christian faithfulness were apparent to many. We were then born into civil disobedience, or more rightly, into Christian obedience. Our witness to the rest of the church was that as citizens of God's Kingdom, we are to be in opposition to culture and civil government, not in collusion with it.

Secondly, we are called to uphold the peace of Jesus Christ through adherence to what has become known as the "peace position" of the Church of the Brethren. While this has never been universally accepted among all the members, it is still the element that makes us a historic peace church.

Thirdly, we are called to model the servanthood of Jesus Christ, and even of suffering servanthood, which is the specific way in which we exhibit radical discipleship.

These three elements—separation of church and state, the peace position, and radical discipleship through service to the world—combine to form one unified calling. This is the special and unique witness for which the Church of the Brethren has been called into existence.

While I may be having some difficulty coming up with *ultimate* concerns, I am not without concerns for our denomination. I will mention just one. Our nation has just come through what has come to be called a "popular war" in the Middle East. While I am saddened that anyone would consider a war to be popular, I am not so much concerned that society in general considered this war to be popular. What concerns me is that this war has been popular within the Church at large and even within many congregations of the Church of the Brethren. It has been so popular that many of our pastors, myself included, have suffered repercussions bordering on persecution from their own congregations. This is because some of us have tried to uphold the peace position and refused to enter into the nationalistic orgy of celebration and victory. We have tried to witness to the fact that all war is sin.

When we see symbols of the state such as American flags and yellow ribbons being brought into our meeting houses, and our members supporting the war by displaying bumper stickers and lapel pins, it is time for us to be seriously concerned about the integrity of the witness of our church. The state of the church is sound, but the state of the Church of the Brethren is a contingency. There is a large "if" question. The state of the Church of the Brethren will be sound if we are faithful to the purpose to which we are called.

Let me conclude as simply as I can. I believe that as long as we continue to be a free church, a peace church, and a servant church, God will continue to lead us and to provide the resources we need. If, on the other hand, we fail to do the task to which he calls us, God will simply take the calling away from us and give it to another.

III

David Rittenhouse

We have been asked to share some of the things that concern us about the Church of the Brethren. I think that it is in order to look at some of the hopeful signs as well.

I would like to refer us to a scripture from Matthew 22, "Thou shalt love the Lord thy God with all thy heart, with all thy soul, and with all my mind. This is the first and great commandment. And a second is like unto it, Thou shalt love thy neighbor as thyself." The love of God and the love of neighbor are at the heart of where I believe the church should be. If we can keep this in mind, I believe that it will take us a long way in getting along together and at being in harmony with one another.

The Church of the Brethren has always emphasized this relationship of love, and I see this as one of the hopeful signs in our denomination. It is interesting that when Peter denied the Lord, Jesus did not ask him to promise not to curse anymore or not to deny him anymore, but he asked him if he still loved him, or if he did indeed love him. Peter, having responded with, "Lord, you know that I do," was then commissioned to care for his sheep.

Moving to some of my concerns, I would start with a word of caution for those who are in the group called "evangelicals." Evangelical means different things to different people. I am hearing a great deal of talk today about what some are calling "the evangelical turn." It is a concern of mine that this will not awaken a new legalism. I think there are people who are afraid of that, and I share that fear. We do not want to see a time of new legalism. Legalism, old or new, does not represent the Church of the Brethren at its best.

We also want to be careful that we don't side with the fundamentalists as we seek to become a people who take the scripture seriously. To me the Brethren have never really been fundamentalists in the sense that our view of the scripture was memorized formulas and calendars and that we could only talk about those formulas and calendars. There is a temptation—and this is one of my concerns—that people in looking for friendship and in looking for support turn to a forceful popular religion. I hope that we have a church that is biblically evangelical, not one that has a fundamentalist view of the Bible.

For me a Biblical person can always talk about what the scripture is really saying. We are open to really look at the scriptures and see fresh things. The older Brethren used to say we teach from the scripture and we are willing to be taught by it. That would be a concern and a hope together.

While the above are real concerns to me, the biggest concern I have is the reality that we live in a self-indulgent age. We are like the prodigal son who said, "give me what is mine. I want to do with it what I please." This takes different forms, but it is in harmony with the self-realization psychology of our general school system: the fulfillment of self, the realization of my potential. It is centered not on the worship of God but of man. This is at the heart of humanistic thought: man is the center, and that I am the center of life. I think this is why we have so many broken marriages; this is why we have so much immorality. It is the wide approval and acceptance of the self-indulgent spirit that concerns me.

I believe that we must strive for God-directed lives and a God-directed church. What needs to happen is that in our worship of God and in our discovery of what God has said to us in his Word and in Jesus Christ, is that we live our lives in obedience. This I strive for, often unsuccessfully, in my own life. We have had too much of self-centered feeling. There comes a time that what I feel like is not really important. The most important thing is, "What does God have to say about it?" That might be about peace, or it might be about marriage. To me morality is revealed from God. He guides us in what is right and wrong. We do not decide it. I think we have often gotten in trouble because we feel like people themselves may decide what is right and wrong instead of trying to find out through his Word what God had decided.

So I pray that again we would be a people who are willing to be instructed by the Word, that we would be teachable by the person and the life of Jesus and by the clear teaching that he left us. And I pray that we would conform our lives and our conduct to the life and teachings of Jesus, even against our feelings.

In addition, I would like to say something about where I feel I am. I am sure other people were like brother Steve who said he did not know which faction or group he was representing. I feel that we are just Brethren and that we all share that feeling of being together.

Let me also express an appreciation for the Holy Spirit group and the influence of the charismatic movement in the church. I have a fear that in discovering what we understand to be a new truth that it would make us lay aside what we have traditionally known as the old truths. If it is from the Lord, there should be harmony in it. I do not have to leave a church of the Brethren and become a Pentecostal in order to have room for the Holy Spirit in my life. There is as much of a temptation to be self-indulgent in what is called Holy Spirit worship as there is in any other kind of license. So I think it is healthy that there is a turn in the charismatic circles toward becoming involved in missions, to talk about compassionate deeds, and to look for stability and for balance. I think this is a healthy thing. It is both a concern and an appreciation about what is happening.

Also, in my associations with the Brethren Revival Fellowship, I am happy that there is a new openness. The fact that they would include me in some of their activities shows that they are more open than they used to be. While there is an identifying and a clarifying of positions, there is still openness to appreciate the faith that we share. I hope that always continues.

Now I would like to say that these are the things I feel in my heart. I want always to be able to share just where I am with my deepest convictions and emotions. I do not want to imply that every one else has to be where I am. Yet I want to give witness to where I am. And I want also to hear where other people are. I do not want to argue. I used to like to argue. I am trying to get over that. I want to be able to state a position, to witness to a position, and also to hear the positions of others. And I think that is the mood of this meeting and this conference. I believe that we should forcefully and as eloquently as possible share how we feel about the church and what our beliefs are. Yet we should also be able to hear each other. Now I think I will leave it there.

IV

Karen Carter

At the Church Growth and Evangelism dinner at Annual Conference, popular evangelist Terry Hershey passionately pleaded with us Brethren, as did Jesus with the Pharisees: take off your tinted glasses, tinted by old interpretations and old definitions of what God requires of us; take them off so that in the clear light of Jesus you can see one another as human beings created in God's image. "Ultimately," Hershey said, "we will not be judged by our words, but by our love."

I grew up in Hitler's Germany. People who were arbitrarily deemed "unfit" for Hitler's master race were made despicable through propaganda: Jews, Gypsies, homosexuals, and mentally retarded. First, such persons were excluded from positions of influence, then from society, and finally, rounded up and shot or exterminated or placed in death camps like Dachau and Auschwitz.

We need a kinder, gentler church!

The Jews had to wear the yellow "star of David" on their clothes; the homosexuals, the pink triangle, for easy identification for discriminatory purposes. When Hitler marched into Norway and demanded the same practice there, the King of Norway and many of his subjects wore the yellow star of David also. This effectively thwarted Hitler's persecution plans. At Annual Conference, many of us joined the gay community in wearing the pink triangle as a sign of solidarity with them. Besides solidarity, it proves a valid point: you cannot tell the homosexual from the "straight" because many of them do not fit the stereotype at all.

The fact is, we do not know who is gay and who is not. As Ralph McFadden said in his article in the winter, 1991, issue of <u>Brethren Life and Thought,</u> "if we [gays] could just turn purple," we would be utterly surprised to see the number of homosexuals in our midst. They are among our staff, our musicians, our artists and writers, committee members, pastors, our spouses, our own sons and daughters. The reason for not knowing who they are is that we have not been able to accept them as children of God.

We need to work diligently in our churches and in our Annual Conference program to apply the same standards and expectations of faithfulness to Jesus Christ to homosexuals and to heterosexuals: fidelity within covenantal relationships. If sexual relationships are to be confined to marriage, then marriage must be an option for homosexuals as it is for heterosexuals. For both, the homosexual and the heterosexual, love and justice needs to be the character of all relationships. Stewardship of time, talent, substance, peacemaking, and all the rest of our beliefs need to be nurtured and practiced by all of our members, regardless of their sexual orientation. We shall know them by their fruits, and we are wise to leave the judgment of the final harvest to God.

At an Insight Session on homosexuality at Annual Conference, I shared briefly how my congregation worked at this issue. I have been overwhelmed at the number of people who have shared with me, both at Annual Conference and later, their own pain: spouses, parents, friends, and siblings of gays, and gays themselves, all alienated because of feeling pushed out of the church. No matter where you are on the issue, you can quote scripture in support of your argument.

When we began our pastoral work in 1961 south of the Mason-Dixon line, there were many Brethren who could "prove" to us from the Bible that God has marked our black brothers and sisters and that they are inferior to the white Brethren. Those of you who are over fifty will probably remember such incidents. "Wash me and I shall be whiter than snow."

Let me close with a scripture which in the context of homosexuality has turned me around 180 degrees. It is Acts, Chapter 10, Peter's experience on the rooftop in Joppa. You will remember the scripture in which Peter had a vision on the rooftop of a house in Joppa. A sheet came down from heaven with all manner of animals on it, including those explicitly forbidden by the Jewish faith. A voice said, "Rise, Peter, kill and eat." Peter was shocked at such a request. It went counter to everything he had been taught, and something Jesus in his teachings had not drawn into question to Peter's knowledge. Peter refused, basing his refusal on his religious upbringing and his obedience to the Bible. The voice repeated and admonished him: "Do not call unclean what I have cleansed."

Today, we are in need of a Joppa experience.

V

Terry Hatfield

We are in a time of unprecedented trans-cultural, political, and economic change. The world will never be the same as our memories or the realities of the 1940s, 1950s, or 1960s. The next two decades will place us in the cockpit of starship earth, where long looks in the rear view mirror will not be terribly helpful for the streaking journey ahead. And there is no going back.

Nothing, not even the church, has the power to turn the tide of the spectacular and equally frightening pace and face of a reordering world. The church will change, dramatically change, for the better or for the worse. But it will change.

We have not responded well to the "value" changes of our culture of the last few decades. They caught us by surprise. We could not understand why "church" was not working any more. Why the "tried and true" of institutional life was failing us. Why the ranks thinned, even as we attempted to be more relevant, more tolerant, more like the culture. We adapted to the social and political agenda of the times. At times we blindly championed the "causes" which fit the agenda even though they could not be easily fitted to the prophetic or service motifs of the church.

As Paul Grout recently said about the result of this methodology in relation to our peace witness, "This has tragically led many of those who claim to speak for peace to rely on an empty illusion. This has tragically led many of those who claim to speak for Christ to abandon the way of Christ. Is there a Church of the Brethren left that faithfully combines both?"

Can we, as Dale Stoffer suggests, bind up the results of the three-way wound of the 1880s division which "carved up the original heritage of the church by emphasizing different parts of the dialectical tradition?"

We do not hold as dearly to the principals of community, nonconformity to the world, and a simple self-denying lifestyle as do the Old Order German Baptist Brethren. We are much more like American Baptists than Anabaptists.

We do not hold as dearly to "upholding individual freedom of conscience, active evangelism and mission in the world, and a life of individual piety" as do the Ashland Brethren. We are much more like conformed Pharisees than radical pietists.

We do what we do well, that is, emphasize certain aspects of the heritage: the peace witness, openness toward different expressions of the faith, social concerns, and commitment to Brethren heritage. But like our ecclesiastical siblings, we are trying to keep the balance of our being on one leg of a three-legged stool in an unbalanced world.

We have, therefore, neither kept the unity nor the holiness which should mark us as disciples of Christ.

To pursue unity through a celebration of a diversity which does not honor Jesus Christ as the salvation of mankind, or to redefine "holiness" to fit our own worldly or perverse behaviors, will result, I deeply fear, in the removal of the lamp stand from our midst.

I believe that a renewed form of radical pietism must be introduced to who we are. Only then can we be true to the Christian faith and to our Brethren heritage.

Those aspects of pietism which I believe are essential to our future hope as Brethren include:

1) An emphasis on new birth or conversion which clearly holds up Jesus Christ as the Son of God and the only Savior of the world.

2) A movement from that rebirth to a genuine new life in Christ; to a mystical union with Christ, a looking constantly toward Christ in spiritual discipline and the practice of ethical sensitivity and virtuous living.

3) A subscribing to the Word of God, the Bible, as the foundation of faith and the authority of all truth, with emphasis on the evangelistic and practical aspects of the faith.

4) An optimistic and unyielding call for repentance and reform in the church whenever it loses touch with the practice of simple apostolic Christianity and the movement of the Holy Spirit or when it bows to the idols of this fallen world.

Evangelicalism, on its far right, is individualistic, judgmental, and narrow. Liberalism, on its far left, is individualistic, judgmental, and narrow.

The Church of Jesus Christ by its biblical design and the Church of the Brethren by its commitment to the New Testament as its creed and rule must have in its essentials, which are few but crucial, unity; in non-essentials, which are many and important, liberty; and in all things, charity, which is very difficult.

VI

Earle W. Fike, Jr.

George Bernard Shaw once said, "The only person who behaves sensibly is my tailor. He takes my measurements anew every time he sees me. All the rest go on with their old measurements." Someone assumed who we were to invite us to be part of this panel. I want to begin with some current measurements which may help you understand why I will share the concerns and hopes which you will hear.

For me, there are at least five critical marks of the Brethren. They may not be uniquely Brethren because I believe they are also Christian. But they are a part of our spiritual genetic pool and a part of my developmental environment. And they seem to me critical whatever our state of transition.

1) We are a people who have confessed our sin, accepted Christ as Lord, and have proposed to live in keeping with the spirit and teaching of the New Testament, have proposed to be faithful members of the Body of Christ, and have sealed those commitments in Christian baptism.

2) We are a people who work for integrity between word and deed. When persons asked Alexander Mack how the Brethren were to be recognized, he

said, "By the manner of their living." Not a word about what they believed; no mention of creed; no mention of what they underlined in the New Testament; no mention about future pronouncements at Annual Meetings. I grew up looking for integrity between worship and life, not the practices or formulas which guaranteed eternal life.

3) We are a people of unfinished faith. Brethren have no creed other than the New Testament. For some, that is not enough; they want it more defined; more clear; less open-ended; more manageable. I grew up appreciating the strength of that tradition, and I still rejoice in it.

4) We are a people committed to living in community. Because faith is unfinished, always in process, our life together can never be judgmentally divisive, ought never to create fences which delineate who is in and who is out. We need each other in our quest to be faithful while remaining open to new leadings of the spirit. That is, integrity in relationship with one another is as important as integrity between word and deed.

5) We are a people committed to service. "In as much as you have done it to one of the least of these" are words to mature and grow by; words to test our own kingdom-work; and not words to test the validity of another's faith conviction.

Now a few observations. I am not a joiner. I am not a member of the BRF, the BPF, the OEP, or the ABC. Early on, I determined that my commitment to Christ, my ministry, would be worked out and expressed within the church, so I belong to the Body of Christ known as the Church of the Brethren. By nature, I am more a transformer than a revolutionary. I believe new life can emerge from the old. I grew up trusting the community process, and therefore I have tried to let my concerns, my insights, my dreams for the future be worked at from within the community structures. I am what some would call a centrist, subject to criticism from those who feel I am too traditional and also from those who feel I carry the tradition too lightly. I am, however, willing to raise questions with and be in dialogue with any individual or group who attempts to undermine or work outside of the spirit and intent of the above convictions about who the Brethren are.

You are not my tailors. You are my brothers and sisters. But I hope my concerns and hopes about the Church of the Brethren will be registered in the light of these present measurements.

1) I am happiest about the Church of the Brethren when we use our time-honored traditions for community decision making; most unhappy when we try to find ways to circumvent or operate outside those covenants. It is sometimes slower, but I believe our heritage in representative decision making allows for prophetic voices to bear witness among us to bring about change. At the same time this protects the community from strong but questionable individualism. The arena of conference dialogue is germane to who we are. The procedures for relating to one another are important. They are, however,

not written in concrete. They can be changed by community agreement. They ought not to be circuitously ignored.

Specifically, I will be happy when the church comes to some consensus on the nature and style of its missionary effort, even if it takes on more than one form. I am unhappy when, as in our present effort to plant churches around the world, some seem to seek to bypass our traditional ways of respecting one another and working collegially.

Specifically, I was happy when young people stood up and bore witness and influenced the delegate body to a seven to one support of those who refused to register for the draft, even when a plurality vote of church members would likely have rejected it. It is our way of doing business, strong in witness, persuasive rather than mandatory in opinion, open in acceptance of those who conscientiously disagree.

Some people would call such decisions and such a style of doing business as weakness, fence sitting, and uncertainty about what we believe. I am happy when the church continues to struggle in the ambiguity of what it is to be faithful. I think it comes to us out of trying to live in the spirit and teaching of the New Testament.

2) I am not happy with where the Church of the Brethren is in evangelism, nor am I sure we know where we want to go. I am most happy when we focus on how we can be faithful to Jesus Christ rather than emphasize the orthodoxy of what we believe. I am most happy when we are clear that we are saved by the grace of Christ, and I am terribly concerned when we begin to focus on a legality and Pharisaism that needs phrases and words and unity of belief in order to be comfortable. Jesus was not concerned with whether persons were conservative, evangelical, or liberal. He asked all the people in their self-imposed boxes the same questions. Rather than helping them to define who their neighbor was, he asked them if they were a neighbor. Rather than saying when the kingdom would come, he suggested they be ready at any time. He even had the audacity to ask them to live as if they were already in the kingdom, suggesting that "it is among you." If we respond to evangelism with new vigor and emphasis—and I believe we should—we should not do it because we want to grow or because it works for others. We should share the good news of the Gospel of Jesus Christ as God gives us grace and insight to understand it.

3) I am happy as we begin to have strong emphasis on bearing witness to and receiving new persons in our church from other countries and cultures. I am sad when we speak out of both sides of our mouth. Who we are theologically and historically will certainly allow us to witness to and receive new persons from other cultures. But who we are will not allow us to filter them through our culture and require them to go through our own Germanic forms of circumcision in order to be acceptable. It appears to me that some who speak loudest on evangelism also exhibit the most fear about the threat of being adversely watered down and diminished by outside influences. We cannot be open to the moving of the spirit in Koreans, Africans, Dominicans,

and Hispanics and then be upset because a Friday evening worship service does not fit our usual patterns of worship. If we are true to who we are, we must be as open to what others may bring as to what we have to share. And if we are true to the New Testament, we will find a way to do that. For a Biblical precedent, review the Jerusalem Council minutes!

Now to some things I would like to see happen.

1) I wish we would budget our resources and do fewer things but do more of them well. Our resources cannot and should not take on all the issues which need Christian commitment.

2) I wish we focused less on equal geographical representation and more on the skills and tested leadership abilities of those we elected to significant positions.

3) I wish the Church of the Brethren would spend less time doing theological and spiritual navel gazing and more time putting its dialogical and emerging faith convictions to work in the world.

4) Since the health of the church is mostly exhibited in the local parish, I wish denominational organizations looked at the parish as a unit to serve and support rather than as a source of support.

5. Finally, I wish we were a "Good News" denomination, not a portion of Christ's body lugging around a poor self-image with a sad heart.

In summary, I believe the path of faithfulness we have chosen means we will always live in the tension of wanting to strengthen our hand by clarifying what we agree on, while at the same time carrying a commitment not to make those agreements into creeds. It means we will always live in the tension of wanting to celebrate what we hold dear while at the same time remaining open to the new movings of the spirit among us. I am not satisfied with what the church is, but I am excited about the time in which we live. I am pleased with our heritage which commits us to search and grow and respond to new light. It provides a flexibility which allows us to be in mission in precarious times. And our polity has built in safeguards which prevent power-seeking and/or individual ram-rodding of pet ideas. And I am excited because I believe that if we focus on being faithful rather than naming and labeling the faithful, if we focus on sharing God's word rather than collecting Church of the Brethren merit badges, I think God has some significant things for us yet to do. I think we can do them. I believe we will. I believe we may learn how to rejoice and be glad in our kind of service to God!

VII

Dawn Ottoni-Wilhelm

To share with you my concerns and hopes for the Church of the Brethren today seems to be a task too great for any one person alone. Like the story of the six blind persons each holding fast to some piece of the elephant and each asked to describe the animal as a whole, so also may we be assured that each of our descriptions will not wholly explain what we so earnestly grasp. We are each limited and blessed by our particular perspective, and integrity demands that before I share my concerns and hopes, I first confess to you some of the experiences that have informed my particular perspective.

I was born of immigrant families and reared in Detroit, Michigan, during the 1960s and 1970s. There I learned something about wealth, poverty, racism, sexism, and violence. Mine was an ecumenical introduction to the Church, my family being part Catholic, part Lutheran, and not at all Brethren. I was exposed at a young age to diverse and rich religious experiences through the congregations that served our part of Detroit, and I learned quickly something of the tensions that exist within and between different denominations, the hypocrisies, and the marvelous ways that churches may act as God's instrument of love and justice. When I found my church home among the Brethren some eleven years ago, I joined this body because I respected the integrity of the Church of the Brethren, its long heritage of following Christ in word and in deed. I and my husband have been active members of four different congregational settings in the Church of the Brethren: suburban Detroit, suburban Philadelphia, rural Lancaster County, and, presently in State College, Pennsylvania. It is in large part through my work as a hospital chaplain, rather than as a pastor of two of these congregations, that I have developed my particular concerns and hopes for our church.

I have three concerns for the Church of the Brethren. They are, I believe, related to one another.

First, I am concerned that most of us, both lay persons and leaders alike, are terrible communicators! Most of us are more comfortable with an uncomfortable silence than with speaking the truth in love. I am speaking of the silence that does not know how to speak with persons who visit our churches, especially to persons whom we quickly learn do not share our heritage or at least have family in some Brethren congregation.

I am speaking of the silence that weighs heavily through countless committee and board meetings. Perhaps fearful of confrontation, this silence can only erupt later on the church parking lot. I have heard the sharpness of this silence in many homes that I have visited as our members are unwilling to recognize and to share the sorrows and the joys of their lives, buried beneath the surface of their busy schedules. Silence does not necessarily communicate hostility, nor does it necessarily communicate that a deep understanding exists between two or more people. But silence *does communicate confusion.* At this time in our church's history, we are particularly confused about who we are and what we will be and do. Surely this confusion is related to our difficulties in communicating and communing with one another.

Second, I am concerned about the divisiveness that permeates our congregations. Within my support group of Brethren pastors in Lancaster, there was not a congregation among seven that had not experienced a significant division within a five-year period. Perhaps this is due to our unwillingness to speak openly and confront others directly or to our fear that we, ourselves, may have to change radically. Whatever the reason, we Brethren today seem particularly plagued by a divisive spirit.

Finally, my greatest concern is that we are now a dying denomination. As the youngest pastor here tonight, I have wondered more than once when I and my children will witness a major split within our denomination, its gradual dissolution, or its adoption by another denomination. As a chaplain, I have witnessed and shared in the deaths of over 200 people. I know what death looks like. I recognize the panic and denial I see among our members and leaders. I cry for our lack of faith in believing that it is *only as each of us dies* (to our pride, to our insistence on our own ways), that God may begin the work of re-creation among us.

I have tried to speak frankly and honestly of my concerns for the Church of the Brethren, and this has certainly been bad news indeed. So, what is the good news? What are my hopes for the denomination?

Initially, I had thought to tell you that I hope our church members and leaders would become better communicators, less divisive, and stop dying! Then I thought that I should wish that the church could be more like me and my Italian family: meeting together every Saturday to share pasta, talk, laugh, and argue freely, solve difficult family problems, sometimes to become angry, but to return the next Saturday, always trying to make room for new people and new perspectives. Then I realized this was quite vain. As I have prayed for ever greater love for our church and for one another, God's wisdom has taught me that it is best that the church not be created in my image, or in anyone's image, but in God's image. My hope, then, lies in our faith in God and in our becoming more spiritually attuned to God's life and will among us.

First, I hope we will grow spiritually by deepening our will to love God and one another. We are to be rooted and grounded in love, not looking to conform to others but to be continually transformed by the Spirit of God in Jesus Christ.

Second, we may have faith that as we become more spiritually mature, more genuinely loving, more prayerfully grounded and biblically literate, we will hear God's call to service. Surely this call will grow out of our strengths and gifts as God has given them to us.

For example, I find it unlikely that God will call a group, such as ourselves who generally find it difficult to communicate verbally, to became leaders in evangelism worldwide. Although each of us is responsible for sharing God's truth as we know it, still I am far more hopeful that God will call us to draw upon the wondrous strengths that we have been given and have valued and nurtured in order to serve the world. I refer to strengths of commitment to family life and an active concern for peace and justice. I am hopeful that as we become the denomination that God created us to be, we will be filled with a sense of joy, renewal of purpose and identity; thankful for who we are and what we are called to do in the kingdom of God.

As my grandmother told me before my first date, "Keep-a you eyes wide open!" We who are people of the faith know that the struggles and losses we are experiencing now are not the end of God's story for us. As Paul encouraged the church in Romans, Chapter 8, we would do well to remember that hope that is seen is not hope, but if we hope for that which we do not see, then we may wait for it with patience. Brothers and sisters, "Keep-a you eyes wide open!"

PART II

AN OVERVIEW OF BRETHREN CHANGE IN THE TWENTIETH CENTURY

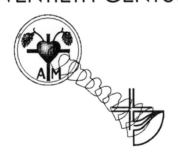

1

From Urban Village to Urban Society: The Church of the Brethren and Modern America

by Stephen L. Longenecker

Designed to provide a background for the research oriented papers of the conference, the presentation by Longenecker discussed several major influences underlying change among the Brethren. He draws on the excellent study by Stephanie Grauman Wolf of the development of the Germantown, Pennsylvania, community during the eighteenth century. He shows how the conditions of urbanization, industrialization, and modernization contributed to serious problems for the Germantown and Philadelphia German Baptist Brethren churches. As compared with rural congregations where sectarian distinctiveness was more easily maintained, the urban environment made separateness from the world much more difficult. Progressive tendencies in doctrine and practice brought frequent Annual Meeting censure of the Philadelphia Brethren in the nineteenth century. Loss by a sect of its self-definition as "social outsiders" appears crucial in the struggle to resist acculturation. Longenecker notes parallels in the history of the Mormon, Quaker, and fundamentalist groups in this respect.

I

Among America's first urban societies, according to Stephanie Grauman Wolf, a prominent social historian, was eighteenth-century Germantown, Pennsylvania. Although only a village, Germantown possessed many characteristics of urbanization, including economic specialization, secularization, diversity, social and spatial mobility, pragmatism, and tolerance. The shops and manufactories lining Germantown Avenue, exemplified by the Christopher Sauers' press, created a miniaturized urban society, foreshadowing what became typical in modern America.[1]

The Church of the Brethren, which transplanted itself from Europe into this tiny city, never sank deep roots in its first seedbed. Stephanie Wolf claims that in Germantown the Brethren influence dwindled because they tried to "maintain a closed community in the midst of an open society." Only in the isolation of the backcountry, she concludes, could their separatism withstand the allurements of assimilation.[2] In the next century the Germantown congregation and its neighbor, Philadelphia, which Germantown Brethren organized in 1817, struggled even more. Germantown went without a resident minister for twenty years and at one point also had no deacons.[3] When Wilbur B. Stover arrived in 1891 to serve a short pastorate, he remarked that without the cemetery "there [was] not much left."[4] In 1888 Philadelphia sold its building at a loss because a steep decline in membership made it difficult to meet mortgage obligations.[5]

Although several urban fellowships of Brethren have prospered, this has been the exception rather than the rule. In 1888 D. C. Moomaw, an elder from Roanoke, Virginia, complained that Brethren labor in cities consistently "yielded meager fruits,"[6] and little has changed since that assessment. The Philadelphia and Germantown congregations became typical of the urban experience among the Brethren.

While these two urban congregations struggled to remain robust, they often found themselves outside the mainstream of Brethren attitudes. In the 1840s the Philadelphia fellowship permitted a woman to preach, Sarah Righter Major, whom a committee of elders nearly benched when she moved to the mid-west.[7] In 1869 a committee appointed by Yearly Meeting discovered that the Philadelphia and Germantown congregations had departed significantly from standard love feast practices, discontinuing the supper and the salutation.[8] In 1876 another committee from Annual Conference investigated charges that Philadelphia had adopted "popular and fashionable religion" and had "abandoned the practice of the brotherhood." The delegation subsequently censured the Philadelphia Brethren for basket offerings taken during worship, a baptismal pool in the meetinghouse, Sunday School picnics, instrumental music during worship, and for employing a paid minister who was not "called" from the congregation but who nevertheless enjoyed "pre-eminence" over older, elected preachers.[9] The accusations were so serious that conference took the unusual step of printing them in the Minutes.[10] The following year the District Meeting of the Eastern District of Pennsylvania declared that Germantown and Philadelphia were "more or less out of order,"[11] and in 1896-7 the Germantown congregation decorated its remodelled meetinghouse with Greco-Roman columns, a strong contrast to the austere architecture of most meetinghouses. These episodes demonstrate that, as Wolf suggests, the Brethren's first urban congregations found nonconformity difficult and, thus, frequently fell on the periphery of the denomination.

II

By losing their self-image as social outsiders, urban Brethren relinquished a self-definition that vibrant fellowships often possess. First-generation Mormons, for example, in some ways resembled their contemporaries but still saw themselves as outsiders. Practicing revivalism, absorbing magic and the occult, and foreseeing a divine mission for their nation made Mormons similar to other Protestant Americans, and Joseph Smith, their founder, claimed to seek restoration of the universal church and to end division in Christendom. He worked nonetheless to make his fellowship nonconformist. Smith's writings consistently warn of God's harsh judgment on the rich, powerful, and educated. The Book of Mormon depicts wealth and oppression of the poor as the source of evil, and the prophet Nephi condemns latter-day churches with "fine sanctuaries" that will be built and financed by unscrupulous persons, "puffed up" with pride, who "rob the poor." When Mormons settled in Nauvoo, Illinois, the city fathers welcomed them with a charter containing considerable autonomy, so Smith immediately distinguished his fellowship from the larger community with marriage for eternity, plural marriage, and baptism for the dead. The secret Council of Fifty and ritual borrowed from the Masons clashed with popular notions of republican democracy and further separated Mormons from the mainstream. In Missouri Smith organized the covert Band of Danites, who allegedly evened the score with enemies of Mormonism. Many of Mormonism's unique practices courted persecution, which became part of its heritage.[12]

Fundamentalists, like the Mormons, had much in common with the mainstream but developed a self-perception of nonconformity. Fundamentalists suspected that prestigious intellectuals and theologians increasingly held them in contempt but claimed that rejection by the elites was an asset. J. Frank Norris, after suffering expulsion from the Baptist General Convention in 1924, asserted that his work had "prospered" because his new status as an outsider attracted more support for his work. While in the pulpit, he often read letters, which critics surmised that he authored, attacking him. Other fundamentalists, such as William Bell Riley, J. Gresham Machen, and Carl McIntire, allowed their opponents to claim the ground of insider, which they willingly seized. Harry Emerson Fosdick, a prominent liberal, remarked that in battles with the conservatives he felt fortunate to have "powerful backing from those by whom one would most choose to be backed." Rockefeller money, specifically, backed Fosdick in his ministry at New York's Riverside Church. Fundamentalists, as Timothy L. Smith has remarked, portrayed themselves as a "beleaguered minority with their backs against the wall," thereby turning middle class WASP's into outsiders.[13]

Nineteenth-century revivalists also rejoiced that they were outsiders. Francis Asbury, the first Methodist bishop in America, believed that preachers who "labor for the poor" should "suffer" with them and avoid the clothes, bearing, and financial security of gentlemen.[14] Lorenzo Dow, a popular Methodist itinerant, was, according to one eyewitness, "not only uncouth in his person and appearance, but his voice was harsh, his action hard and rectangular." But the observer also noted that Dow "understood common life."[15] Revivalists often portrayed themselves as simple folk without the refinements of society; one revivalist insisted that,

> larnin isn't religion, and eddication don't give a man the power of the Spirit. It is grace and gifts that furnish the real live coals from off the altar. St. Peter was a fisherman—do you think he ever went to Yale College? When the Lord wanted to blow down the walls of Jericho, he didn't take a brass trumpet, or a polished French horn: no such thing; he took a ram's horn—a plain, natural ram's horn—just as it grew.

This preacher concluded that when God "wants to blow down the walls of the spiritual Jericho," he bypasses the "smooth, polite, college larnt gentlemen" and selects instead "a plain, natural ram's-horn sort of man" like himself.[16] Other revivalists found nonconformity in a strong reform movement which included temperance, abolition, and social welfare, and underscored that America did not yet walk the straight and narrow.

Occasionally, but not often, fellowships reverse their drift into the mainstream. Late eighteenth-century Quakers, many of whom had become wealthy, powerful, and worldly, rebuilt the hedges, as they called them, that separated their society from the world. They withdrew from politics, reinstituted Meeting discipline, and, in a fellowship declining in numbers, disowned slaveholders. They stressed the insidious nature of wealth, rejecting the beliefs of many mid-century Friends that riches were evil only when used improperly. Reformers, such as Anthony Benezet, welcomed the American Revolution because it might force Friends, especially those "encumbered with the clay of this world," to redefine priorities, and they also strongly suspected that fortune corrupted children, who never knew the earlier, simpler life of their now wealthy parents. Further opportunity for nonconformity came from a more vigorous antislavery witness, which had previously been a minority position among Friends. At mid-century Quakers owned slaves in proportion equal to the larger population, but reformers now encouraged manumission and disowned uncooperative slaveholders. Friends abstained from rum because of its link to the slave trade and boycotted products of West Indies slavery, including indigo, a blue dye; Quaker women used walnut leaves instead and sometimes redyed old bedspreads that had been already blued with indigo. As Quakerism became more nonconformist, eccentrics, whom previously had been considered embarrassments, received tolerance. In 1738, for example, Friends disowned Benjamin Lay, a hunchbacked vegetarian who lived in a cave and abstained from tea and wool, but by the 1760s John Woolman, who wore undyed homespun, refused to use silver tableware, and avoided sugar to protest slavery, had become a role model.[17]

Thus, eighteenth-century Quaker reformers, nineteenth-century revivalists and Mormons, and twentieth-century fundamentalists demonstrated the importance of nonconformity in American religion.[18] As Senator Mark Hatfield, an evangelical, advised a Congressional prayer breakfast, Christ's followers usually find themselves with "miserable minorities" rather than "comfortable majorities." The threat, then, that early modernization posed to the Philadelphia and Germantown congregations, by jeopardizing their outsiderness, was indeed significant.

III

Nineteenth-century modernization, however, touched the entire society, not just the embryonic urban centers. Although change came later to rural areas, by the 1830s many Americans became convinced that the increasingly commercialized, competitive, and industrial society endangered old values. Gunsmiths at the federal armory in Harper's Ferry, Virginia, complained that labor discipline and the machine dehumanized them, cheapened their skills, and eliminated the artistry inherent in their craft. In 1830 a zealous foreman suffered assassination, and in 1842 the installation of a clock in the workplace with a mandatory ten-hour workday sent workers on strike.[19]

Although most artisans avoided dislocation until late in the nineteenth century, the new mobile, heterogeneous world nevertheless threatened many Americans. Antebellum reformers, for example, targeted perceived threats to traditional values. Communes harnessed individualism, and temperance advocates promised to cleanse society of immoral, debilitating behavior. Abolitionists often charged that slavery encouraged immorality, including laziness and licentiousness. Others found stability in health regimens, phrenology, or the Graham cure. Phrenologists diagrammed the shape of the cranium to reveal thirty-seven distinct personal traits, called "faculties," each occupying a unique position, or "organ," on the head. Phrenology became popular because it provided answers during a period of uncertainty. The Graham cure was the theory of Sylvester Graham, a clergyman from Connecticut, who believed that most illnesses stemmed from stomach irritation. He advocated a rough diet of fruits, vegetables, and coarsely ground grain plus the famous cracker that bears his name. His cure also encouraged people to exercise, bathe (which most Americans avoided), wear loose clothing, ventilate their homes, and avoid sexual excess. Thus, to survive or even to succeed in the industrial world, Graham suggested discipline. Self-control, he taught, was the answer to the age of anxiety.[20]

Others, however, feared that reformers destroyed rather than protected the old order. Abolitionists became the focal point of northern, middle class anxieties because their national organization and avalanche of printed propaganda menaced local, traditional authority. During the 1830s northern mobs, which frequently included bankers, lawyers, and other "gentlemen of property and standing," according to the contemporary phrase, physically attacked abolitionists. These rioters, many of whom belonged to old, distinguished families, worshipped with orthodox denominations, and held local political office, were tied to the local, pre-industrial economy, and consequently feared the abolitionists whose organizational methods paralleled the new mercantilism and challenged the traditional order.[21]

Contemporary Brethren, like the phrenologists, the "gentlemen of property and standing," and temperance men and women, sought an orderly world. Yearly Meeting became increasingly active, and the number of queries to it swelled significantly during the 1820s and 30s, a pattern that prevailed until after 1860.[22] Conference ruled on a variety of topics, ranging from tobacco to lightning rods and the procedure for love feast, but the bottom line was that in a confusing and modernizing world the denomination sought order and tighter discipline. Rulings against fashionable dress, celebrating the Fourth of July, college education, benedictions with uplifted hands, and Sunday Schools reflected attempts to maintain the hedges between themselves and the larger world. A decision in 1847 against borrowing from banks to drive cattle or transport grain to urban markets was an especially sharp rebuff to commercialization. Towards the close of this period the Meeting added another layer of ecclesiastical structure by creating district conferences. Although geographic dispersal of the denomination offered a pragmatic reason to create greater formality, spatial mobility characterized the sprawling society that also concerned other antebellum Americans. New threats, flowing from modernization, stimulated new responses by Yearly Meeting.

By late in the century Brethren debated new issues, such as dress, evangelism, and education, that stemmed from increased contact with the larger society and led to schism. Like all Americans, the entire Brethren denomination, not just the fellowships in Philadelphia and Germantown, felt the encroachment of modernization.[23]

IV

The consequences of change for early America and the Brethren suggests that recent trends may have had a similarly significant impact, especially in the vital area of nonconformity. Education, for example, is critical in determining American religious behavior; those who are better educated tend to be less religious. Has the increased availability of education weakened walls that once separated Brethren from the larger society? Did the agricultural revolution, which made labor intensive farming obsolete, force Brethren from the isolation of rural farms and expose them to the allurements of assimilation that tempted their brothers and sisters in colonial Germantown? To what extent did the transportation and communication revolutions further stretch the bonds that bound Brethren communities? Is it more difficult for a small communion to maintain itself in an environment of high spatial mobility? How has the modern nation state touched the Brethren? Did the civil rights crusade and the peace movement entice Brethren into mainstream Protestantism, or did all those Pennsylvania Brethren who faithfully voted Republican in the 1950s find the conformist, Judeo-Christian civil religion of that period more convincing than liberal activism? Did William Sloan Coffin or Dwight David Eisenhower do more to destroy denominational loyalty among the Brethren?

In addition to external pressures, internal decisions must have shaped the denomination's recent trends. Did the great ecumenists of the mid-twentieth century lead us into the valley of the shadow of mainstream Protestantism? Or are their successors a bungling generation, a cohort of quibblers dissolving into self-destructive factions?

Sometimes it's easier to know where we are going if we know where we have been. Modernization, which created anxiety for many Americans in the previous century and made nonconformity more difficult for the Brethren, has now engulfed society. We need, then, to study what happened to the Church of the Brethren as it moved from an urban village to an urban society.

[1] Stephanie Grauman Wolf, Urban Village: Population, Community, and Family Structure in Germantown, Pennsylvania, 1686-1800 (Princeton, N.J.: Princeton University Press, 1976), 327-37.

[2] Wolf believes that the Mennonite experience in Germantown was similar to the Brethren. See ibid., 151-3.

[3] S. R. Zug, History of the Church of the Brethren of the Eastern District of Pennsylvania (Lancaster, Pa.: Church of the Brethren Eastern District of Pennsylvania, 1915), 103-4.

[4] Stump's quotation is in Elmer Q. Gleim, From These Roots: A History of the North Atlantic District (Lancaster, Pa.: Atlantic Northeast District Historical Committee, Church of the Brethren, 1975), 113.

[5] Council Minutes, October 15, 1888, in Roger E. Sappington, The Brethren in Industrial America (Elgin, Il.: The Brethren Press), 25.

[6] Moomaw is quoted in Carl F. Bowman's forthcoming history of the Brethren which The Johns Hopkins University Press will publish. Professor Bowman graciously allowed me to preview a draft of the manuscript.

[7] Roland L. Howe, The History of a Church (Dunker) with Comments Featuring the First Church of the Brethren of Philadelphia, Pa., 1813-1943 (Philadelphia, Pa.: published privately, 1943), 53, 57; and Sappington, The Brethren in the New Nation: A Source Book on the Development of the Church of the Brethren, 1785-1865 (Elgin, Il.: The Brethren Press, 1976), 234.

[8] Minutes of the Annual Meetings of the Church of the Brethren: Containing All Available Minutes from 1778 to 1909 (Elgin, Il.: Brethren Publishing House, 1909), 277.

[9] Ibid., 341-3.

[10] In 1877 Conference created several committees to investigate problems but did not include the specific complaints in its minutes; see Minutes, 355-6; and Sappington, Brethren in Industrial America, 235.

[11] District Meeting Minutes, May 11, 1887, quoted in Howe, History of a Church, 490.

[12] Nathan O. Hatch, The Democratization of American Christianity (New Haven, Connecticut: Yale University Press, 1989), 117-120; and R. Laurence Moore, Religious Outsiders and the Making of Americans (New York: Oxford University Press, 1986), 32-37.

[13] Moore, Outsiders in American Religion, 164-69.

[14] Asbury is quoted in Hatch, Democratization of American Christianity, 85.

[15] Samuel Goodrich's description of Dow appears in Hatch, Democratization of American Christianity, 20.

[16] Ibid., 20.

[17] Jack D. Marietta, The Reformation of American Quakerism, 1748-1783 (Philadelphia: University of Pennsylvania Press, 1984), 55, 104-5, 107-8, 110-28.

[18] Other fellowships that illustrate the importance of nonconformity are orthodox Jews, immigrant Catholics, several African American denominations, and the Pennsylvania German Anabaptists. Laurence Moore discusses all of these except the German traditions.

[19] Merrit Roe Smith, Harpers Ferry Armory and the New Technology: The Challenge of Change (Ithaca, N.Y. and London: Cornell University Press, 1977), 256, 270-4.

[20] Ronald G. Walters, American Reformers, 1815-1860 (New York: Hill and Wang, 1976), 3-13, 75, 120, 147-50, 156-63, 171.

[21] Leonard L. Richards, "Gentlemen of Property and Standing": Anti-Abolition Mobs in Jacksonian America (New York: Oxford University Press, 1970), 131-55.

[22] Mendy Howard, a student aide at Bridgewater College, tabulated Yearly Meeting queries between 1775 and 1840; see <u>Minutes</u>. For a tally of queries in the remainder of the century see Carl F. Bowman, <u>Beyond Plainness: Cultural Transformation in the Church of the Brethren from 1850 to the Present</u> (diss.: University of Virginia, 1989), 181; and Sappington, <u>Brethren in the New Nation</u>, 286.

[23] Bowman's manuscript describes in rich detail the attempts of the nineteenth-century denomination to define separation and preserve nonconformity. See also his dissertation, <u>Beyond Plainness</u>; and Sappington, <u>Brethren in the New Nation</u>, 286.

2

The Therapeutic Transformation of Brethren Tradition

by Carl Bowman

Based on careful research into Brethren change, Carl Bowman describes the visions of the church and discipleship held by the founders of the denomination and compares them with the views held in the late twentieth century. Rejecting the idea that Brethren should revive outdated practices, he nevertheless shows how far we have departed from the beliefs and practices which early Brethren believed were at the heart of the faith. He shocks us into the discovery that in their zeal to reshape the denomination into a contemporary mold, the Brethren have reinterpreted and transformed—sometimes in major and disturbing ways—the fundamental beliefs of the founders. He reveals that this distortion of the Brethren heritage allows us today to comfortably accommodate our beliefs to the prevailing cultural themes of individualism, religion as therapy, moral relativism, permissiveness, and an attitude of ultra-openness. While the old order had its dark side, he suggests the same is true for the new order. Only in critically examining both our history and our contemporary situation—the old and the new—may Brethren find their way in faithfulness into the new century.

About 1930, Rufus D. Bowman, General Secretary of the Board of Christian Education penned an old-style Brethren tract that posed the vexing question, "What are those precious things in our heritage which are worth conserving?"[1] True to the modernist spirit of the age, elder Bowman supplied a definite answer. The Church of the Brethren was founded upon three unalterable principles: the New Testament as its rule of faith and practice; the ordinances as a means of grace; and no exercise of force in religion. Total commitment to the New Testament required the rejection of all human creeds and abstract theologies. Brethren could have no theology, Bowman explained, other than that of truth seekers striving for unfettered knowledge of Biblical truth. Their principle of "no force in religion" required a posture of "tolerance toward those of differing convictions," and granted every member the freedom to follow his or her own conscience in matters of faith. Even though Bowman acknowledged that Brethren had sometimes departed from these ideals, he was convinced they were finally returning to the tolerant spirit of Alexander Mack and the founders.

A half century later, S. Loren Bowman wrote that "getting away from authority" was a goal of the early Brethren. They were "disgusted" with the abuses of power in the churches of their day and sought to establish "an intimate, direct, personal faith relationship to Christ, based upon free adult choice." Toward this end, they founded a fellowship where decisions were made by consensus and each respected the "freedom of conscience of another, with no coercion in matters of faith."[2] But this vision was dashed by internal dissent and the difficulties of transplantation to the new world, causing Brethren to retreat from diversity's "promise of enrichment" toward conformity's promise of security.[3]

Today, the official Brethren periodical, *Messenger*, ritually reprints the morally correct confession that, "To hold in respect and fellowship those in the church with whom we agree or disagree is a characteristic of the Church of the Brethren." Month after month, *Messenger's* pages bear witness to church openness by heralding the good news that Brethren are noncreedal truth-seekers. In a 1991 issue, for example, Paul Keller proclaimed that a sense of finality, of having arrived at the truth, "is a state of mind the early Brethren were determined to avoid." They were "dissenters from certainty,"[4] and those who succumb to certainty's seduction violate the founding spirit. The Church of the Brethren, Keller points out, "stands as a living reminder that there can be commitment without domination" and "conviction without dogma." In fact, one of our unique contributions as a denomination is in the area of noncreedal-ism—Brethren long ago realized that "written authority can be injurious to your mental and spiritual health."[5]

In sum, the overriding message is that *the ancient Brethren were precociously modern.* Tolerance of individual variation, openness to change and a commitment to democracy formed the core of the historic legacy. Noncreedalism, freedom of conscience and "no force" in religion were founding tenets of the faith. What a wonderfully comforting fantasy! If the real ancient Brethren ever had nightmares, these specters of progressive openness, celebrated diversity, and unfettered individualism must have been the haunts. It is absolutely amazing what the spiritual heirs of Alexander Mack's Schwarzenau Brethren can do (and tolerate) in his name.

The Brethren Vision

Those who peer beneath such gilded sheens to examine the true historical record are sometimes surprised at what they find. To begin with, Mack did not write a pamphlet called *"Rites* and Ordinances" as many believe. Donald Durnbaugh pointed out years ago that the German word *rechte* in Mack's

Rechte und Ordnungen actually has the English meaning of laws, rights or statutes, not rites. When challenged by Pietists to justify the organization of the Brethren movement, Mack did not throw up his hands and invoke the gospel of noncreedalism. Rather he sat down with a pen and summarized Brethren convictions in a tract not so humbly entitled "the laws and orders of the house of God, as commanded by Jesus, and recorded in his last Will and Testament." He began by admonishing the reader . . .

> [W]e see how strictly God commanded his people to observe the laws which he had made known by his servant Moses. So we may very readily believe, that God will be still more strict to have observed all that he has in these latter times revealed to all the world by his beloved Son.[6]

Years later, Alexander Mack, Jr., referred to the pamphlet as being issued not by his father, but by the church at Schwarzenau, to instruct those who were seeking after truth. It was reissued by the colonial church during the 1770s to provide "a statement of truth" for instructing young people. While the pamphlet never became an official creed, it was studied intensely and accepted as an explicit account of the Brethren faith.

In 1778, the earliest recorded Annual Meeting minute proclaimed that ministers who had taken the attest (oath of allegiance to the U.S. government) would be disowned unless they confessed their error, and that ordinary members who had done likewise would be set back from the Holy Kiss, from church council, and from communion until they repented. Brethren, the ruling stated, were to obey "the Spirit of Truth, which teaches we shall not touch the unclean thing, nor be unequally yoked together with unbelievers."[7] This is not an isolated example of Dunker resolve. From the beginning members were expected to follow the decisions of church council. By the end of the eighteenth century, they were especially expected to heed the Annual Meeting, the united council of the entire church, whose rulings were seen as descending from the line of apostolic decisions recorded in scripture. Annual Meeting's exacting "mandatory decision" of the 1880s, sometimes portrayed as a creedal aberration, simply sharpened the earlier Brethren precedent that those who disobeyed Annual Meeting should be barred from communion until they "do better and become obedient."[8]

But if the Brethren vision was not a progressive one of openness and inclusiveness, what was it? An *old* vision, or as Mack put it, the Brethren embraced "no new church, nor any new laws; but in simplicity and true faith . . . desire[d] to remain with the old church which Christ instituted through his blood, and to follow the commandment which was from the beginning."[9] This ideal of restoring pure, primitive Christianity led Brethren to seek: a childlike faith and love for Christ; obedience to New Testament commands, large and small; oneness of faith and practice; and separation from the sinful ways of Christian pretenders. I have argued elsewhere that these four tenets—*childlike faith, obedience, unity* and *separation*—were the core commitments of the Brethren faith, guiding it in a relatively continuous fashion from the church's founding until the end of the nineteenth century.[10]   To pretend that there was no variation in application of these commitments during the church's first two centuries would be folly.   To argue that there was consistency of commitment, on the other hand, is true to the historical record. These four themes permeated Mack's original writings.

Childlike faith—A childlike faith was the spiritual wellspring from which the Brethren movement flowed.   It was their deeply pietistic faith that led Brethren to strive for obedience, unity, and separation in the first place. Their uncritical devotion pervades eighteenth-century Brethren hymnody, poetry, and historical records.   Mack counseled his brothers and sisters that all their "sighs and desires" should be for this,

> to love thy God, who created thee, and Jesus Christ, who redeemed thee with his precious blood, with all thy heart, with all thy soul, and with all thy mind, yea above all things in the world, whether they be beauty, or riches, or whatever may come in sight or hearing.   And in this love, fear God with a *childlike heart*, contemplate all his commandments day and night; keep them with a pure heart, let them be thy counsellors, and pray continually for the Holy Spirit, who will guide thee into all the commandments of God, and into all truth.[11]

This passage and many like it reveal that the early Brethren, in adopting Anabaptist doctrines and church organization, did not forsake the fervent spirituality that was their motivating force.

Obedience—"[T]o the unbeliever," Mack said, "nothing seems to be commanded,"[12] yet genuine regeneration is "nothing else but real and genuine obedience towards God and all his commandments."[13]   Anyone who resists in only one thing will be "justly punished for his disobedience."[14]   By its fruit, Mack reminded Brethren, ye shall know the tree.[15]   As Brethren admonished and disciplined one another in their struggle to remain obedient, they remained mindful that correction had to be offered in a spirit of Christian love.   As Alexander Mack, Jr. so eloquently put it, "dear brethren, let us . . . be careful, and above all preserve love for then we will preserve light.[16]   Yet Brethren understood that such a love could not ignore sin any more than God would ignore it; to do so would be not only hypocritical, but dangerous.   The posture that "I will maintain my own opinions, and you can maintain yours, and we will love one another and be brethren," though merciful in appearance, showed a total disregard for Christ's commands.   "[W]e have but too long stood in such a . . . love," Mack confessed, "while we were yet among the Pietists."   In leaving them, the Brethren had learned a love that reproved evil, and yielded an exacting obedience to the rules of God's House[17]—they had abandoned that species of "free love" that covered all and condemned none.[18]

Christian unity—Many "free-loving" Christians believed there was no need to obey the letter of the scripture.   Such persons, Mack observed, were so confused that no two of them could agree regarding doctrine or the beginning of a Christian life.   "[W]hat a curious spirit that must be," he mused, that would "write such different laws into the hearts of men."[19]   Among true Christians, on the other hand, "no disorder or false liberty exists, but it is all order and union."[20] All who possess the one true faith "are also all of one mind as to the rules and practice of faith."[21] Brethren drew a clear distinction between the Spirit of Christ and the Spirit of Error. All who possessed the former were united by one faith, one baptism, and one Spirit, for it was God's will "that his own should all be one, even as the Father and the Son are one." The spirit of error, on the other hand, separated people from God's law and divided them into a multitude of separate opinions.[22]

Separation—Implicit in the Brethren emphasis upon unified obedience was the idea of separation from sin. Whoever wished to partake of the Lord's supper in a worthy manner had to be "separated from the body of Satan, the world, from all unrighteousness, and from all false sects and religions . . . ."[23] Scripture commanded Brethren to exclude from communion "all sinful, offensive and self-loving spirits,"[24] for *he that eateth and drinketh unworthily, eateth and drinketh damnation to himself, not discerning the Lord's body (I Cor. II: 28,29).* Anyone who displayed an independent spirit or caused division was to be placed under avoidance until they yielded to the church. In fact, excommunication was one of the first sub-headings in <u>Rechte und Ordnungen</u>.[25] No true church, Mack proclaimed, could exist without it. Public confession usually sufficed to restore transgressors, but when they remained unrepentant, offenders were either set back from communion or disowned. This was done "not on account of their sin, but for their pride and obstinacy; because they reject the counsel of God's Spirit."[26] Failure to discipline wayward members was believed to reflect a lack of concern for their eternal salvation.[27] The church was to remain a faithful bride, untainted by the sins of the world, awaiting the return of the Bridegroom.

Matthew 18—If one had to pick the single most influential scripture governing Brethren church life from their emergence right up until the 1930s, it would be Matthew 18:15-22. Alexander Mack, Jr. wrote that it was Matthew 18's directive to confront a brother about his faults that had produced misgivings among some Radical Pietists. Their total rejection of formal church structure had left them no recourse—nowhere to go—if an offender refused to hear an admonition. For this reason some returned to the established churches, sensing too much liberty among the Pietists, while others looked to the primitive church for their model of church governance.[28] The Brethren solution was the latter—to reject both excessive liberty and the established order in favor of a "primitive" order. Matthew 18 instructed them to exercise their apostolic authority to *bind and loose*.[29] They had been entrusted with the keys to the Kingdom (Matthew 16:19), and were charged to *prove all things; hold fast that which is good; and abstain from all appearance of evil* (1 Thes 5:21-22). Both the church and heaven, Brethren believed, would be tarnished if they took this responsibility lightly. After all, the divine authority to judge the saints had been bestowed by Christ and confirmed by His apostles—"*Do you not know that we shall judge angels? How much more things that pertain to this life?"* (1 Cor 6:3). From the 1730s until about the 1930s, applicants could not join the church unless they accepted Matthew 18's order of church governance.[30] If they would not labor for righteousness by correcting others and allowing themselves to be corrected, they would "be dealt with accordingly." Nothing more needed to be said.

This brief review reminds us that the historic Brethren vision—not only during the nineteenth century, but from the outset—was *not* the vision of noncreedalism, no force in religion, and freedom of conscience that is popularly portrayed. Direct individual interpretation of scripture may have been characteristic of mainstream Protestantism, but not of dissenters like the Brethren who were community-based in both their hermeneutic and ecclesiology. Behavioral standards and constraints were much more exacting among groups influenced by radical Pietism and/or Anabaptism (like the Brethren, Mennonites and Amish) than among more established Protestant communions. Christopher Sauer, Sr., once wrote that the first generation of Brethren erected a fence around themselves by admitting and expelling, conducting themselves less honorably than even the Mennonites.[31]

The Reconstruction of Tradition

If faith, unity, obedience and separation were central to historic Brethrenism, what are the *rechte und ordnung* of contemporary Brethrenism? What are today's rights, obligations and commitments?

Christian unity is still a powerful symbol, but its meaning has been literally turned inside-out. When Christ prayed, as recorded in the gospel of John (17:21), that *they all may be one*, the ancient Brethren believed that *they* referred to the Brethren, and that *one* meant alike. Most contemporary Brethren, on the other hand, see *they* referring to the church universal and *one* referring to harmony and coordination among denominations. Unity used to be the rationale for defining and enforcing the Dunker order. Now it is the motive for opening church membership and communion to those from other denominations, and for shattering restrictions and rulings that make some feel secondary or unwelcome. Unity as harmony and acceptance has displaced unity as singleness and sameness—all are now welcome at the Lord's table.

When the District of Nebraska requested the formation of a Church Unity Commission in 1929, it was unity with other Christians, not just Brethren, that they had come to have in mind. Conference responded by reminding the Nebraska Brethren that "the most precious and practically vital part of Christian unity" was that which existed "within the denomination itself," for this was the basis of true spiritual unity with God.[32] Although no Unity Commission was authorized, unity's domain was already being questioned. By the 1950s, its meaning had been inverted, with Annual Conference endorsing the Dunker heresy that *all* Christians belonged to one, invisible church.[33]

Groups that used to be written off as "popular" or "nominal" Christians were referred to as "fellow Christians."[34] The Love Feast was described by Annual Conference as a "Christian family rite."[35] The Church of the Brethren put itself on record as building an "ecumenical fellowship" following the will of Christ.[36] The same symbol of "Christian unity" that had once bound Brethren to ideals of sameness, exclusivity, purity, and preservation now opened their hearts to the end "of exclusive religion," of the era when "Brethren as the peculiar people, possess either a preferential or an exclusive gospel."[37] By 1960, some were decrying denominationalism as the ultimate sin, separation from the world as mental illness, and the idea of conversion to distinctive Brethren doctrines as a prideful perversion of the Gospel.[38] The 1958 paper on church extension took the landmark step of dropping the rebaptism requirement and accepting Sunday morning Eucharist, all in the name of unity. The very idea that unity once could have served as a rationale for "strict" standards and disownings seemed beyond all comprehension.

To the extent that <u>no force in religion</u> was invoked by the early Brethren, it had to do with *limitations upon the state's authority* vis-a-vis the church. Governments should neither compel citizens to join a church, nor prevent them from joining the church of their choice. Religious commitment could not be forced, but had to spring from faith. If citizens were not at liberty to follow their own consciences with respect to membership, churches would be populated by the uncommitted, making a mockery of Christianity. Following in the footsteps of Anabaptists and Radical Pietists, the Brethren championed <u>freedom of individual conscience</u>—only true believers who had counted the cost and were willing to yield their self-will should take up the yoke of church membership. "No force" and "freedom of conscience" also implied that the church should follow its own path in matters of faith, even when it violated worldly standards.

What "no force" did *not* imply was that the church should refrain from disciplining its members. Neither did freedom of conscience imply that members were free to interpret and apply Christ's commands according to the whims of personal opinion. Whenever individual discernment openly contradicted scripture or violated the collective discernments of council, it was considered to be inspired by something other than the Holy Spirit, and it was the church's responsibility to correct it. As the President of Bethany Seminary wrote in 1945, the rightness or wrongness of an act for the early Brethren "did not depend upon the individual's conscience but upon God's Word as revealed in the New Testament. . . . The statements which we so often hear today, 'Let your conscience be your guide,' 'Follow your conscience,' are not in harmony with our Brethren heritage."[39] The ancient Brethren prayed as a body for "conscience toward God" to do what was right, understanding that this placed constraints upon the individual. While there was freedom in some matters, there was no freedom to violate basic doctrine and practice.

But as was true of "unity," these traditional symbols were transformed. Twentieth-century Brethren have converted rehabilitated versions of "no force in religion" and "freedom of conscience" into banner motifs of contemporary Brethren culture. A key figure in the reconstruction of "no force in religion" was Martin Grove Brumbaugh. His 1908 proclamation that the founding doctrine of "no force in religion" meant it was wrong to force "anyone to join *or to leave the church of Christ*"[40] cast a dark shadow over the church trials and disciplinary measures that were still common at the time. Like others who were fighting against Dunker distinctiveness, Brumbaugh argued that disownings, etc., were departures from the founding spirit. Never mind the fact that Mack himself had insisted upon the necessity of excommunication, Brumbaugh's message was that twentieth-century Brethren who practiced the same were adopting the very force tactics that early Brethren had struggled to overcome. The crux of Brumbaugh's history lesson was that Christian persuasion and toleration should be the church's guiding moral precepts.[41]

Similar messages carried by other influential and educated messengers (such as J. S. Flory's portrait of an early Brethren enlightenment and D. W. Kurtz's campaign for Brethren democracy) contributed to the twentieth-century rejection of Dunker distinctives and the waning of traditional concepts of church authority and discipline. The logical culmination of their joint trumpeting of "no force" and "freedom of conscience" was reached in the 1948 peace position, heralded by many as the strongest peace stand in the church's history. But first a little historical background.

Since the eighteenth century, Brethren had insisted that no member should engage in armed conflict. Baptismal applicants were consistently required to affirm this position (known as defenselessness or nonresistance) before being received as members. The insistence on doctrinal conformity was so taken-for-granted that membership certificates issued during World War I for military exemption purposes could state unequivocally, "'Not to go to war, nor to learn the art of war,' has been one of the conditions of membership of the Church of the Brethren from its beginning." In 1935 the church extended its peace witness by proclaiming "that all war is sin; that it is wrong for Christians to support or to engage in it; and that war is incompatible with the spirit, example and teachings of Jesus." The statement again reminded Brethren that it has been "the practice of the church through the years to require of applicants for membership a pledge not to engage in war nor learn the art of war."[42] No mention was made of any freedom of conscience to depart from this pledge.

Yet it was only three years later that the church declared its willingness to deal leniently with those who performed military service, even though it continued to insist that they were "not in full accord with the faith and practice of the general brotherhood."[43] In spite of the newfound tolerance, Conference still declared unequivocally in 1939 that "Brethren cannot fight and kill. . . . The church has the right and authority to declare her position on war and *her members are under obligation* to buttress such declarations with a peace mind, demonstrated in service.[44] So in 1940 there remained an air of uncertainty as to where servicemen stood. They could remain members but were somehow out of "full accord" with the church. In spite of the official stance, no less than eighty percent of Brethren draftees rendered full, combatant military service during World War II, with only 8.5 percent rejecting military service altogether.[45] The incongruity between the official position and the reality of mass military participation was worked through in the 1948 peace statement which reiterated the position that all war is sin, while relaxing behavioral expectations for members, based upon a liberal reinterpretation of "freedom of conscience."

Just as Brumbaugh and other progressives had reconstructed "no force in religion" a couple of decades earlier, the 1948 peace statement remodeled Brethren understandings of freedom of conscience by declaring that the *"church itself respects the right of individual conscience within its membership and has never set up an authoritative creed."* Carrying this logic to its natural conclusion, the paper asserted: "Inasmuch as the church believes in the right of individual conscience, it recognizes that various positions on war and military service will be taken by its members." And whether their convictions led them into military service or alternative service, the church pledged to "maintain a fellowship of all who sincerely follow the guidance of conscience," offering them spiritual nurture, a fellowship of prayer, and material aid. While the statement identified rejection of military service as the "consistent" and recommended option, it no longer claimed that members were obliged to choose it, and no longer spoke of those who rendered military service as being in less than full accord with the church.[46] Indeed, the assertion that Brethren had "never set up an authoritative creed" misleadingly suggested that the church had always granted freedom of conscience on such matters, while the opposite was in fact the case.

By the 1960s, reworked versions of old symbols had become the bellwethers of contemporary Brethren culture. Symbols that once proclaimed the separation of church from state and the limitations of *state authority* over matters of conscience (no-force-in-religion and freedom-of-conscience), now proclaimed the moral autonomy of individuals and limited *church authority* over individual conscience. Symbols, meanwhile, that once condemned differences *within* the church (Christian unity), now softened differences *between* Christian communions. Other symbols were subtly modified in support of the new moral code. "No creed but the New Testament," for example, was translated in the minds of many Brethren into noncreedalism, period. Continuity at the level of cultural symbols preserved the appearance of loyalty to Brethren tradition, even in the presence of radical normative realignment. The symbolic shells were sustained while their moral content was purged; new Brethren "wine," so to speak, was poured into old Dunker "wineskins." Ironically, traditional symbols became instruments of change. The metamorphosis has been so complete that newcomers today raise their eyebrows in puzzlement at the very mention of a bygone "Brethren's order." Younger generations are perplexed at the thought that the "noncreedal/no-force/freedom-of-conscience" Church of the Brethren could have once "dictatorially imposed" peculiar customs upon its members.

The New Order

What has been the final product? A forward-looking, radically open, and inclusive Church of the Brethren. A church that strives to meet human needs by enabling, accepting, healing, nurturing, empowering, fostering friendship, and calling all to equal participation. A church that is skeptical of authority and hierarchy for fear that it will trample the conscientious spiritual quest of its members. A church that has overcome the alleged "dark side" of its past, the side that called for sameness, obedience, and self-denial; that "trampled" individual rights in favor of exacting standards; that defined the church as a community of saints responsible for correcting and disciplining its members; and that separated from the world and saw the inclusive embrace of the mainline as fundamentally unchristian. This dark side is amazingly absent from contemporary Brethren dialogue and rapidly fading from collective memory. Intolerance, exclusivity, uniformity, narrowness, and stagnation have become the mortal sins of new order Brethrenism. Judgement and separation are dirty words. Obedience and discipline have been warmly repackaged as commitment and discipleship, which are bathed in even warmer images of reconciliation, openness, love, acceptance, and spiritual growth. Redemption is preached more than regeneration, and grace more than duty or obligation. Today's Brethren do not consider themselves saints, and they suspect anyone who does. They are too modest to see themselves as being closer to perfection than other Christians, and too independent to humble themselves before church authority. How can anyone presume to judge when, as Annual Conference recently put it, all views "are limited and change with our own experiences," when no one has "captured the kingdom?"[47]

In order to demonstrate their inclusiveness, new order Brethren revel in symbolic variation. Would you like beef, or cheese & crackers at Love Feast? Organ, guitar, or handbells during church? Baptism or affirmation of faith as a path into the church? Should a man, a woman, a mainliner, a BRFer,[48] a black, or a Hispanic be elected as Moderator—or should there be some kind of rotation? Should God be referred to as He or She? By breaking down old boundaries, attitudes, and prejudices, the church strives toward the inclusion of all. By providing symbolic variation—some image or motif for each to identify with—it finds "unity in diversity" and challenges all to grow into deeper and richer understandings of the faith.

Excommunication for unrepentant sin, a basic tenet from 1708 up until the early twentieth century, is an unthinkable defilement of new order Brethrenism. What is more, the words "counseling" and "discipline" have been purged from Brethren manuals of organization, for *discipline* communicates "negative, unloving, and punitive overtones," and *counseling* implies "pressuring" and "advice giving" rather than assuming the role of responsive listener. Since 1976, they have been replaced by the more congenial and positive words *discipleship* and *reconciliation*.[49] Even Matthew 18:17, the historic basis for church discipline, has been reinterpreted as calling for "openness" and "unending compassion."[50]

The cardinal virtues of New Order Brethrenism are openness, inclusiveness, diversity, and dialogue, grounded in reconstructed versions of unity, no-force-in-religion, freedom-of-conscience, and noncreedalism. These excerpts from recent speeches, articles and Annual Conference statements illuminate the tone of the new moral order.

- What we need is a heavy dose of inspiration—a luminous view of how the New Testament can energize our lives. What we do not need is more "certainty." That, by definition, is a sure route to irreconcilable conflict.[51]

- Individuality requires freedom. Respect for freedom is seen in our traditional Brethren belief in "no force in religion," and so we avoid patterns of enforcement which violate the freedom of individuals and local groups.[52]

- [D]iversity is God's pattern in creation. God's delight in variety is expressed in countless ways. . . . It is the way of the world to try to force individuals into a uniform mold.[53] [L]et us celebrate the diversity and complexity of the challenges we face. Let us focus on the healing process. Let us praise God for the healing that does occur.[54]

- Divorce as a tragedy is not to be judged. . . . Congregations are encouraged to discover ways in which the church can support, sustain, and redeem the brokenness of the people involved.[55]

- "An inclusive attitude is key," says Marianne, who cringes at the terms "family" Bible camp and "family" Memorial Day camp. By the word choice, some people [singles] are set aside.[56]

- I have become a Church of the Brethren member because the Church of the Brethren has no creed. . . . I do not look for the Church of the Brethren to come up with a definitive statement . . . on which we then decide who is in and who is out—who belongs and who doesn't. . . . I prefer a framework that can be inclusive, and that can be changed on one matter at a time, from year to year.[57]

- I've always kept my mouth shut when any group says the Creed. . . and that's what I committed myself to seventy years ago when I was baptized [as a Brethren]. . . . No one's gonna tell me what I have to believe.[58]

Generations of twentieth-century Brethren have fought the good fight against control, exclusion, and sharp definition. Much has been gained;

Brethren *are* more open, inclusive, and free than the Dunkers of old. Healing *has* occurred. People *are* being nurtured. But as the twenty-first century dawns, are Brethren open enough to see a dark side to the new order (just as they found a dark side to the old)? Does a dark cloud drift ominously behind the silver lining?

Therapeutic Culture

Consider for a moment American life in general. There has been a chorus of criticism in recent years of its excessive individualism and me-centeredness, and its general lack of purpose and commitment. Both society at large and the churches more specifically have been the targets of such criticism. Americans, we are told, are driven by expressive individualism (the pursuit of personal satisfaction) and utilitarian individualism (the pursuit of personal gain), and have refashioned religion to service their personal needs.[59] They have a hard time grasping a vision of anything larger than themselves, that calls them out of themselves and obligates them to engage in activities that might not feel good, but move them toward a sacred goal. Ethics have been individualized and contextualized to the point that no one is sure what is bad, or if they are, they can not apply it to concrete situations.

Robert Bellah and colleagues, well-known proponents of this critique, argue that Americans are genuinely concerned about values, but cannot say what those values *are* or how they should be applied. Americans are sensitive towards another's feelings but ambivalent about the substance of their beliefs and actions. They care more about the quality of a dialogue than about its contents or consequences. What matters most is that everyone listen and have an open chance to participate. All of this, we are told, yields a *quasi-therapeutic blandness* in American mainline religion. At worst, it deteriorates into Sheilaism: each person constructs his or her own religion, tolerates everyone else's, and the Bible becomes one more resource to draw upon in the process.

Some commentators, such as Kenneth Gergen, actually celebrate Bellah's nightmare of infinite moral openness. Gergen suggests that the very idea of pivotal conflicts between good and evil may one day dissolve upon a lush plain of unbounded tolerance and integration of perspectives. In such a world "warfare becomes a nonsensical proposition."[60] There would be nothing left worth killing for. I don't know about you, but I find this scenario of ultimate indifference unnerving.

In a widely read critique of contemporary faith, Philip Rieff charges that the triumph of the therapeutic in American culture has leveled vertical authority, snapping "every rung of the old ladder languages of faith."[61] In the name of acceptance and healing we have lost sight of virtue and smashed all sacred barriers. What were once unchallenged evils have become platforms for rituals of liberation. According to Rieff, modernists (being non-judgmental) tolerate no revealed, eternal or commanding truths, but have become actor-managers, prepared to select from a broad repertoire whichever beliefs and values are best adapted to the situation at hand. More cynically stated, *the modern therapeutic outlook has no true Gods, but it knows the value of a good god-term when it sees one, and "will use all so long as none are true."*[62]

While traditional American culture was a *culture of restraint* that demanded sacrifice and united people by means of shared convictions, contemporary culture is a *culture of release* that celebrates personal liberation. Its governing symbols are *anti*creedal, of infinite plasticity and absorptive capacity. Abandoning the ideal of victory for the correct commitment, modern therapeutic culture seeks a way of using and integrating all commitments. It transforms what were once merely means—dialogue, openness, searching, etc.—into ultimate ends. The expansion of possibilities replaces the limitation of possibilities as the design of salvation. The longing to be saved is supplanted by the longing to be comforted. "I believe," the cry of the ancient ascetic, is drowned out by "I feel," the cry of the contemporary therapeutic. We can finally live free at last, says Rieff, enjoying all of our senses except that of the past.

Is there substance to this critique? Have we really, as Rieff suggests, become liberated to the point where we live out our lives in a technological Eden—as unremembering, honest, and friendly barbarians? Do therapeutic symbols point to a land where the only remaining truths are the freedom to live unencumbered lives and the assurance that grace will save us? When we enter this land of boundless liberty, will we find that no bright light exists but only a night that we never really sought?[63] This is the nightmare that haunts the new moral order.

The Dark Side of the New Order

Most new order Brethren have either heard or themselves recited the sins of their Dunker forbears: they were legalistic and rigid; too focused upon externals and too confining in their treatment of individuals; they were narrow and exclusive in many of their practices. Most are also convinced that the old order of sameness and separation is inapplicable to the modern age. During the last seventy-five years, much energy and initiative have been devoted to overcoming it. The church has matured, achieving a level of Christian witness and outreach that far surpasses the achievements of the ancient order. Most Brethren, even those who look upon bygone days with nostalgia, believe this to be true. But is there also a seamy side to openness and inclusiveness?

The works of Rieff, Bellah, Lasch, Gergen, and others suggest a series of cultural conflicts on which all traditions must stake out a position. *How should today's Brethren work through the underlying tensions of tolerance versus truth, freedom versus constraint, and inclusiveness versus consensus?* If our ancestors erred on the side of unbending truths requiring self-denial and submission, do we err on the side of acceptance? If they were too quick to shut people out, are we too quick to get them in? One way of thinking about the difference between the old and new moral orders is that *they entail radically discrepant understandings of truth, authority, virtue, and community*, as represented in the following table.

OLD AND NEW MORAL UNDERSTANDINGS

Understanding of...	Traditional Moral Order	Contemporary Moral Order
Truth	Universal & permanent	Particular & variable
Authority	External - constraining, obligating, commanding, redeeming	Personalized - liberating, enabling, healing, nurturing, satisfying
Response to Authority	Obedience, self-denial, humility, being called-out from the world	Gratitude, growth, empowerment, conscientious decision-making
Virtue	Purity emphasis - conformity to right practices and doctrines, avoidance of sin	Process emphasis - openness, honesty, support, and tolerance in dialogue and relationships
Community	Exclusive - based upon shared, binding commitments	Inclusive - based upon mutual support and acceptance

To consider the Brethren case in light of the generalized critique of contemporary culture raises some nagging concerns. It suggests that "Christian unity" and "noncreedalism," as broadly interpreted by new order Brethren, can easily deteriorate into moral indifference and relativism. "Freedom-of-conscience" and "no-force-in-religion" can degenerate into the individualization of authority—the substitution of personal choice for a sense of religious obligation. Perhaps the problem with our culture and also our church today is not one of excessive constraint or definition but of *a therapeutic preoccupation with healing and support that unwittingly undermines commitment to any truth or morality bigger than our own backyard.*

And the critics bring a great deal of evidence to bear upon their argument. Seven out of ten Americans believe there are few moral absolutes, that what is right or wrong usually varies from situation to situation. American junior and senior high school students typically say that the most believable authority in matters of truth is their own personal experience. When asked the most important criterion for choosing a career, the most common responses of American school children are to "make a lot of money" (30%), for "personal satisfaction" (27%), and for "fun and excitement" (16%). (Only ten percent say that "helping others" and eight percent that following "God's will" are most important.) Sixty-five percent of high school students admit they would cheat on an important exam.[64] Although one might hope that Brethren would stand apart on such matters, one of the principle findings of the 1985 Brethren Profile Study was that Brethren are very diverse and independent, and similar in many respects to the surrounding society. They are so independent, in fact, that only one out of every four Brethren believe their young members should be counseled against joining the armed forces. Only a third of the membership believe it is wrong to fight in any war. Less than four in ten support the idea that the Brethren community has a right to challenge the way they live. And as many as eight out of every ten Brethren agree that the correct position for persons to take on most moral issues is *whatever they decide upon* after careful soul-searching and reflection.[65] Have we embraced too fondly the contemporary moral order?

The progressive battle for personal and spiritual liberation that was waged for most of the twentieth century has been won. It is over. The chains of constraint are shattered and the shalt-nots have been vanquished. The battle of the next century is not one for greater liberation, but for definition, for a vision that sees beyond personal feelings and opinions. If yesterday's struggle was to transcend human creeds, perhaps today's is to transcend an *anticreed* of dogmatic openness—to transcend an exaggerated no-force, freedom-of-conscience, inclusively noncreedal morality that denies the very possibility of correct doctrine. If yesterday's battle was to overcome sectarianism and carry Christianity into the world, perhaps today's is to rediscover the lines separating Christ from culture and to excavate the non-mainline elements of the Brethren vision. Perhaps . . . perhaps.

If the critics of therapeutic culture have a point worth hearing, and if any of these "perhaps" are worth considering, then we can still learn from the ancient Brethren. They excelled in the very areas where we come up short: clarity, instruction, a sense of calling, and the articulation and defense of a shared understanding of the Christian faith, which was put into practice even when it called for a departure from comfortable convention. Was there something in the role of an unpaid elder; an annual visit; a specific set of membership criteria; a public confession; decision by consensus; an order of the Brethren; the virtues of self-denial, obedience, mutual admonition, nonconformity and nonresistance; or the simple rituals of kneeling for prayer, a kiss of charity, or an icy outdoor baptism from which we can learn today? Can they help us to transcend the dark side of New Order Brethrenism? "Oh," you may yawn, "another nostalgia buff who wants to return to the good old days of beards and backwoods Brethrenism." "No," I respond, "just one who views heritage as a rich deposit for mining visions of the future."

History can never be transposed like a song on the piano. It can, however, serve as an inspiration for crafting new melodies. Christopher Lasch recently wrote in The <u>True and Only Heaven</u> that progressives share an important trait with those who nostalgically seek a return to the past: both "find it difficult to believe that history still haunts our enlightened, disillusioned maturity."[66] Both oversimplify the past—progressives by writing it off as backward and ignorant, and nostalgics, by freezing the past into an idealized state of unchanging perfection. Neither, according to Lasch, engages in the positive exercise of memory. Memory, while it may also idealize the past, does not do so in order to condemn the present. *Seeing past, present and future as continuous, memory draws hope and vision from the past in order to enrich the present and face the future.*[67] Perhaps a humble willingness to reassess the dark side of new order Brethrenism and the bright side of the old order is a first step towards finding a future where faith—defying therapy—still requires us to count the cost.

[1] Rufus D. Bowman, Our Dunker Ideals (Brethren Publishing House, nd.), 2.

[2] S. Loren Bowman, Power and Polity Among the Brethren (Elgin: Brethren Press 1987), 19.

[3] S. Loren Bowman, 1987, 119-120.

[4] Messenger, April 1991: 27.

[5] Paul W. Keller, "Truths Not So Self-Evident," in Messenger (April 1991), 26-29.

[6] "Rights and Ordinances," in Brethren's Encyclopedia (Columbiana, Ohio: Henry Kurtz publisher, 1867), 17-18.

[7] Annual Meeting Minutes 1909, 5, (Annual Meeting of 1778).

[8] The binding nature of Annual Meeting decisions was reaffirmed in 1842 and again in 1850. The fact that decisions were binding does not imply that they could not be reconsidered.

[9] Alexander Mack, Rites and Ordinances (Ashland: Brethren Church, 1939), 91-92.

[10] Carl Bowman, "Beyond Plainness: Cultural Transformation in the Church of the Brethren from 1850 to the Present," Ph.D. dissertation, 1989, University of Virginia.

[11] Mack (1939), 69, italics added.

[12] Mack, (1939), 78-79.

[13] Mack, (1939), 88.

[14] Mack, (1939), 85.

[15] Mack, (1939), 78-79.

[16] Mack, Alexander, Jr., in Mack, (1939), 98.

[17] Mack, (1939), 91.

[18] Mack, (1939), 48-49.

[19] Mack, (1939), 55.

[20] Mack, (1939), 49.

[21] Mack, (1939), 50-51.

[22] Mack, (1939), 54.

[23] Mack, (1939), 32.

[24] Mack, (1939), 41.

[25] Mack, (1939), 40.

[26] Mack, (1939), 36-37.

[27] Mack, (1939), 48-49.

[28] "Rights and Ordinances," in Brethren's Encyclopedia (Columbiana: Henry Kurtz, Publisher, 1867), 22.

[29] Mack, (1939), 41.

[30] Dale R. Stoffer, "The Background and Development of Thought and Practice in the German Baptist Brethren (Dunker) and the Brethren (Progressive) Churches (c. 1650-1979)", Ph.D. Dissertation, Fuller Theological Seminary School of Theology, 1980, 291. Citing the Chronicon Ephratense (p. 244), Dale Stoffer reports that George Adam Martin persuaded Brethren in 1737 to adopt the Matthew 18 reading as a part of the baptismal service.

[31] From a letter printed in Donald F. Durnbaugh, ed., The Brethren in Colonial America (Elgin: The Brethren Press, 1967), 36.

[32] COB Full Report (1929, 94).

[33] (1965), 110.

[34] (1956), 150.

[35] COB Minutes (1956), 151.

[36] (1951), 84.

[37] (1965), 110.

[38] (COCU) on page 673.

[39] Rufus D. Bowman, Seventy Times Seven (Elgin: The Brethren Press, 1945), 130-131.

[40] Martin G. Brumbaugh, "The Conditions in Germany about 1708," in Two Centuries of the Church of the Brethren (Elgin: Brethren Publishing House, 1908), 21; italics added.

[41] Brumbaugh, (1908), 22-23.

[42] 1935 Annual Meeting Minutes in COB Minutes (1946), 110-111.

[43] 1938 Annual Meeting Minutes in COB Minutes (1946), 144-145.

[44] 1938 Annual Meeting Minutes in COB Minutes (1946), 147.

[45] Rufus D. Bowman, Seventy Times Seven , 38.

[46] 1948 Annual Meeting Minutes in COB Minutes (1956), 101-102. Italics added.

[47] 1979 Annual Conference Paper on "Biblical Inspiration and Authority," reprinted in Joan Deeter, A Study Guide (Elgin: Brethren Press, 1980), 30.

[48] Acronym for Brethren Revival Fellowship.

[49] See COB Minutes (1980), 200.

[50] COB Minutes (1980), 202; italics added.

[51] Paul W. Keller, "We don't need more 'certainty'," in Messenger (Vol. 140, No. 10, November, 1991), 26.

[52] 1979 Annual Conference paper on "Biblical Inspiration and Authority," reprinted in Joan Deeter, A Study Guide (Elgin: Brethren Press, 1980), 29-31.

[53] 1979 Annual Conference paper on "Biblical Inspiration and Authority," in Joan Deeter, A Study Guide (Elgin: Brethren Press, 1980), 29-31.

[54] Ibid., 7.

[55] 1977 decision on Marriage and Divorce, in COB Minutes (1980), 304-305.

[56] Rosalita J. Leonard, "Singled Out," in Messenger (Vol. 140, No. 6, June, 1991), 14.

[57] Excerpted from Karen Carter's statement during the business session of the 1991 Annual Conference regarding the query on "The Nature of the Church" (transcribed from a recording of the business session).

[58] Excerpted from E. Paul Weaver's statement during the business session of the 1991 Annual Conference regarding the query on "The Nature of the Church" (transcribed from a recording of the business session).

[59] Robert Bellah, et al., Habits of the Heart (Berkeley: Univ. of California Press, 1985).

[60] Kenneth J. Gergen, The Saturated Self: Dilemmas of Identity in Contemporary Life (New York: Basic Books, 1991), 254.

[61] Philip Rieff, The Triumph of the Therapeutic: Uses of Faith After Freud (Chicago: Univ. of Chicago Press, 1987 edition), ix.

[62] Rieff, (1987), xi.

[63] Philip Rieff, The Triumph of the Therapeutic. Many of the word images and contrasts in this and the preceding paragraph are taken directly from Rieff, although they have been paraphrased and recombined from various sections of his book.

[64] "Girl Scouts Survey on the Beliefs and Moral Values of America's Children," conducted by Louis Harris and Associates for Girl Scouts of the United States of America during the Fall of 1989, Robert Coles, Project Director.

[65] Carl Bowman, "The Brethren Profile Study," unpublished data collected in 1985.

[66] Christopher Lasch, <u>The True and Only Heaven</u> (New York: W. W. Norton & Co, 1991), 118.

[67] Ibid, 82-83.

3

Recent Developments Within the Church of the Brethren: Their Influence on the Future

by Allen C. Deeter

Focusing on the period from the 1950s, Allen Deeter selects five areas of change in the church which have been crucial in affecting the contemporary situation. His careful analysis of these changes and their effects reveals an understanding arising out of experience and careful observation. Events still fresh in memory are set in their larger context, and insights regarding consequences are shared. Several important lessons for Brethren may reside here including the down side of our generous ecumenical sharing of several unique service and outreach programs in the 1950s and 1960s, a sharing which certainly enriched Christendom but also weakened our own sense of ownership. In addition, Deeter comments on the weakening of denominational cohesion through growing factionalism, changes in the role of ministers, and the effects of demographic trends. He suggests that changes in Brethren identity appear to be especially crucial to our future. His comprehensive summary of events is a valuable source of insights to both contemporary scholars as well as church leaders.

In August 1960, a conference very similar to this one was held at Manchester College on the Nature and Function of the Church of the Brethren. As one reads the papers that were presented and later published in Brethren Life and Thought, one is struck by the quite different mood of the times and of the Brethren participants. Edward K. Ziegler, editor of Brethren Life and Thought, introduced the articles with an enthusiastic note of optimism: "The church is alive . . . . In the Church of the Brethren we have moved from isolationism, from smug pride, from complacency, to a new and more becoming humility. We are accepting responsibility and our small and lowly place in the whole church of Christ."

The period of 1958 to 1965 marked the high point in Church of the Brethren membership, slightly over 200,000. The period since 1965 has been one of more or less steady decline with a current membership of 150,000. The

Brethren live predominantly in rural areas and parts of the country where there has been less population growth. But the context of the thirty plus years suggests that more than just demographics are involved in the numerical decline. During the same period that Brethren have declined twenty-five percent, the nation has experienced more than thirty percent population growth.[1] What impact have changes among the Brethren had on the decline in membership and, more importantly, on who we are as Brethren? How have the changes resulted in new directions for the Brethren? While no definitive answers can be suggested, an attempt will be made to assess these changes in relation to overall development, health, and strength of the Brethren as we prepare to enter the twenty-first century.

At least five major changes have occurred with significant impact between 1960 and 1991. They are key changes in growing awareness of increasing diversity, professionalization of ministry, and redefined roles of clergy, staff, and laity, organizational transformation, the "greying" of our membership, and, in summary, in the sense of our own identity. Certainly, there have also been other significant changes, but this paper will focus on these five.

I

First, there has been a greatly enhanced awareness of the increasing diversities among the Brethren. Organizations, such as the Brethren Revival Fellowship, Brethren Renewal Service (formerly Holy Spirit Renewal group), Evangel 21, the Womaen's Caucus, and Brethren Mennonite Council for Gay and Lesbian Concerns, have become increasingly prominent. Moreover, persons who represent particular concerns have been quite persistent in making sure their concerns are heard and acted upon. For example, from the period of the Vietnam War, the Brethren Peace Fellowship, Brethren Action Movement, and, recently, SHALOM! have symbolized the strong concern of Brethren pacifists to reassert, in a more activist mode, resistance to war. Out of this concern came draft-card burning, non-registration, refusal of induction, and great involvement in the continuing anti-war movement. In sharp contrast in some churches, antipathy was aroused not only by failure to support government policies but by the association of the anti-Vietnam War movement with counter-cultural lifestyles and attitudes. There was a polarization in many Brethren churches over payment or non-payment of war taxes, anti-war preaching and activism, and the meaning of patriotism (flags in churches, articles in Messenger, speeches at Annual Conference), especially as related to various church-sponsored actions and resolutions in opposition to government policies. Similar stridency and polarization has arisen over many of these special concerns, outspoken individuals, and groups.

While these diverse subgroups gathered strength and momentum, numerous queries of concern were proposed and debated in congregations, districts, and at Annual Conference. Significant challenges emerged to church leadership and policies, to seminary education and various forms of preparation of ministers, and to current organizational structures. Human sexuality, abortion, the definition and roles of ministry and laity, the roles of women in the church and society, and the authority and inspiration of the Bible became hot issues. The issues themselves have grown out of changes in the Brethren, and they fostered significant additional changes. Annual Conference committees submitted reports that were significantly modified or returned for further work. In some cases, study committees were dismissed or replaced as their work was rejected. The impact of all this has been an increasing awareness of diversity and tensions within the Church of the Brethren. Some have predicted that these differences have become so great that some splits or departures are inevitable. Others insist that the Brethren gifts for tolerance and compromise will win out.

II

A second major change has been in the professionalization of ministry and staff and changed roles of laity and definitions of ministry. These changes have been in process for many years but have peaked in the past thirty years. These changes have been motivated by concerns to be true to our heritage, to achieve efficiency and effectiveness of leadership in a church with an increasingly educated and professionalized laity, and to have increasing contacts and cooperation with mainstream churches and the ecumenical movement.

Proportionate to our size, the Brethren have provided an unusually large number of leaders and staff for local, state, national, and world councils of churches. National staff have increasingly held key elected and committee assignments in the National and World Councils. While these involvements have been supported by many members, local churches, the General Board, and Annual Conference, some Brethren have vocally objected, sponsored queries, and often written to Messenger, complaining of these official relationships to ecumenical bodies and involvement of Brethren in them.[2] Not only the fact of ecumenical involvements has been criticized but also the influence these involvements has had. As we moved closer to mainline churches, we have imitated their standards and understandings of ministry and lay roles.

Even among some of those supportive of these ecumenical involvements, there has been concern that ecumenical priorities, as well as management and leadership styles, have increasingly influenced Elgin staff and Brethren leadership. This is often perceived as a radical change from the family model of decision-making and leadership (often with its traditional paternalism) to a governmental or business management model. Nearly all of the staff and some General Board Commission chairs have been sent to management training seminars early in their tenure. More attention has been given, some say, to the machinery of management and the possibilities of merger than to the programs and mission of the church.

The high point of Brethren ecumenical involvement and concern for merger was reached in the mid-1960s as the Fraternal Relations Committee evolved into the Interchurch Relations Committee with an Annual Conference mandate to explore cooperation, discussion, and possible affiliations with like-minded churches. Yet the 1966 Annual Conference decisively rejected by a 4 to 1 vote the invitation from the Consultation on Church Union to move from observer/consultants to full participants in the on-going process of merging of the mainline Protestant churches. Instead, full cooperation with Councils of Churches at all levels was reaffirmed and alternative explorations of merger with like-minded groups of Anabaptist heritage encouraged. An associated relationship with the American Baptist Convention has continued, though it has meant little more than fraternal visitors and a few shared programs.

The understanding of ministry among Brethren has emphasized two roles. On the one hand there is the universal priesthood of each believer, who is to serve and lead, and on the other hand a called out professional ministry, which is to subordinate itself to lay leadership, or at least to a democratically determined consensus of the entire church. This increasing emphasis on lay leadership is a radical change from the pre-1960 era. No longer is there a predominance of elected leadership from the colleges and pastoral ministry.[3] No longer does a District Elders body determine fitness for ministry. No longer are District and Annual Conference delegate bodies and committees dominated largely by ministers who determine policies and who were able to balance and hold together diverse concerns and groups.

With the concern to involve more Brethren, particularly younger people and more women, the traditional Brethren ways of making decisions, achieving harmony, and maintaining continuity are gone. This is most evident in the way Standing Committee and the delegate body at Annual Conference are chosen and function. Gone is the ever-presence and dominance of certain experienced and often revered leaders. Fresh faces and voices emerge at every Conference. These new persons provide input, leadership, and sometimes serious objections to reports, General Board decisions, and staff directions. As often as not, these new voices speak not just for themselves, or their congregations or districts, but for one of the interest groups noted above. Fairer representation has not necessarily helped to unify or to clarify Brethren priorities. It has contributed to further change and greater involvement of women, youth, and minorities. It undoubtedly moves us closer to our stated belief in the priesthood of all believers.

One factor in this move to greater lay impact on decisions is the elimination or change of status of a large number of formerly ordained ministers, whose current work is not pastoral or requiring a ministerial credential. Thus, by this new definition, many who were ordained "ministers" are now "laity." More importantly the ranks of those "ordained but not currently functioning as ministers" has not increased. While many of the formerly ordained ministers agree that this redefinition of ministry (and restriction of types of ministry recognized by ordination) was overdue, others feel rejected. A more creative solution to this problem of ordained ministers not serving as pastors (or primary pastors) might have been to conceive of them as "free ministers" serving in unpaid team ministry, in keeping with a long Brethren tradition.

One wonders about the impact on the number of young people being licensed. The former conception of an ordained "called forth" ministry, which served the church even outside its official structures encouraged many young persons, who did not necessarily see themselves as future pastors, to consider a specially "called out" ministry. Many of these went to Bethany, and often tried pastoral and other ministries in the course of their training, or immediately after. But if their sense of calling led them into other vocations, especially with the Brethren colleges or in "helping professions," they were not asked to relinquish their ministry or see their role as less a calling or less appreciated by the church. Many of these ministers served the church in a wide range of capacities for their entire lives, including filling the pulpit, giving local, district, and national leadership, while working for church-related or secular humanitarian organizations.

In passing, the closing of the Bible Training School in connection with Bethany Seminary's move created a vacuum. Various official correspondence and satellite courses (TRIM, Education for a Shared Ministry, and Associates of Arts degree at some colleges) and the unofficial Brethren Biblical Institute sought to provide training for pastoral ministry for those who lacked a college and/or seminary education.[4] The problems of enrollment and support of Bethany may be more related to this decision to close the Training School and to a more diverse student body, including many non-Brethren, than has been widely understood. It may now appear to some that Bethany is less focused on preparing pastors for the Church of the Brethren, and more on respectability as a graduate school, serving an ecumenical clientele as much as the Brethren.

A serious shortage of trained pastors had developed even before 1960. Reports by the General Brotherhood Board in 1954 and in 1959 by an Annual Conference Study Committee on Ministerial Recruitment and Conservation indicate a shortage of trained ministers and efforts to overcome this.[5] The shortage has since grown more severe. The transformation of many Brethren congregations (especially newer ones) into community-based rather than traditional-Brethren-families-based has encouraged bringing in many pastors, as well as non-Brethren-background lay members, from outside. Many new elements and emphases have entered with them. Together with whole new congregations of Hispanics and Koreans joining the Brethren today, not only diversity but widely differing patterns of worship, preaching, and beliefs have entered the church. Some of the influences toward charismatic, Pentecostal, and evangelical beliefs and concerns have also entered through the influence of attractive religious TV and radio programming. In the effort to cope with this additional source of diversity, district ministry commissions are increasingly following instructions of Annual Conference to insist upon formal training and/or supervision over the ministry of new, or untrained, pastors who undertake an apprenticeship of sorts while reading specified materials on Brethren heritage and polity.

In the pre-1960s era, ministerial camaraderie and prominence in leadership was often based on common experience in Brethren colleges and the seminary and training school. In district, regional, and national organizations these friendships tended to moderate differences and work to develop a primary loyalty to the whole church more than to subgroups. There was certainly competition for funds and support by groups such as the seminary, colleges, retirement homes, Brethren Service, and missions. But the motivations and goals of these interest groups were less diverse than those of today. The differences that existed were expressed in terms of ideology, theology, and organizational independence. There were numerous efforts to coordinate and cooperate in fund-raising even as new arrangements for a unified Brotherhood budget and definitions of the appropriate areas of independent fund-raising were being developed in the period around 1960. There has long been the ambivalence of pride in our ability to keep reasonable harmony on the one hand along with diversity and frustration in our inability to move ahead together on many issues and concerns because of these major differences on the other. But the glue provided for many decades by a more homogeneous ministry and lay leadership is less evident today.

III

Third, certain organizational changes have also been significant. The elimination of the regional structure and of the Elders Body, the combining of Brethren Service and Foreign Missions, the instituting of the unified budget, and effort to lessen the competition for funding and support of various projects and church agencies have each brought unintended side effects as well as expected results. A good case for the wisdom of each of these has been made for these changes. But they have brought in their wake additional changes of great significance.

Eliminating regional offices, boards, organizations, and committees has undoubtedly increased the roles of Elgin and of the districts and may have eliminated some wasteful and unnecessary processes. It also tended to centralize more tasks and communication in Elgin, while throwing more responsibilities on the districts, the district executives, and local leadership. Some of the decisions and responsibilities now carried by Elgin staff and General Board were previously handled or at least shared by regional staff and committees and district officers. These regional and district representatives were often better known, seen more often, and perhaps more responsive to local concerns. They also buffered or absorbed some of the criticism for policies, actions, and initiatives not appreciated locally.

Each of the regions was centered in one of the Brethren college communities. Regional Conferences, men's and women's fellowships, youth and young adult organizations, and camping program organizers often met at the campuses. Leadership from college faculty, staff, and students was heavily involved. Annual Conference recommended even greater use of college faculty in Christian education and congregational development. The church and colleges contributed to each other strength, sense of identity, and belonging. Leaders throughout the regions were nurtured at the colleges and learned to know and support the colleges. The church and colleges helped each other recruit students, train church people, and recruit pastors for the churches and teachers for the colleges. A 1960 General Board "Statement Concerning the Church and Its Colleges" detailed this cooperation and Annual Conference passed it with appreciation and a recommendation that local churches carry out its recommendations.[6]

Both the church and the colleges lost by the elimination of the regions. But other factors also contributed to their distancing and lessened interdependence. The colleges felt the need to broaden their constituencies and, in some cases, to lessen the influence or control of the church in order to do so. The colleges needed more students and greater financial resources to build new facilities, modernize their campuses, and expand their offerings. The church sought to serve Brethren students in non-Brethren institutions and began campus ministries on state university campuses. The sense of uniqueness and religious/moral superiority of the Brethren campuses gradually eroded. Fewer Brethren students went to the Brethren colleges. The percentage of Brethren students in Brethren colleges fell dramatically. Brethren college graduates aged twenth-five to fourty-four in 1984 were one-third the number of those graduating from non-Brethren institutions. Moreover, the percentage going to Brethren colleges has dropped by more than half between 1920 and 1990.[7] The colleges gradually hired fewer Brethren to their faculties. In at least one situation, a bitter struggle emerged over control of the college. Thus, the church and the colleges grew further apart.

The combining of Brethren Service and Missions, along with the unified budget, reduced various inefficiencies and tensions concerning resource allocation. It also changed in major ways the local church members' awareness of involvement in and ownership of outreach projects. The 1960s were a time of increasing awareness of the paternalism and unintended "colonialism" of much the church's overseas work. The ecumenical church and mainline Protestant denominations were moving quickly toward indigenization of mission programs. Much of the relief and rehabilitation work of Brethren Service in Europe was being phased out as Europe was increasingly able to care for refugees and those incapacitated by World War II. Missions schools and hospitals were gradually being turned over to local government and/or indigenous church ownership and management. Many long term missionaries and service workers were returning to the U.S. While there was some cutback in funding for these projects, the lesser visibility of individual project support meant greatly reduced awareness in local congregations of these overseas ministries. The earlier constant flow of missionaries on leave among the churches and camps and of Brethren Service volunteer returnees had made the church very conscious of our denomination's work abroad. In the 1940s and 1950s Brethren had a strong sense of ownership of our mission programs, CROP, Heifer Project, Church World Service, International Christian Youth Exchange, programs we pioneered and then turned over to others in our concern to broaden their base and indigenize.

The relocation and building projects of many churches during the 1950s and 1960s tended to become the focus of Brethren efforts, replacing the attention given to overseas efforts. Increasingly, the Vietnam War and domestic civil rights and "Great Society" issues replaced Brethren Service and Missions as causes for the Brethren. Thus both internal church and external societal changes made great impact on the Brethren, our sense of ownership and involvement in the outreach of the church, and Brethren priorities. The loss of focus of attention on overseas service and missions seems to have paralleled a turn to domestic concerns.

IV

A fourth change among the Brethren is clearly evident: the greying or aging of our membership. This carries with it many accompanying changes, as noted in Carl Bowman's questionnaire-based study. At the same time in 1985, that the median age of his Brethren representative sample was determined to be fifty-four and that over thirty percent were over sixty-five, only sixteen percent of the general adult population of the United States was over sixty-five. For example, while a large number of Brethren are currently in or near their peak income years, many others are living on retirement incomes. The difficulty in years ahead of increasing giving may relate to the demographics of aging as much as to the overall decline of membership.[8] In part, this is a phenomenon related to our still predominantly rural and middle class membership. Income is lower and population shrinking in areas where Brethren live and work.

There are countervailing tendencies among the new Brethren such as the Hispanic and Korean congregations. The number of children is larger and average age of these new Brethren is certainly younger. But these congregations, and other new congregations planted in areas where they may attract more young families, will not, at least not soon, compensate for the loss of numbers and giving. Death, high costs of care of the elderly, and population mobility deplete the Church of the Brethren of financial resources. As Brethren and others in higher density Brethren areas move to where the jobs are in the

Sunbelt, large cities, and the far West, they often will not find established Brethren congregations. Nor are many of those who move sufficiently motivated to help establish new Brethren fellowships.

There are more than demographic and financial support implications in the aging of the Brethren. The style of response to various issues, the willingness to tolerate differences, and the moral and political issues which take primacy may be different for older Brethren. Older Brethren and certainly many of their children may also be more accommodated to certain societal norms and attitudes. It may not have been true in the past, or in certain conservative areas today, where Brethren guard their sense of uniqueness and separation from "the world" more closely. But for many today growing older tends to make us more tolerant, less idealistic, and broader in our experience and perception of the key problems of life and our world. More traditional Brethren in the past tended to stress an attitude of, if not an actual, separation from society. Rarely today do Brethren seek to create islands of moral and spiritual rigor and mutual accountability. Only among the Brethren Revival Fellowship and a few other conservative congregations does this Brethren tradition live on today. Even this more conservative group of Brethren find themselves allied with more liberal Brethren in seeking transformation of many areas of the wider society, as well as in the personal transformation of religious commitment, moral discipline, and conversion of "the unsaved" at home and abroad.

Moreover, not all Brethren liberals and middle-of-the-roaders are so committed to ecumenical merger, or even cooperative efforts, that they want to see the Church of the Brethren absorbed into a larger Christendom. In fact, some who formerly favored merger or the primacy of ecumenical endeavors now see evangelism, missions, and projects with exclusive Brethren identity as the primary tasks for today. Thus, an apparent Annual Conference majority has emerged which is ready to move again to the project emphasis in fund-raising, in staff-time commitment, and in involvement of our volunteers and local congregational life. The emphasis on relationships and therapeutic self-healing and self-examination, whether ecumenical or personal, which characterized the 1970s and 1980s among Brethren, and its leadership particularly, seems to have declined. Most do not want Christian unity and cooperation both within our denomination and with other Christians suffer decline, yet focusing on the outward-oriented tasks of missions, evangelism, and certain kinds of societal transformation seem more urgent.

The Brethren since the 1920s have sought to be compassionate, to aid the needy, prevent war, and cooperate with other Christians in disaster relief and hunger prevention. We have sought to be reconcilers and bridge builders and to serve Christ in the best way we knew in terms of the needs of the times. Brethren have been increasingly compassionate in relation to personal moral issues such as divorce, remarriage, mental and physical health problems, poverty, homelessness and hunger, aging, and the breakdown of traditional support systems. Youthful idealism often allied with moral legalism, as well as traditional Brethren strictness and discipline, seem to be much less prominent among the Brethren generally but particularly among the older, more highly educated and urbanized Brethren.[9] Nonetheless, in Carl Bowman's 1986 investigation, Brethren rejection of non-prescription drug use, extra-marital and homosexual relations was very strong and widespread, with 92%, 89%, and 85% of the sample considering these acts as "always wrong." Brethren were more nearly equally divided on abortion and the drinking of alcohol.

V

All of the above four areas of change relate to what is perhaps the greatest change among Brethren: the issue of Brethren identity. It is not accidental that Joan Deeter has titled the recent booklet commissioned to describe us, Who Are These Brethren? Carl Bowman's Profile of the Brethren as reported in Messenger ends with the question, "Who are the Brethren of 1986?" And Emmert Bittinger's revised edition of Heritage and Promise, which tells the Brethren story, devotes the final chapter to the issue of Brethren identity.

Reflections on the loss of Brethren identity in our recent developments may help us as we live and work together to discover who we are. Despite valiant efforts of our historians and sociologists, we have continued to be cut off from our roots. It is not so much a matter of the information being unavailable. We have had since the 1950s an amazing renaissance of scholarship into our heritage and present condition. It has rather been our preoccupation with, and our immersion in, the modern world, our struggle to achieve success and acceptance in this world (both secular and religious), and our fixation on elements in our past which have made total assimilation difficult if not impossible. (Perhaps we should thank God for these remnants of non-conformity.) To be non-resistant, or more actively pacifist, in an era of more or less constant hot and cold wars which force many of us to choose sides, support or reject causes, etc., has not been easy.

To try to live out traditional Brethrenism in a time of immense change and a scintillating media driven culture, while earning our living, being educated, and finding our recreation and involvements in community affairs as full participants in most aspects of our culture, is to expect the nearly impossible. Fanatics and saints may be able to live such partitioned and disciplined lives, in the world but not of it, but ordinary folk find it nearly impossible. So our "cut-offness" from our roots is of both the heart and head. It is a matter of where our loyalties and world view have become established. Our distance from our roots and their inaccessibility is built into each of us by our high level of acculturation. We, as Brethren, have not easily accepted a civil religion of the least common denominator and the "cheap grace" of media and everyday conversational Christianity, but accepted it we have in larger measure than we realize. So, we are cut off from the nourishment of our roots by inattention. Colored glasses filter out from our vision the difficult parts or inconvenient beliefs, practices, and attitudes.

Many of us have a nostalgia for our past, but few would want to return to many aspects of it. It is too inconvenient. Some of us would like to preserve simplicity of life in the midst of our very complex entanglements. But for most Brethren the "simple life," being different from mainstream Americans and Christians, is no longer important or even meaningful. For a majority, participation in war, litigation, drinking, have lost their significance. You can be a "good Brethren" without rejecting these things for yourself or others. Or, if you cannot, you find your spiritual sustenance and fellowship elsewhere.

It has been suggested that we may come to suffer from a "paralysis of diversity." It is remarkable how little this has happened up until now. In part, this seems to be because of our tolerance, our live and let live, serve and let serve, witness and let witness way of carrying out our calling. But it may also be because there is a high level of seriousness about being faithful to our calling and witnessing to the faith that is in us. Even the most humanistic or liberal Brethren who remain with us, want to share our witness, as they perceive its imperatives. All of us want to better understand the "mind of Christ" and the implications of God's will for us in this time. There is a common thread of commitment and intensity among Brethren, new and old.

A good case could be made for the Brethren, who came out in the middle of the three-way split of 1881-1882, to this day being the great compromisers and adapters. Compared with the Mennonites, who have more than twenty-two distinct groups, the Brethren have only five emerging from their original movement. And the Church of the Brethren among these groups has had only one additional splitting until now. The great question for our time and the foreseeable future is whether this ability to compromise and stay together, which has been our genius, can continue indefinitely.

The increased awareness of our differences, and perhaps actually greater differences than we have had or been aware of previously, has made the task of keeping the Church of the Brethren together much more daunting. As noted in the professionalization of ministry and increase of lay leadership, many of the personal relationships and heavy influence of revered and long-term leaders, which helped keep the Brethren together, have now been lost. Personal relationships, and the family atmosphere of our conferences and worship, help restrain the stridency and bitterness of the debates and the centrifugal pull of our diverse opinions and causes. The Church of the Brethren is still small enough that Annual Conference often seems as much like a family reunion as an occasion for business and inspiration. And the Brethren *have* brought new members into significant roles in leadership, worship, preaching, and decision-making, however slow and paternalistic we have been in doing this.

Organizational changes among the Brethren have institutionalized the diversity. The spread of decision-making between the constantly shifting personnel of Annual Conference and Standing Committee is balanced by the more stable General Board and staff, with five to ten years of service in most of the key positions. At one time, in the 1920s to 1940s, many thought that staff leadership and the independence of the diverse boards and committees, allowed for too little Annual Conference and local or lay control. The recent attempt by the church structural reorganization committee to throw much more of the decision-making and administrative supervision of program on Annual Conference and short-term elected officials failed to gain general support. Instead, the present balance of policy-making by the Annual Conference and General Board with the possibility of program initiatives from any local congregation through District and Annual Conference, and the program development and administration through staff, was reaffirmed. Moreover, formerly open struggles for resources and priority among the diverse interest groups have been minimized. Unified budgets, district assessments, and coordination of fund-raising have helped. Thus, the Brethren genius for reconciliation and compromise has worked, not only at the personal and inter-group level, but in the way we have evolved in our polity and process.

Similarly, Brethren publications such as <u>Messenger</u>, <u>Brethren Life and Thought</u>, Brethren Press books, and church school materials have featured a wide spectrum of opinion and points of view. <u>Messenger</u> has seemed particularly effective in throwing a sympathetic light on the great diversity of groups and individuals who are Brethren today. Annual Conference Central Committee has featured our diversity in speakers, insight sessions, worship leadership, and invited guests. While these diverse elements have often made some uncomfortable, they have also enabled us to see first-hand what makes up our diversity ethically, culturally, in styles of worship and preaching, and in theological emphases. The General Board report has also creatively presented the work of the church in its manifold witness and service. It is unfortunate all cannot experience this.

If a more theologically-focused analysis had been attempted, I would have examined an hypothesis about liberal/conservative trends. It would appear that twentieth-century Brethren have always had a wide range of opinion. But the shift from the 1940s to 1990s seems to have been from a predominance of middle-of-the-road and liberal theologies in the direction of conservatism, by way of neo-orthodoxy (and perhaps existentialist-influenced theologies) for the most highly theologically trained Brethren. The old saw that Brethren were theologically liberal but socially and ethically conservative could almost be reversed today. Contemporary Brethren seem highly and increasingly accommodating (liberal) socially and ethically (equality, the legitimacy of litigation, acceptance of war, divorce, remarriage) but increasingly conservative in their theological beliefs, preaching, congregational life, and certain key values (identifiably Brethren projects, emphasis on evangelism and missions, abortion). These issues seem relevant to what our emerging identity is likely to be.

Just as missions, education, service, and evangelism helped the Brethren of the nineteenth century evolve into today's Brethren, these same programmatic emphases may help unify us and keep alive our witness to the world in the 1990s. As suggested earlier, the great threat to Brethren denominational health, especially in the 1950s and 1960s, was the turn inward. We were preoccupied with building our edifices and solving our personal and group complexes, as domestic and national problems, such as poverty, racial injustice, war, and crime impinged upon us. The turn again to focus our energies on the larger world and particularly in welcoming other groups into our midst, and creating specifically Brethren instrumentalities for carrying our witness to the wider world may yet heal us.

It is a good question as to how much the "ecumania" among us was based on embarrassment (or self-hatred) and desire to escape our peculiarities, and how much it was based on genuine concern for Christian unity and a wider, deeper base for our witness to the world. To many among us it now appears that much in our earlier efforts at evangelism (often trying paternalistically to bring others into existing congregations and worship patterns),[10] service (through sending workers and large amounts of money to other organizations), and ecumenical cooperation and merger discussions has been self-defeating. The uncertain sense of ownership of these 1960s and 1970s programs and processes has not helped us develop a sense of who we are and whose we are. Much of the activity of the Church of the Brethren in the last 30 years has enabled many us to come to the opinion that there is little or nothing distinctive or worth preserving in the church of the Brethren. It has made joining other groups, as people move, or become disenchanted, very easy. The vast variety of new Brethren, with the questions they raise and the vitality they bring, force us to redefine ourselves and to turn away from an ambivalent pre-occupation with our past, our Germanic ethnicity and cultural peculiarities, and our particularistic lifestyles and rural middle-American orientation.

The things we can unite on are programs to serve a needy world and to witness to the Christ who heals, unifies, saves, and creates community where little existed before. We will discover who we are as we work and witness together and perhaps save our denominational life in losing it in the tasks to which Christ calls us today and in the years ahead. We cannot do less than follow where Christ leads, grow in and celebrate His grace and love among us.

[1] Donald F. Durnbaugh, ed. Church of the Brethren, Yesterday and Today (Elgin, Illinois: Brethren Press), 203-204.

[2] William R. Eberly, ed. Minutes of the Annual Conference of the Church of the Brethren 1965-69 (Elgin, Illinois: Brethren Press, 1970), 152, 175, 147-248, 289-91, 296-297.

[3] Roger E. Sappington, "The Concept of the Elite in the Church of the Brethren," Brethren Life and Thought, vol. v, Autumn 1960, 4-12.

[4] Minutes, *1955-64*, 212-222.

[5] Ibid., 64-68.

[6] Ibid., 151-161.

[7] Yesterday and Today, 209-210.

[8] Ibid., 201 ff.

[9] Ibid., 217-223.

[10] James Lehman, Thank God for New Churches (Elgin, Illinois: Brethren Press, 1983) pp. passim.

4

Recent Trends From the
Long Term Perspective

by Vernard Eller

A creative and provocative thinker, Eller stresses the commitment to radical discipleship which comes out of the Pietist and Anabaptist movements from which the Brethren came. He argues strongly that the Brethren have compromised, weakened, grown tired of, and finally abandoned that commitment in favor of a less costly form of discipleship which he calls cheap grace. It is incongruous, he suggests, that just as the tradition of radical discipleship is coming to be recognized by theologians and biblical scholars as a valid part of the witness of Christendom, that the Brethren should abandon it in favor of accommodation to the prevailing pattern of churchly life. Still, all may not be lost, for a small remnant may succeed in keeping that vital tradition alive.[1]

I

There is general agreement among students of church history that Christendom divides into two distinct versions of the gospel. How the two are to be defined and explained is a matter that still needs attention, at least a bit of which we can give now.

Those who are familiar with my previous writings will recall that I no longer give much weight to the supposedly nonpartisan sociological researches of Troeltsch, Weber, and H.R. Niebuhr. Sociology is simply too peripheral to gospel interest to get us to the heart of the matter. Rather, the fundamental issue must be: which tradition uses the New Testament as a jumping off point for churchly revisionism and which marks a seriously intended effort at gospel fidelity.

Obviously, the sociological distinction between "church" and "sect" is inadequate here. I am all for dropping that lingo, though I am not sure I have the right terminology to use in its place. I do believe the term "radical discipleship" is as good as can be done for the fidelity line. For the other, the best I can offer is the term passive blessedness. Here, being a good Christian amounts to going to church and allowing that sacral institution to bestow its ministrations of grace and instruct you as to what you should believe and do.

He probably is not of any help with our terminology, but Dietrich Bonhoeffer is perhaps the teacher who best gets us to the distinction. He explicitly condemns the churches as purveyors of cheap grace, and he explicitly identifies the New Testament teaching as that of costly grace. However, I do not know that he ever recognizes that there is an ongoing Christian tradition, namely, radical discipleship, which is dedicated to costly grace.

To my mind, the greatest error of the sociologists was in assuming that radical world denial was the equivalent of world hatred, or world rejection. Yet, when the medical doctor diagnoses a patient and tells him that his smoking has him fast on his way out of this life, nobody accuses the doctor of being an enemy of the patient, particularly when that doctor goes on to explain that there is a way out of the predicament. In the very same way, the radical Christian critique of the world can be understood as the most constructive and loving thing to be done for that world.

So, ignoring the sociologists, I prefer to trace the line of theological church historians who, quite apart from their personal Christian proclivities, spot the churchly line as revisionist and the radical discipleship line as at least seeking fidelity.

II

My interest has led me to seek to discover how radical discipleship has expressed itself in church history in those groups, movements, and individuals who best exemplify the radical tradition in thought, word, and deed. In many instances there is a clear linkage between one exemplar and the next. We are dealing with a real Christian tradition and not a theoretical construct. And that tradition includes some truly authoritative thinkers; it is not the motley collection of *Schwarmergeister* Luther accused it of being. This tracing of historical developments shows that the Brethren are directly in the line of radical discipleship. A description of the belief-structure of classic Brethrenism[2] will now be attempted.

I think we can assume that the tradition of radical discipleship holds an important place in the eyes of God. Of course, faithful obedience to the Lord is right and good for its own sake. Yet I am convinced that our tradition also has a special calling, a unique role to play in God's overall plan for the world he so loves. Let's hark back to the analogy of the physician used earlier.

Consider that, if our physician has any true love and concern for his patients, the one thing of which he must be most careful is not to simply join them in the self-destructive lifestyles that are at the heart of their problems. He must both maintain and display a personal regimen that is conspicuously different from theirs—healthwise different. It is, indeed, this demonstrated difference that gives him the right to counsel his patients as to how they might improve their health. And I am suggesting that, in his moral education of both the churchly and secular world, God wants a radical-discipleship tradition he can point to as exemplar and model.

Yet, playing the role model is a most strenuous assignment. For one thing, it is not easy to maintain fidelity when all the pressures are the other way. For another, people do not take kindly to the judgment that it is their own chosen and enjoyed lifestyle that is killing them. And of course, the suggestion that they must undertake the arduous disciplines of a totally different lifestyle comes to them as very bad news indeed. It is, of course, cheap grace versus costly grace we are talking here. And always the big temptation of the radical-discipleship tradition will be to give up the task and take the easy way out, to alleviate the tension by simply joining the world in its preferred lifestyle.

Against this background, I want to argue that, for the first two centuries of its life, the Church of the Brethren did a creditable job of making its radical witness. That is to say, it did practice its Christian anarchy, that is, nonconformity to the world, being not of the world, whatever you might call it. However, now, during our third century, we have grown tired under the strain. Deciding it is not worth the cost to stand over against the world, we have compromised, accommodating ourselves to the world on one front and another.

III

For the remainder of my time, then, let me point out the major instances in this century where I feel the Brethren have traded away their costly-grace, radical-disciple, New Testament witness in the process of getting more comfortable in and acceptable to society, the worldly church as well as the worldly world.

1) Perhaps the first of these moves was our going from the free ministry, constituted of leadership chosen from out of the faith-community's own numbers, to importing paid, professionally qualified outsiders. Whether or not this simply had to happen for the sake of church's continuance, the move was made, not out of fidelity to New Testament norms, but as an accommodation to the fashions of the world.

In the process, there was introduced into the life of the congregation a serious bifurcation of its gospel egalitarianism. Now, every member is on the same footing except the one who is there because he is paid to be there, that being how he makes his living. Individual congregations may handle this pastoral disparity either poorly or well. But poorly or well, it is still a falling away from the gospel ideal. The great tragedy comes in the fact that now the people do not themselves have to be the Bible students, theologians, and thinkers who, through their own discernment of the Spirit, define and mold their own faith-community. No, they have brought in a professional to take care of such matters—a typical worldly move.

2) From perhaps the second quarter of this century until now, what I consider a major defection from the gospel norm is the thronging of Brethren into the social gospel movement. Clearly, in the New Testament it is assumed that the chosen lifestyle of humanity is so utterly self-destructive that there is not a chance, as it were, that society might lift itself by its own bootstraps, turn itself around, and reform itself into social salvation. No, for either the salvation of the individual or of society, the only possible Savior to whom to look is the Lord God and his Christ.

American Christendom, however, was of a quite different mind. This was an age of incredibly naive optimism. The course of history was assumed to be expressed in the statement, "every day, in every way, I (along with everybody else and society as a whole) am getting better and better." The faith to which the Brethren flocked saw society's lifestyle, not as self-destructive but as self-perfecting. What Christians were to do was simply to introduce the "Strong, Righteous Man of Galilee" as leader of the world's moral development. (By the way, neither that nor the hymn, "O Young and Fearless Prophet," are adequate as biblical titles for Jesus.) But through our own Christian piety, then, we would represent righteous living and model it to the world, until, as the hymn has it, "So shall the wide earth seem our Father's temple." Our Christlike example would be welcomed as God's means of bringing his kingdom and the saving of the world.

A catch of lines from the favorite hymns of the era will reveal the entirely self-confident mood of the times: "God has no hands but our hands to do his work today," implying that we had better get at doing what He cannot; "'Are ye able?'" said the Master. 'Yes, we are able—our spirits are thine!'"; "Who will build the world anew?" implying, we good Christians will do that very thing for you, Lord. "Rise up, O men of God! His kingdom tarries long." The clear implication is: so we will have to "bring in the day of brotherhood and end the night of wrong"; "True hearted, whole hearted, faithful and loyal." That is us in a nutshell.

Now the sad mockery of such human self-confidence is this: although the Brethren, along with the greater part of American Christendom, came into this century with purple dreams about leading the world to social health and salvation, the church is presently coming out of that century at the low ebb of reputation, recognition, and acceptance on the part of the world. The moral flow of the century has been the very reverse of what we thought to give it. Yet my point here is that our original move into the Social Gospel, rather than representing radical discipleship, was nothing more than a convenient accommodation to the optimistic world-spirit of the times.

3) My third example is the one presently giving me the greatest concern and grief. Our radical tradition had always been clear on what is Jesus' teaching regarding divorce, adultery, and all marital-sexual infidelity. Further, that teaching was seen within the context of the fundamental biblical theme of covenant. Immediately following the account of God's irrevocable covenant

relationship with the whole of his creation, the Bible tabs the marital covenant as the highest of human relationships. By the same token, the scorning of covenant is the root sin and the most serious of human wrong doings.

Out of their radical discipleship, the Hutterites claim now to have lived four hundred years without one incident of divorce. In a recent issue of the Fuller Seminary Bulletin there was an article by a prominent African Presbyterian pastor from Kenya. As contact person for World Vision, he is also informed on the African church scene generally. He is forty years old and says that, during that time, he has never so much as heard of a divorce among African Christians. The congregations are so organized as to keep an eye on the marriages in their midst. As soon as there is any sign of trouble, the church itself is on the spot to deal with the difficulty. And it seems plain that, for the first 250 years of their history, the Brethren generally could be numbered along with the Hutterites and the Africans. Our people were so thoroughly taught that divorce is simply not a Christian option, that marital problems had to be solved, not just given up on.

And it is not merely that the Brethren divorce rate has skyrocketed over the last twenty years. The sky rocketing has been prevalent in the pastoral leadership, the General Board staff, and faculty of the Seminary, among the very people to whom the church most looks for teaching and modeling as regards covenant fidelity. Among us, divorce no longer carries any moral stigma, nor is it seen as an impediment to one's practice in the pastoral or teaching ministries.

I do not think our situation can be explained in any other way; we have deserted our radical calling and accommodated ourselves wholly to the standards of the world. Our abject failure in the *practice* of covenantal fidelity certainly destroys the credibility of any witness we ought to be making in that regard. I trust you understand that my concern is not so much with the divorcees as it is with the fact that the church now treats divorce just as does the world itself: seeing it as quite normal and taken for granted.

4) I think there is a direct spin-off from the preceding and to the emphasis we are now to consider, namely, the peace witness upon which we so pride ourselves. Much more than we do, we need to recognize that all of Jesus' peace teaching, I think unanimously all, is directed to his committed followers as instruction on how they are to be peaceable and reconciling in all of their personal relationships. If you will, Jesus teaches that peace must begin at home; if you can't manage it there, there is little chance of your accomplishing it anywhere else.

The peacemaking we definitely do not get from Jesus is that which we are perhaps most prone to practice: namely, to come on as a worldly left-wing political cause group, denouncing the worldly powers for their violence and instructing them as to how they could pacify themselves if they would just listen to us. Yet notice that, when Jesus had his chance to advise Pilate, he chose to say nothing at all; what good would it do?

So think, if you will, of two young adults from good Brethren families who are very much in love with one another and who accordingly commit themselves with the covenant vows of marriage, vows made not just before God but with the prayer that his own covenantal fidelity become the guarantee of theirs. But if Brethren cannot live faithfully in what should be the easiest and elemental of all peaceful relationships, and increasingly resort to the violent sundering of covenant, what grounds have we for lecturing George Bush on how he should be able to live peaceably with Saddam Hussein? "Physician, heal thyself," would be the perfect retort. Perhaps we need to read the whole of Luke 16:10, "Whoever is faithful in very little is faithful also in much; and whoever is dishonest in a very little is dishonest also in much."

I am not saying we should entirely drop our public peace testimony. I am asking whether we haven't jeopardized our radical commitment to the Prince of Peace by accommodating ourselves, rather, to the worldly dodge: "Why do you see the speck in your neighbor's eye, but do not notice the log in your own eye? . . . You hypocrite, first take the log out of your own eye, and then you will see clearly to take the speck out of your neighbor's eye." We have some radically obedient peace work to do at home before going public as a peace church.

5) Finally, lest I leave the impression that our accommodation to the world is always toward the side of liberalism, let me close with an accommodation from the other side. It is plain that in the radical church of the New Testament, evangelism and church growth showed itself as a quest for the quality of intimate community, centering upon the practice of costly disciple-ship. Consequently, concern over the number of adherents and the congregation's institutional success simply were not in the picture. Nevertheless, the models of church growth now being proffered to the Brethren are decidedly not those of the New Testament. They are clearly those of accommodation to the world.

Now, we are being told, a congregation's way to success is to start with a stellar powerhouse pastor, a CEO, if you will, who takes pains that everything be done his way. Allowing anything to happen outside his game plan could derail the whole effort. Next, it is important to enlist everything possible in the way of modern media to advertise, promote, and sell that which this new business, church-business, has to offer. And thirdly, the church must take pains to tailor its ministries to what the clientele want, and to what will meet their perceived needs, and to what will keep them happy. Here, it is with the church as with the world, that the customer is always right; not, as with the gospel, that it is the Lord Jesus who is always right. And obviously, the end goal of this concerted effort is the creating of a mega-church, something that early Christianity went for three hundred years without getting as much as a start toward.

Again, it should be apparent that all these accommodations to the world represent, according to Bonhoeffer, a turning away from costly grace in favor of cheap grace. We have relaxed our earlier tension of standing against the world simply by accommodating to it. Yet it can be argued that, at the same time, we have compromised the possibility of our being of any real good to the world. Surely, what the world needs least is our affirmation that the way in which it is going is indeed the way of right and truth.

Even after I considered this paper complete, there came a news story from the Associated Press reporting the findings of an extensive poll on the current religious beliefs of Americans. It gets right to the nub of our argument.

In the first place, it says, believers increasingly feel that "being part of a local church is not a necessity." And that, if I may say so, represents an extraordinarily cheap form of cheap grace: a Christianity that doesn't even ask one to be involved with other people.

Secondly, the poll shows people leaning toward the idea that one person's understanding of God is just as true as anybody else's. This may be the ultimate form of cheap grace; it does not ask for as much as the discipline of rightly dividing truth from falsehood.

In the third place, eighty-three percent say that "people are basically good," and sixty-three percent think "the purpose of life is enjoyment and personal fulfillment." Perhaps it is the same people, but at least the same sixty-three percent, who agree that "when it comes right down to it, your first responsibility is to yourself."

The essential contradiction between this popular view of life and that of the radical gospel is revealed in what might be Jesus' most concentrated utterance (Mk 8:34-36, NSRV), "If any want to become my followers, let them deny themselves and take up their cross and follow me. For those who want to save their life will lose it, and those who lose their life for my sake, and for the sake of the gospel, will save it."

Yet consider to what degree the contemporary church has fallen in with the world. We actually seek to exploit the worldly misunderstanding to our own churchly advantage by confirming people in their quest for "a life of enjoyment and personal fulfillment" and convincing them that the church of Jesus Christ exists to no other purpose than to give them what they seek for themselves. We offer this, when what Jesus said was, "Seek first God's kingly rule and his righteousness?"

IV

Notice here, then, that nowhere have I expressed any concern about the institutional survival of the Church of the Brethren. That is the last thing I worry about. In fact, I am quick to agree that the accommodations to the world we have already made and are in process of making may well be our best means of assuring that we do survive, yet survive simply as one denomination out of the largely indistinguishable mass.

Most Brethren will not even notice that a change in our station has taken place. Many others will feel quite comfortable with the switch. Some have never seen any reason for our trying to be different in the first place.

I personally have no intention of trying to fight the move. I see it as already accomplished. The most that I hope to do is make the Brethren aware of what they are doing as they do it. So I invite you to examine again the Mack Seal on classic Brethren beliefs and decide for yourself to which we have remained faithful and which we have traded away.

But to me, the Brethren have come to a situation of great irony. Just at that time in Christian history when the works of such people as Kierkegaard, the Blumhardts, Barth, Brunner, Bonhoeffer, and Ellul have brought the tradition of radical discipleship to its greatest visibility and credibility ever, why, of all times, should it be just now that the Church of the Brethren tires of the tension and so jumps ship to join forces with the already world-compromised side of Christendom?

As a well known thinker once stated it, "If salt has lost its taste, how can its saltiness be restored? It is no longer good for anything."

And does this mean, then, that things are all over for us? No, let us not be guilty of making the same mistake Elijah did. Even if we can never manage to be a denomination of radical discipleship, we need not be hindered as individuals, clusters, groups, and perhaps even some congregations from committing ourselves to a genuine radical discipleship. After all, the Lord who did speak of lost saltiness also spoke the encouragement of "Fear not, little flock." So my choice is to continue to speak to and work with the little flock within both the Church of the Brethren and other churches.

Anabaptists

Obey Jesus

Restitution of the early
Christian life and
Church order.

Outward Obedience
"What does it profit to
speak much of Christ
and his word if we do
not believe him and
refuse to obey his
commandments?
Again I say, awake and
tear the accursed
unbelief with its
unrighteousness from
your hearts, and
commence a pious,
penitent life as the
Scriptures teach. . . .
We are referring to a
penitence possessed of
power and works, such
as John the Baptist
taught saying: Bear
fruit that befits
repentance."
Menno Simons

Brethren

"That which the Holy
Spirit ordained for the
faithful was written
outwardly. All
believers are united in
it, for the Holy Spirit
teaches them inwardly
just as the Scriptures
teach them
outwardly. . . .
Therefore, when a
believing person whose
inner ears are opened
reads the Holy
Scriptures outwardly,
he will hear as the Lord
Jesus intends his
teaching to be
understood. He hears
that which the apostles
want to express in their
writings. He will also
be impelled, through
his inner hearing, to
true obedience which
makes him obey even
in outward matters.
Outwardly, he reads the
Scriptures in faith and
hears the inner word of
life which gives him
strength and power to
follow Jesus."
Alexander Mack

Radical Pietists

Love Jesus

"O for a closer walk
with God"

Inner Experience
"To sum up, my feeling
is briefly aimed therein
that one must seek
Jesus in one's heart as
the only true foundation
of salvation and the
heart must be
completely purified
through the true living
faith in Jesus. In case
it is wished to perform
in true singleness of
heart also those
outward actions which
the first Christians did
in addition to these
inner unmovable bases,
I cannot consider this a
mortal sin if one only
remains in impartial
love toward those who
cannot feel in their
minds this necessity for
these outward acts.
The freedom of Christ
suffers neither force nor
laws."
E. C. Hochmann

"Some *felt powerfully drawn* to seek again *the footsteps* of the first Christians.
They *passionately yearned* to avail themselves in faith of the *ordained testimonies of Jesus Christ* according to their right value. At the same time, it was
emphatically *opened to them in their hearts* how necessary is *obedience in
faith* if a soul wishes to be saved."
The origin of the Church of the Brethren as described by Alexander Mack, Jr.

EXHIBIT A

DISCIPLESHIP: anti-intellectualism; anticreedalism; voluntary personal decision; inward commitment; devotional immediacy.

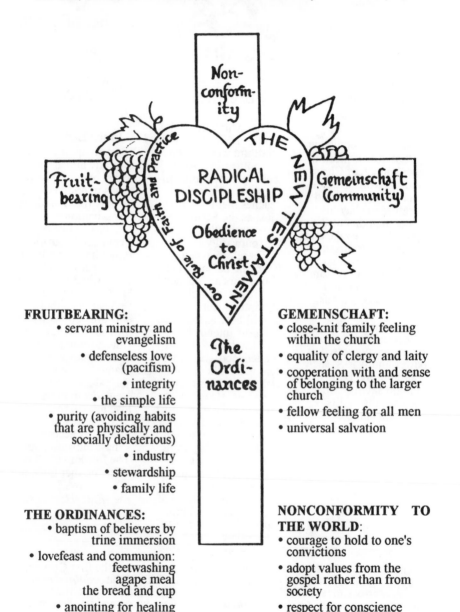

FRUITBEARING:
- servant ministry and evangelism
- defenseless love (pacifism)
- integrity
- the simple life
- purity (avoiding habits that are physically and socially deleterious)
- industry
- stewardship
- family life

THE ORDINANCES:
- baptism of believers by trine immersion
- lovefeast and communion:
  feetwashing
  agape meal
  the bread and cup
- anointing for healing
- laying on of hands

GEMEINSCHAFT:
- close-knit family feeling within the church
- equality of clergy and laity
- cooperation with and sense of belonging to the larger church
- fellow feeling for all men
- universal salvation

NONCONFORMITY TO THE WORLD:
- courage to hold to one's convictions
- adopt values from the gospel rather than from society
- respect for conscience
- not afraid to be "peculiar."

EXHIBIT B

[1] Several exhibits and papers were provided to illustrate major points from this essay. Some of these were lengthy. Those who are interested in obtaining them may request copies. Only two exhibits are included, the Mack seal and its interpretation.

[2] Classic Brethren belief is symbolized by the Mack Seal which is interpreted in my paper, "We are Committed. . . ." See Exhibits A and B in this chapter, depicting the Mack Seal.

Response to
An Overview of Brethren Change

by Warren S. Kissinger

One overarching and unifying theme of these three papers is the reality of Brethren change. Change has had, and is having, momentous implications for us as Brethren. It staggers and confounds us to the extent that many of us feel like Abraham in going out and not knowing where we are to go.

Carl Bowman presents us with a scenario in which traditional Brethren beliefs and practice have been misconstrued through the subtle impact of modernity—a modernity which for Brethren has distinct theological, ethical, psychological, and sociological implications.

Allen Deeter has provided us with a notable analysis of change in the Church of the Brethren during the last thirty years. He does so under five categories: growing awareness of increasing diversity, professionalization of ministry and staff, organizational transformation, the "graying" of our membership, and our sense of identity. Allen Deeter's paper I found to be broadly descriptive and informational. It reflects an objectivity characterized by minimal value judgments.

In Vernard Eller's presentation, I discern a different temperament. Here firmly held opinions and value judgments are unmistakable. In both Carl Bowman's and Vernard Eller's papers, there has been a "fall" insofar as the Brethren are concerned. The fall results from the Brethren embracing false gods instead of giving allegiance to the one who led them out of their Egyptian captivity through the pristine waters of the Eder River. The fall has been marked by a distortion of the Brethren vision through liberal theology and an acceptance of the values or non-values of our secular, therapeutic culture. By utilizing the techniques and strategies of our contemporary world, we have baptized (presumably by a trine immersion) professionalism, secular practices, individualism, church growth, and success.

These provocative papers, which have spoken admirably to the phenomenon of Brethren change, open before us a myriad of questions and possibilities from which we can only pick and choose in the brief time allotted to us.

Let me attempt to sketch a few tentative reflections. I still find the Troeltsch-Niebuhr typologies useful in describing our situation sociologically and theologically. According to the changes discerned in the three papers this morning, we have moved as Brethren from church to sect to church in Troeltsch's view, or from the Christ of culture to Christ against culture and back again to the Christ of culture in Niebuhr's framework. Our perennial struggle as Brethren and as Christians concerns our relationship to culture. How do we relate to the visions and values of the culture of which we are a part? To what extent have we become acculturated?

Our dilemma is characterized by the fact that our faithfulness and our discipleship (no matter how radical it is) is always only a partial and limited response to the gospel. H. Richard Niebuhr observed that all our faith is fragmentary, but we do not have the same fragments of faith. We need to correct, but also to be corrected. This is a Kantian perspective which holds that we can never fully comprehend or fathom reality. To use St. Paul's figures, we always see as in a mirror dimly, and we know only in part.

Our purpose in this conference is to try to discern the trends and implications of the transitions in which we find ourselves. It is to more clearly discern who we have been, who we are, and where we ought to be going. To use Niebuhr's categorization again, it is to describe and to appropriate more fully the fragment of faith that has been entrusted to us.

One mark of our finitude is that our faith to a larger degree than many of us realize or are ready to admit is historically and culturally conditioned. Much as we may want to idealize and romanticize the eight who came to Schwarzenau, we must view them both as faithful in their discipleship but also as being children of their time and place. And so it has been from their day to ours.

Given the traditional Brethren stance against creeds and systems of theology, their emphasis on following Jesus and on love of neighbor and service, and their affinity for the good life as expressed in the Sermon on the Mount, I am not at all surprised that in this century they have been strongly influenced by the social gospel and liberal theology. Nor am I surprised that today many Brethren respond favorably to the tenets of liberation theology, black theology, and feminist theology. The fragment of faith that is ours has been filtered through tinted lenses and is historically and culturally conditioned.

All our systems and theological formulations are fragmentary. They are relative and conditioned by our historical and cultural context. Our temptation is to attempt to transcend our finitude by absolutizing the relative and by investing the finite with infinity. It is painful and disconcerting to realize that we are always on the way toward the goal and that our faith is partial and fragmentary. But to make our fragmentary faith absolute is to fall into idolatry. We need a sense of perspective and of humor lest we take ourselves too seriously and become lost in intellectual, moral, and spiritual pride. Karl Barth ranks among the most impressive theological systematizers of all time. But he was able to laugh at himself. In a charming insight, Barth said that the angels must laugh as they see old Karl coming with his push cart full of the Dogmatics, each one thicker than the last and each trying to contain the truth of God and about God.

In recent years, there has been a pronounced interest in and analysis of philosophical and theological language. Language is symbolic and points toward and becomes transparent to truth and reality. But how often do we invest our theological categories with an ultimacy which is idolatrous. Theologies come and go and are invariably influenced by philosophical systems, be they those of Plato, Aristotle, Augustine, Aquinas, Kant, Hegel, Kierkegaard, Whitehead, Heidegger, or Ellul to name a few.

The term "discipleship" has become a familiar category among contemporary Anabaptists and Pietists. But the term is probably more dependent upon Bonhoeffer's <u>Nachfolge (Cost of Discipleship)</u> than it is upon our Anabaptist and Pietist forebears. And how much of the contemporary controversy regarding the inspiration and authority of the scriptures grows out of the fundamentalist-modernist controversy in this century, instead of being grounded in Paul, the Church Fathers, and the Reformers.

I wish that I could foresee a new day of unity and concord for the Brethren, but I cannot. As we move into an increasingly urbanized and heterogeneous environment, our fragment of faith will continue to reflect dichotomy and tension.

There is one area of our contemporary life which as I see it has profound implications for our discipleship and our fragment of faith. I refer to our economic situation, our wealth, our aggrandizement, our consumerism, our materialism, our willingness to embrace the gospel of worldly success. Our Germanic penchant for hard work, thrift, punctuality, and orderliness has made us epitomes of the old saw that "while we purposed to do good, we have also done very well." All of us here today, as are the Brethren in general, are persons of wealth in the midst of a poverty-stricken world. We are fat and full among brothers and sisters who are lean and destitute. One can only speculate what subtle transitions have taken place in our psyches and our moral sensitivity as we are continually bombarded by those apologists who equate the good life with more and better things. What does costly discipleship mean in a culture mesmerized by creature comforts, a preservation of life at any cost and a denial of the reality of death? It may come as a surprise to many of us that the New Testament has more to say about the ethics and theology of wealth than it does about homosexuality and sexual ethics. The communist attempt to organize social and political systems has been tried and found wanting. However, the Marxist notion that material and economic forces are the real determiners of history is very much alive among us.

As for our sexual and marital transgressions, there is real cause for concern. Our peace witness, our fidelity to covenantal relationships, and our word being as good as our bond have been compromised by our actions. The Christian ideal is to strive for consistency and to bring our words and our deeds into a meaningful relationship. But having said that, we must also note that some of our most courageous and prophetic exponents of peace and justice and nonviolence have not been paragons and models of sexual and marital virtue.

One would always hope that private virtue and social righteousness and justice would be in harmony with each other. But alas it is not always so. Some of the most impressive exemplars of radical discipleship and of costly grace have not always been models of private virtue. And on the other hand, many paragons of private virtue have evaded the demands of radical discipleship by a surfeit of wealth, comfort, and self-indulgence.

At this point I must plead for forgiveness for stepping over that indistinct boundary between academic, objective respondent and homileticist. How shall we understand and witness to the fragment of faith that is ours? In speaking to new converts to Brethrenism across the years, I have been intrigued by what influenced them to make their decision. For many, it was not our theological formulations or our biblical hermeneutic but our peace witness, our service projects and insistence that faith and works must be in a meaningful dialog, and our emphasis upon simplicity and integrity. But I am also acutely aware that many have departed from us because in their view we were theologically amorphous, not Bible-believing Christians, not charismatic, not eschatological-ly concerned, not evangelistic, or not missionary minded.

So how shall one describe our fragment of faith, and how shall we continue to be faithful to it? The Great Commandment has both a vertical and a horizontal dimension, a theological and an ethical. We cannot resolve the paradox, and therein lies the tension and the stress. By God's grace, we must continue to make our way between an ethical humanism on the one extreme and a theology of divine sovereignty and transcendence which obliterates human thoughts, words, and deeds on the other. Such will be our burden and our joy until that day when we shall see clearly and know fully.

PART III

TRANSITION IN SIMILAR OR RELATED DENOMINATIONS

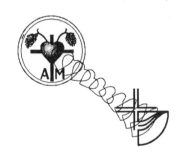

5

The Old Order Brethren
In Transition

by F. W. Benedict

Well-known as an author and publisher, Benedict shares some valuable observations regarding the impact of contemporary society upon his communion, especially those situated on the fringe of large urban areas. The Old German Baptist Brethren are the "old order" branch of the Brethren movement. Assumed by many to be impervious to change, the OGBB are undergoing minor yet significant modifications as they live and work in these modified settings. Especially useful are his observations—from an insider's perspective—into how change occurs in several dimensions, both mental and behavioral. Even its most subtle aspects, to Benedict, have far reaching significance. Some of these responses, such as the formation of private schools, are efforts to conserve the youth for the church. Other changes, including the shift from farming to various professional, business, and skilled labor occupations, the willingness to patronize restaurants on Sunday, the impact of rising standards of living, etc., are not easily countered. He suggests that no longer is the issue simply a matter of participation or withdrawal, but rather, how shall the OGBB participate in the world?

The title of this paper will incite considerable interest from many Old Orders. Among a few of them it may cause some confusion and anger. Among others it may cause feelings of inadequacy and terror. To me, it is the facts as I see them. The paper does not have the advantage (or disadvantage) of much formal study, nor is it based upon scientific principles and surveys. We may consider it a few random observations preliminary to a more formal study. I choose the method of simple illustration to make a few points, and I hope the method is informative and perhaps a bit entertaining. I chose to be no crusader, but rather an observer and commentator. Alas, with this approach, I may have no friends in the end!

As the Annual Meeting was coming to a close and the large worship tent was being taken down, I saw him about a hundred yards away, slowly moving northward across the meeting grounds. In spite of the warm weather, the man, now almost fourscore and ten, was dressed in full Dunker uniform and hat. He was easily identified: tall, bearded, very thin, yet quite agile and erect for his age. He walked slowly and gracefully. I had never met him, yet I had heard much about him and had a little correspondence with him.

I suppose it was true that he lived in one of the plainest homes in the brotherhood. He was careful to observe many of the smaller strictures of Annual Meeting. Yet there was a difference. The brother showered you with love. He did not dwell on trifles in conversation. You felt quite at ease in his home. I had never heard criticism of him. All this I learned from others.

I felt it urgent to cross the meeting grounds to meet him. Upon exchanging the kiss of peace and telling him who I was, he became very animated in conversation with many expressions of love, good will, and appreciation for the wonderful meeting and the fellowship of the church. We lingered in conversation a little longer than usual. When we were ready to part, he moved toward me saying, "Brother, let me kiss you again—you know, we may never meet again!" As he slowly made his way across the grounds, I wondered. Am I observing the passing of an era? Did the brother represent the best of Nead and Kinsey? Am I seeing the passing of Shoup and Hess and Montgomery and Benedict?

In order to better understand a subculture, it is necessary to enter the thought world of a people who consciously choose a world view based upon a different order of values than that chosen by most people. Some of the labels and definitions common to the "world" are misleading when applied to the Old German Baptists. The Old Order Brethren are composed of liberals, conservatives, and moderates. Sounds familiar, right?

Wait a minute—let me explain! If you trim your beard, have white sidewall tires, drive a light colored car, appear in public sometimes without the broad-brimmed hat, frequent restaurants, vacation at popular resorts, attend religious seminars, etc., you could well be an Old Order liberal. On the other hand, if your hat brim is three or more inches wide, if you have a black Chevrolet, if your beard is untrimmed, if you seldom appear without the "full order" of dress, if you eat meals only in homes, if you would not be found visiting a church of another denomination, if almost all of your association is with Old Orders, etc., why, you just might be an Old Order conservative. If you are a mixture of the above and are careful to offend as few people as possible, then you are an Old Order moderate!

Let us define briefly the ideology of the Old Orders. Theologically speaking, most Old Orders would be more comfortable with fundamentalism (minus the extreme patriotism) than with religious liberalism. To the outsider it may appear that a set of rules plus some odd traits would be sufficient to ensure salvation for the Old Orders. This is an extreme over-simplification. The truth is, the Old Orders may be freer to make choices than are many other people. Perhaps society's pressures toward conformity are greater than the Old Order's pressure to conform to traditions.

A central principle of the Old Orders may be summed up in a statement that The Vindicator has carried in each issue of the paper for over one hundred years. It is a statement of purpose, one phrase of which reads, "It admonishes to . . . a deeper work of grace in the heart." This may be what is popularly called Christian growth. Old Orders are still convinced that a proper understanding of the traditions of the fathers will not do violence to true spirituality but rather will promote it.

There is, however, another central principle that is not so explicitly set forth in writing. I once visited with a member of the horse-and-buggy Brethren. After a couple of hours, I frankly told him, "I think your group has held to the vision of the Old Orders of 1881 more strictly than any other Old Order group." After a few moments he said, "That is exactly what our aim and goal is!" For a few years that reply has troubled me. Each Old Order group, in its own way, believes itself to be the true inheritors of the Old Order spirit of 1881.

You will note that I have set out two central principles. One principle is spiritual; the other is a vaguely defined posture of nonconformity which lends itself to imprecise personal interpretations. To emphasize the second principle at the expense of the first is to invite trouble. Old Orders have had their share of trouble.

Some earlier Brethren authors have implied that the Old Orders are a bunch of senior citizens with an enraptured fixation on their own noncon-formed navel, people who could not care less while the world goes to hell in a hand basket. I want to say that description will fit just a few persons I have known, and I dare say it will fit a few you have known! Most of my friends are like most of your friends—loving, caring, helpful, and true to the end.

If we Old Orders do not have missions, do we have no concern for lost souls? If we do not have Sunday Schools, do we do nothing about the nurture of children? If we do not have organized prison ministries, do Old Orders have no interest in or do nothing for prisoners? How about organized ministries to the homeless, the hungry, the naked? Do Old Orders have no interest in these needs? If the houses of worship are Spartan and plain, do the Old Orders have no interest in craftsmanship, art, or beauty? I will not answer these questions. The student will find the answers not in books but fror. the Old Order members themselves.

In the lifetime of many Old Orders living today, the membership has moved from a rural lifestyle to that of the professional and artisan, preferably self-employed. A number of families have inherited farms which have only recently been converted to shopping centers, residential areas, or industrial parks. The community colleges make it easy for children and adults to continue higher education. Some speak of the desirability of a college degree. We now have our own private elementary and high schools. These schools combine fine Dunker discipline with the latest in computer technology.

Not only does the increased prosperity pose questions about how to relate to the older image of simplicity and self-denial, but more and more we hear, "how shall we relate to our neighbors?" Let me illustrate.

Recently my wife and I bought our first home. We left the rural tranquility of a large home three miles from town and bought a small brick ranch home in the Peppermint Village section of Union City, Ohio. Perhaps once upper middle class, the area now, because of economic depression, might be described as lower middle class. The houses are close together. We could not have chosen this location if we had children at home. Old Order parents insist on being the primary influence in their children's lives. On one side of us is a Baptist deacon and wife. On another side is someone on disability. Across the way is a family that for a long time has been disintegrating. Down the block is a retired farmer with whom it is said you do not talk religion. Beyond him is a fine couple who go to the Christian Church and who are the epitome of friendliness and helpfulness. Lately my wife, out for a walk, spied at a distance a lady and child who appeared to be different. My wife called out, "Hello, how are you?" The reply was, "Hello, fine thank you, praise the Lord." One of the Wesleyans in this section? We will no doubt find out when we visit their meeting sometime.

Now, did we leave problems behind? I suspect we will have more problems, only different ones. Shortly after moving here my wife said, "I would like a privacy fence from here to here." I said, "No, no." As of now I can wave, "Hi," to the Christian family in their backyard halfway down the block. The Baptist man and his wife came lately for a visit. Children and a few adults use our backyard for a shortcut to their homes on the other street as they probably did when this house stood empty. When one of them passes through, we smile and say, "Hi!" They are usually startled and lately the trespassing has tapered off. The Baptist neighbors are in poor health. Someday, one or the other will need a shoulder to lean on. Their family lives far away. The same goes for some other families around here. Do we need a privacy fence? At our old location we never thought of it. Not only would a fence have a psychological impact on our neighbors, I think it would indicate a psychological shift in ourselves. Do we really want isolation, or is a degree of insulation preferable? As my wife meets someone with a familiar surname, it is not uncommon to hear, "My grandma was a Dunkard, and my ma almost was a Dunkard." How it warms the heart to hear someone say, "Oh, I am so glad you folks moved in here." Do we want isolation? Maybe we will settle finally for a mixture of insulation and openness.

I have given the above illustration as a picture of what the Old Order faces today. He is leaving the relative isolation of the farm. He is somewhat naive and trusting of everybody. It is my conviction that to have an occupation in common with most of one's fellows; to spend most of one's time in the company of one's fellow church members; and to experience in common and in the same way most of life's joys and sorrows is one thing. It is something else to have an occupation shared by only one or two other church members, if any. When men and women work among people of "the world" all day, it is easier to associate in the spare time with them as neighbors instead of seeking out the homes of fellow members. And the children—I remember when most of them came home to do the chores. And then it was supper, homework, and then bedtime. Then, no time was "frittered" away in sports. Now, some excel in sports. Then, physical education was disapproved of because shorts were required. Now, cheerleaders are not unheard of among the Old Orders. Then, no publicity. Now the papers publish the honor students with Brethren names. I am not being judgmental. I am just saying that changed thinking brings different situations, and different situations bring more change in thinking. A few years ago, I visited plain folks around Toronto, Ontario, and was informed that, "We are losing most of our Mennonite young folks. They are leaving and going to Kitchener where they can buy ground and raise hogs. They are determined to hang onto some values." Then the man told me that he himself had been offered a million dollars for his farm for a golf course and for the underground water reservoir. The Old German Baptists have chosen to adapt.

A large Brethren denomination emphasizes the acceptance of diversity, and their choice of moderator may indicate the differing emphasis from year to year.

Is there, among the Old Orders, a class or group or small body of men, or even an individual, who may serve as a prime example of what it means to be an Old Order in the 1990s? I think there is. The strength of the Old Order Brethren today is not in their Annual Meeting, nor in their moderator, nor in one or more influential leaders. Today, the strength lies in the unity of the total body of Elders. From this body a few are chosen for the Standing Committee, and from this committee one is chosen for moderator. The identity of the Standing Committee and the moderator is extremely constant. Only a serious breach of ethics, sickness, or death is likely to remove one of these men from the position. They are hard working, successful farmers or businessmen, apt to teach, who uphold all the order of the church, are usually patient with variations, temperate and moderate. At present, this body is united and bent conservatively. If the student would understand the temperament of the Old German Baptists in the 1990s, then he should become acquainted with several standing committee members. They epitomize the Old German Baptists. I will get my ears pinned back for saying this. I challenge anyone else to name others.

At those points where Old Order tradition meets the modern society, some adjustments need to be made. One of our larger churches gave a seeming anachronous admonition to the members at a business meeting. The members were admonished to avoid unnecessarily patronizing restaurants on Sundays. Much advice was given showing the desirability of members entertaining families in their homes for Sunday dinners. It was shown that the traditional hospitality not only strengthens bonds between fellow Christians, it is very beneficial for the socialization of the children and is favorably considered by neighbors and friends. However, the Old Orders are now accustomed to modern conveniences. The elderly, the youth, and many of the members delight in going to a good restaurant on Sunday. So, why the hassle about eating out? Let us look below the surface.

In this particular locality, a fine restaurant owned by members had many church members for employees. The restaurant closed on Sundays. Then it changed ownership. The local newspaper carried a story on the transaction, commenting on the intention of the new owner to follow the style of the former owner. Privately, the new owner informed the employees that the intention was to stay closed on Sundays. If, however, they had a change of mind later, the Old German Baptist employees would be excused from Sunday work without prejudice. Of course, we all know that Sundays are irresistible to many businessmen. Within a few weeks the new owner had a change of mind. It was soon recognized that if church members would not work at a restaurant on Sundays, yet patronize the same establishment on for Sunday meals, it would appear inconsistent to the neighbors and friends. So, the admonishment to eat in the homes on Sunday was given.

What resulted from this? Can you guess? I made a little inquiry from the youth. After a few Sundays some of the non-member youth went to the restaurant on Sunday. A little later they reported a couple of young members joined the youth group at the restaurant—of course in the church garb. A little later, a few older members were sighted there on Sundays, but these came from churches not in the immediate vicinity and who evidently had not heard of the admonition. Or perhaps they did not feel bound by it. A little later a few local church members, not in harmony with the admonition, bravely ventured to the restaurant on Sunday. Today, the admonition, which carried no penalty, is largely forgotten.

I love to eat out on Sunday. I love to go to a brother's house for dinner and to have others into our home for Sunday dinner. What is the interpretation of the above illustration? It is a very clear example of what is happening to the Old German Baptists everyday, in dozens of places, in dozens of different ways. Their style of life is eroding little by little. Many decisions must be made by each brother and sister. Some of my friends will say they observe nothing of this. I ask us to look away from the few staid churches to those many areas where society has brought modernity to our front doors. While things at this time are by no means at crisis proportions, even now we are undergoing redefinition. The question is: what does it mean to be Old Order in the 1990s? Even the sermons show preoccupation with basic questions that would not have surfaced a few years ago. What is our Christian duty to our neighbors, in our job, in our community?

The outsider sees the surface of things and often is unaware that many incidents among the Old Orders are intimately tied to what church members feel are serious questions of religious identity. Just as important, even those things which appear trivial figure into questions of loyalty to the group and to the goals of the group. I will acknowledge that the Old Orders have a liberal share of legalists. By that, I mean, people who would elevate what should today be a personal preference to a principle that they want to apply to the entire membership. They judge Christians everywhere by their own narrow standards. I submit that this can apply to liberals as well as conservatives.

Old Order youth are raised with the assumption that a strict uniformity is necessary for unity in Christ. Differences in the body appear to many as serious threats to essential unity of the Brotherhood. You will remember that a lack of unity was stressed again and again by the Old Orders as a justification for the division of 1881. I say that not only is some variety desirable, it is necessary. And I think it is a hearty challenge.

Recently an illustration on this came to my mind. Three features of the old sailing ships were the mast, the sails, and the ballast. As you know, the ballast is the weight added to the bottom of the ship to provide stability. The ship may tip over, but the ballast will bring it upright again.

Let us say the young people enter the church after having experienced a spiritual crisis. What was formerly a struggle against the traditions of the church becomes a zealous embracing of the same. Indeed, they may feel that if the ship had more sail, that is, if everyone were more zealous and unitedly more devoted to the traditions, the ship would have more force and success in its journey. The older church members, having mellowed from years of interpersonal relations, have left off the principle of forcing a uniformity of tradition, and by a life of quiet example, portray their unity with the church. These have put down roots. Some are called "pillars" and they may be likened to the mast of the ship which holds the sails firmly in place.

Now, what happens to a ship without ballast? It capsizes. The great body of church members who experience a mixture of ideology and practicality furnish a necessary balance to the church. It is a blessing when the various forces in a body are found in the right proportions. A lack of youthful zeal blunts the body's commitment to ideology. Too little of the strength of patience and experience allows the body to withdraw into extreme sectarianism. The great hidden ballast provides a continuity necessary to study the issues in the light of ideology.

There are more single parents today. When young families break up, the young church members may elect to remain celibate and thus stay eligible to remain a church member. Some of the same pressures upon society at large impinge on the Old Order youth. The association between Old German Baptist youth and the youth of the larger society results in intermarriage, sometimes between youth with conflicting values. Some of these marriages end in divorce, while in other cases the "outsider" becomes a staunch yet generous Old German Baptist. Perhaps their background contributes to an open-mindedness not found in the heirs. Some of these former outsiders are given positions of leadership, thus testifying that the Old Order system can be fair. Our philosophical basis, however, is not sufficiently popular to attract any large number of converts at one time. Thus, the number of converts from the outside is small enough to ensure thorough socialization and poses no threat to the status quo.

In a near-by Old Order church one of the youth in early teens applied for baptism. As is the custom in Ohio, on the day of the baptism, the applicants sit on a front bench with family and friends while they are publicly questioned on their willingness to uphold the "rule of life" outlined in Matthew 18. In this particular case, the girl had many friends on the bench on either side of her, all in their early teens and most of them members of the church. After the meeting, a visitor asked one of the local members, "Is it not unusual, especially here in Ohio, for so many very young people to be members of the church?" After a little pause, the reply was, "Not unusual if you consider they all attend our private school."

In my opinion, our private schools will prove to be one of the bulwarks of the Old Order value system. The school boards are composed of young parents who see the private schools as extensions of the parents' discipline and care for their children. Our schools purposely avoid state certification in order to abide by their own strict charters of organization. I will add that the quality of the schooling is such that where there have been tests administered, results of the private schools have made some public education officials envious. On the other hand, some of the Old German Baptists have bitterly opposed private schools for personal reasons. One credible theory is that the youth in the private schools are too sheltered. But many who choose the private schools are young parents who wish to choose for their children which peer pressure they will face. Many of these parents themselves have just come through the public schools in this time of permissiveness and moral decadence.

While we all like to think that our decisions are made from deep personal study and convictions based upon logical conclusions, we ought to admit that for most of us, and especially children, the forces of society and the influence of our peers are probably the greater factor in our lives. A study ten or twenty years from now of Old Order youth, drugs, marriage, church membership, and the influence of private versus public schooling ought to be made.

Life, however, may be a series of trade-offs. One of my long ago predictions about our private schools may come true. We see the children of the private schools cliquing together. This may be expected. More and more we may see two classes of Old Orders.

I think that a most significant difference in the adaptation of the Old Orders to the larger society, as compared with that experienced by other people, is that the Old Orders never had, nor do they now have, an educated religious professional element to offer guidance to the denomination. In most cases, highly educated Christians seek to be on the cutting edge of change and study to effect change from the general society. They take charge of religious education and attempt to form the world view of their church members. On the other hand, Old Orders do not consciously promote change. It is thrust upon them, or, rather, appears by "accident."

In some ways, Old Orders are individualists. One man may read Dobson or Swindell. Another may be reading Graham or Peale. A man may read only The Vindicator while another may struggle with Barth or Tillich. About the only thing they may have in common is U.S. News and World Report and "Dear Abby."

The Old Orders do make vigorous efforts to hold onto things or strengthen the things that remain. There is much informal social activity among the members. I think it is significant that on several occasions persons have said that when they receive the new directories of church members' addresses, thereafter they seldom use the regular telephone directory. This would indicate that much of their interest and activity revolves around fellow church members. Modern conveniences, such as the telephone and automobile, while at first perceived as threats to the cohesiveness of the Old Order community, have actually become primary instruments of strengthening the brotherhood. Old Orders were quick to use computers for religious publishing and other charitable activities. Modern technology is fully accepted for business uses, and where something new borders on modern entertainment, it is acceptable to consult the local church before adopting the technology.

Whereas once it was natural to associate largely with follow members, now a deliberate choice must be made to do so. It comes as greater cost and personal sacrifice. Many members are doing just that.

I sit in the congregation and see two or three young men clean shaven or with neat beards. They are successful building contractors or entrepreneurs. These men handle hundreds of thousands of dollars, have fine homes, have large recreational vehicles, take long winter vacations, and employ numbers of people. Usually these men have fine principles and stay out of trouble with the church. Some other members are headed for nursing careers, supervisors, certified public accounting, medicine, real estate, auctioneering, banking, education, social work, and postal work; you name it. There are volunteer firemen, school teacher's aids, hospital and nursing home volunteers, and on and on. As yet I know of no one studying law. Just wait! I sit here and observe, and then I remember my visit with the old elder on the Annual Meeting grounds. Is change coming? Has it already come?

A few years ago a brother innocently involved in a lawsuit was temporarily set back from communion unless the local church agreed to suspend the sanction. Today, it is not unheard of that a brother initiate a law suit. Such a brother does not continue in fellowship, but Old Orders take longer to deliberate and decide the merits of each case. Old Orders, today, are more patient with mistakes as much of what was once black and white now appears gray.

One of the greatest single factors for change is the simple association of Old Order members with those outside the church. I have heard the testimonies of persons who took up nursing, attended neighborhood Bible studies, began a factory job, began a business, became a salesman, attended the local college, went to night school, etc. Invariably their experience is similar to my own. Having chosen to associate with members of other denominations with similar interests as mine, I have found some of the finest Christians in the world and have certainly experienced enlarged tolerance and expanded personal vision.

The history of the Old Orders will not lend itself to neat, orderly arrangement. When Laban Brechbill told the story of the Old Order River Brethren,[1] he gave a series of short biographies of outstanding leaders as central to the story. For the Old Order Brethren, unfortunately, much of this is only orally transmitted. Only a little gets into print. It is not the story of denominational impact on the world. It is the story of impact on neighbors, family, friends, and the brotherhood at large.

I do not believe that the Old Orders have greater problems today than they had in the past. An examination of our history will show this. I believe that whereas most denominations actually face new problems, perhaps because basic values are in flux, Old Order problems are the same old ones they have had for over one hundred years. The questions are two: a) how much separation from the general society is necessary for a disciple of Christ, and b) how much unity or agreement among us on the specifics of separation is necessary? The Old Order basic value system is still intact. When we recognize our problems as new ones, we may know assuredly that fundamental change has occurred.

One time we approached the problem of acculturation with at least a similar background and lifestyle. Today, we stand more hesitantly, listening to many voices, still favoring the words of our own elders, halting between self-denial and prosperity, simplicity and complexity. Our choice is no longer between participation in the world and withdrawal from the world. Our problem is how much shall we participate in the world?

Some of my brethren abhor the dividing of the church into parties and characterizing the members in political terms. I do this only for convenience in study. I agree with them that no one can be neatly pigeonholed, that the Body of Christ is a spiritual organism, and that we each are "lively stones" unto God. History tells me that the one absolute, necessary ingredient to unity in the body is that enough persons in the body must be personally motivated by the spirit of Jesus. Without this, everything will fail.

---

[1] Laban T. Brechbill, <u>History of the Old Order River Brethren</u>, Myron S. Dietz, ed. (Lancaster: Brechbill and Stickler, 1972).

6

In Search of a Past and a Future:
The Brethren Church

by Dale R. Stoffer

One of the younger scholars of the Brethren Church, Stoffer shows how his denomination, founded as the progressive branch of the German Baptist Brethren in the 1882 division, entered in the early twentieth century a period of openness to various religious movements. Thus, by the 1960s the church had accumulated a set of incongruous practices and theologies inconsistent with its heritage. After a period of self-evaluation in the 1960s, the church implemented a number of institutional, practical, and theological changes which addressed some of these incongruities. Stoffer suggests four possible responses for other Brethren denominations in a similar situation. The overall impact of the paper suggests that a denomination, by thoughtful evaluation and positive effort, can counteract a trend of theological drift and accommodation. In addition, his own congregation near Columbus, Ohio, has shown that believers who are of non-Brethren background can become committed to a contemporary expression of the Anabaptist-Pietist vision.

During the last twenty years most American denominations have been experiencing an unsettling period of reflection, reevaluation, and restructuring. Undoubtedly, this experience is a part of a larger phenomenon that has left its impact not only on America but also the Western world; we are questioning many of the fundamental assumptions upon which our Western culture has rested for over 1500 years. We have entered a post-Christian era in which a Judeo-Christian foundation is being replaced with a secular one. George Barna, in his book, The Frog in the Kettle: What Christians need to Know about Life in the Year 2000, comments about the impact these developments have made upon the American scene:

> As we enter the 1990s, the way we look at life is already in a state of flux. Our values have undergone a continuing series of shifts since the 1960s, and this made it acceptable to challenge tradition and the status quo. Once the social revolution of that era launched the reexamination of even our most basic moral and social rules, we have constantly explored new avenues of change in our value systems.

We have tentatively experimented with new values and their resulting behaviors and either accepted or rejected those forms after a trial period.[1]

The very fact that we are gathered in this conference is a testimony to the impact that these developments have had upon the Church of the Brethren. But my reason for being here is to share how a related denomination, The Brethren Church, has responded to these cultural changes. I have entitled my paper, "In Search of a Past and a Future: The Brethren Church," because I feel this accurately portrays the state of our church since the 1960s. But before I share observations about this more recent period, I need to lay some historical foundation about our denomination following the three-way division that led to the creation of two new Brethren bodies: the Old German Baptist Brethren and the Progressive Brethren or, officially, The Brethren Church.

One of the intriguing questions of twentieth-century Brethren history is how the Progressive Brethren became conservative and how the Conservative Brethren (the Church of the Brethren) became progressive. The answer to this question lies largely in the theological and cultural movements with which the two denominations have tended to align themselves. I will let Church of the Brethren historians fill in their part of this story, but let me share our story.

Following the division of the early 1880s, leaders of The Brethren Church perceived the church's mission to be to leave behind the eighteenth-century Brethren subculture that they felt had hindered the progress of the church and to move fully into the mainstream of American culture with the gospel of Jesus Christ. They were committed to keeping pace with the times, making use of any available methods that could help them in their evangelistic enterprise. This spirit of openness evidenced itself in several ways. The Progressive Brethren, of course, made full use of methods that had been so sorely criticized by the Old Order Brethren: Sunday Schools and Sunday School Conventions, higher education, revival and evangelistic meetings, a paid ministry, and periodical literature. They quickly became involved with the great interdenominational movements of the late nineteenth and early twentieth centuries: the Women's Christian Temperance Union, YMCA, YWCA, Student Volunteer Movement, Laymen's Missionary Movement, Christian Endeavor, and the Keswick movement. More importantly, though, by the turn of the century the Brethren had made initial contact with liberalism and fundamentalism, the two movements that would shape the history of the denomination through 1940. Liberalism came into the church because a number of leading men were trained in liberal educational institutions and some of these men then became professors at Ashland College. Fundamentalism came into the church through contacts that Jacob C. Cassel, a nephew of Abraham Cassel, and Louis S. Bauman had with fundamentalist leaders.

During the years 1913-1920 these two camps came into direct conflict in the church. The main areas of conflict in the battle were the social gospel, evolution, the nature of Scripture, and prophecy. In the literary debates that filled the denominational periodical, The Brethren Evangelist, three distinct groups can be identified: a small group of vocal liberals, a small group of aggressive fundamentalists, and the main body of traditional Brethren who were conservative but not necessarily fundamentalist. In the clash the main body tended to feel that the liberals were going beyond the limits of Scripture in their accommodation to twentieth century views, but they did not share the militant, aggressive spirit of fundamentalism. The result of the controversy was that the small group of liberals gradually left the church during the 1920s, many of them joining the Presbyterians and Methodists.

This development, which left the church fairly conservative across the board, did not end the problems. During the 1930s Ashland College had become more conservative than at the turn of the century but not fundamentalist as the fundamentalist Brethren desired. During the 1920s and 1930s the fundamentalist Brethren, guided by Louis S. Bauman and the scholarly Alva J. McClain, gained more and more support in the denomination. Bauman and McClain hoped to turn Ashland College into a fundamentalist Bible institute similar to Wheaton College, but the college administration and trustees pushed forward their goal of a fully accredited liberal arts college. Though the fundamentalist Brethren had a strong following in the church, a significant percentage of the church continued to support the college and wanted to follow a conservative, traditionally Brethren course rather than a consciously fundamentalist one. Leaders of the traditional Brethren group were wary of the reactionary, critical, militant trappings of fundamentalism.

Between 1936 and 1939 a power struggle ensued in the church that culminated in 1939 with the control of most of the denominational structures by the traditional Brethren group. The approximately thirty thousand members of the denomination were nearly equally divided between the two groups. The fundamentalist Brethren set up their own institutions without formally severing ties. They called their new seminary Grace Theological Seminary; thus, they have come to be known as the Grace Brethren, while our group is sometimes referred to as the Ashland Brethren. Their official designation was the National Fellowship of Brethren Churches, more recently changed to the National Fellowship of Grace Brethren Churches, and their headquarters became Winona Lake, Indiana.

The division of 1939 affected the Ashland Brethren far more adversely than it did the Grace Brethren. A number of those elements that add vitality and zeal to the life of a denomination were inherited by the Grace Brethren, specifically the youth work, the home and foreign missions programs, and nearly all of the young ministerial recruits. Because most of the seminary students went with the Grace Brethren and due to the fact that World War II followed on the heels of the division (a number of men who later became pastors served in the war), the Brethren Church faced a serious pastoral shortage throughout the 1940s. As a result of these difficulties, the church entered a period of "defeatism, lethargy, gloom," as A. T. Ronk described it, that lasted throughout the 1940s and most of the 1950s. Indicative of this defeatism was a lengthy history of passing resolutions at General Conference without making any attempt to implement them. The problem during this period was a combination of a lack of leadership and an unwillingness, born of apathy and defeatism, to take the prescribed medicine.

By the end of the 1950s a new mood was beginning to appear in the church. The denomination began to make slow and, at times, painful progress. There were a number of components which contributed to this turn around. A revitalized youth program, featuring a summer service program, the Crusader Program, breathed new enthusiasm into the entire church. The church regained its vision for home and foreign missions. Ashland Theological Seminary grew from the smallest seminary in Ohio in 1963 with twenty-two students to the largest, currently with over 500 students (the actual number of Brethren students at the seminary generally runs between fifteen and thirty). It has turned out a steady stream of Brethren men and women who probably have a better understanding of Brethren history and thought than the previous two or three generations of students. Several phases of denominational reorganization have created a structure that has a reduced bureaucracy, greater potential to serve the denomination, and more people involved in ministry rather than administration. Since the 1960s the church has aligned itself with the evangelical movement, especially through involvement in the National Association of Evangelicals. This association has helped to broaden the perspective of the Brethren, though there is always the danger of watering down some of our distinctives in such ecumenical efforts. (Interestingly, The Brethren Church has consistently been among the top two denominations in per capita giving to World Relief, thereby continuing the Brethren concern for one's neighbor in the world.)

Especially important for the progress of the denomination has been a reawakening interest in the historical and theological heritage of the church. Of significance have been the preparation in 1960 of a manual of instruction for new members, entitled Our Faith; the publication in 1968 of a major study on Brethren history by Albert Ronk, History of the Brethren Church; the printing of a more popular work on Brethren history and doctrine, The Brethren: Growth in Life and Thought, by the Board of Christian Education in 1975; the participation of many in the Brethren Church in the historic Brethren Encyclopedia project; and the completion of a Centennial Statement of Faith in 1984, commemorating the 1983 centenary of The Brethren Church. It is this search for our Brethren past that also served as a stimulus for me to work on a doctorate in the area of Brethren thought.

The church has also had to face some difficult theological and practical issues since the 1960s: developing positions on divorce and remarriage, the ordination of women, and the ordination of divorced people; arriving at a consensus on whether to recognize forms of believer baptism other than threefold immersion; and revising and taking more seriously membership commitments. Though these discussions have at times been emotionally charged, the church has developed a greater sense of commitment to and openness with one another and, as a result, an increasing unity within the body. It should also be noted that the topics involved in these discussions indicate that the church is reevaluating its position on issues which have been brought to the forefront by our culture, notably divorce and the role of women.

During the 1980s the church experienced a period of critical self-evaluation of its strengths and weaknesses. Unlike the score of years following 1939, however, the church has sought to overcome its deficiencies through concerted, coordinated efforts. Though the denomination has slipped in membership since 1957, down nearly thirty percent, worship attendance has actually increased during the period, up over twenty percent. The mood in the church is probably as optimistic as it has been for over sixty years. The church has a clearer vision of its distinctive priorities and mission and a developing sense of urgency to fulfill that mission. Alexander Mack, Sr., when asked to speculate about the future of the fledgling Brethren movement, responded with words that can likewise apply to the Brethren Church: "As their faith is, so shall be their outcome."

As I evaluate the theological state of the church, I must agree with an observation that John Stott makes in his book on the Sermon on the Mount: "Probably the greatest tragedy of the church throughout its long and checkered history has been its constant tendency to conform to the prevailing culture instead of developing a Christian counter-culture."[2] Though Stott is primarily concerned about the influence of culture on the church, a similar point can be made about the impact of theological fads on the church, including the Brethren Church. Because of the extreme openness of the Progressives at the end of the nineteenth century and the assumption by some interpreters of Brethren thought that we possess a non-theological tradition, the church has been influenced by nearly every theological movement that has swept across the American ecclesiastical scene. As a result the Brethren Church has been left with an incongruous set of practices and theologies which, in some cases, bear little resemblance to its original heritage. I cite from my dissertation the major examples of these inconsistencies.

First, much of the church has adopted a revivalist-fundamentalist view of salvation that tends not only to view faith as merely a confession of Christ as Savior (assensus) but also to see salvation as connected primarily with this confession of faith. This conception of salvation is completely foreign to the original Brethren view which perceived faith as assensus, repentance (a radical change in one's heart and mind which necessarily leads to a change in life), and faith as fiducia (commitment of one's life to Christ in discipleship) as indispensable conditions to salvation. In this view there is no room for "cheap grace," but the believer by the very nature of his response to God's grace is expected to live a life of total surrender to Christ.

Second, the church needs to fill the void left by the loss of the traditional mystical/devotional piety. From many sides of Christianity today there are calls coming for a reawakening of spirituality in the church. It would seem ironic if the Brethren Church, with a rich heritage of a Christ-centered piety, had to rely solely on other contemporary guides to regain a stronger spiritual sense.

Third, the Brethren Church has inherited a Christian ethic from fundamentalist and evangelical Christianity which tends to identify a number of outward marks which delimit what a Christian should or should not do. There seems to be no integral relationship between this ethic and the initial aspects of salvation. The traditional Brethren conception of the Christian life, however, viewed the salvation process as issuing in a life that conformed more and more completely to the perfection that is in Christ. Thus, the complete surrender and unqualified commitment to Christ found in repentance and faith, the conception of baptism as a covenant before God and His people to live the new Christ-like life, the experience of regeneration which provided the foundation and enabling power for the new life, and the experience of communion with God which manifested itself in a will conformed to God's own will became powerful catalysts for desiring to live an obedient life.

Fourth, if the church is to take seriously its traditional principles of nonconformity, simplicity of life, nonresistance, and self-denial, it must be ready to divorce itself more completely from the current popular conceptions of Christianity and found its faith solely of the Word of God. Progressivism means advancement toward the ideal of Scripture, not acceptance of current theological fads.

Fifth, the church must regain a sense of brotherhood. For too long individualism (both with regard to church leadership and inter-congregational relations) has reigned in the church, blunting the total effectiveness of the denomination.

Sixth, accountability must be restored in all levels of the church. The concept of a covenanted community, founded upon the individual's commitment to a body of believers as a part of his baptismal vows, needs to be revived. What Franklin Littell has said about Free Churches concerning their lack of discipline is apropos: "That the Free Churches, whose original complaint against the establishments was precisely that they practiced no true Christian discipline, should have succumbed to such a degree is a scandal twice compounded."[3]

In the eleven years since I wrote this critique of Brethren thought and practice, I have been pleased with the attempts that the church has made to address a number of these inconsistencies. Several of them, notably the first and third items, are gradually succumbing to endeavors to educate the church about our historic faith and life. Both the Centennial Statement and a new discipleship course, Follow Him Gladly, written from a Brethren perspective, have been instrumental in this regard. During the last five years, the church has also held several gatherings of leaders from both national and local levels to take a hard look at the present status of the church and develop goals and strategies for the future. An important aspect of this process has been the formulation of a denominational mission statement by the General Conference Executive Council. Both denominational organizations and local churches have used this statement in developing goals and strategies. The statement is as follows:

> The Brethren Church is a priesthood of believers steadfast in commitment to its Lord and Savior Jesus Christ and obedient to the New Testament as the guide for faith and practice. The purpose of The Brethren Church, therefore, is to worship the triune God, live as obedient disciples of the risen Christ, nurture the growth of believers to Christian maturity, evangelize the lost, and minister to human needs. Brethren seek to be channels of God's love by being a compassionate community of His ambassadors. To live the Truth as covenantal disciples of Christ, Brethren desire to love and serve all people as neighbors and friends.

These efforts to provide better education about our past and a clearer vision for our future have yielded a greater sense of unity and brotherhood in the church. Many local churches within the denomination have likewise deepened the bonds of fellowship among one another through the implementation of Moderator Warren Garner's 1986 General Conference recommendation to "extend the family ties beyond the local church by establishing triads of love of congregations. The purpose of these triads would be to nurture each other through a series of interactions."[4] During the last five years churches in proximity to one another have gotten to know one another better through such forms of interaction as pulpit exchanges, picnics, and meetings to share music or other programs, and joint youth activities. The "triads of love" have helped to deepen the understanding of what it means to be "Brethren."

Another significant step taken by the church was the adoption in 1988 of a study on the concept of membership. This study called for the incorporation of more discipline and accountability into the life of local churches. To implement this call, the report proposed the inclusion of the following statement in one's membership vows: "will you, in a spirit of love and submission, both give counsel to and receive counsel from your brothers and sisters in Christ."[5] The report further urged the discontinuation of an inactive membership list because it avoided holding members accountable to their vows. Congregations were encouraged to maintain only an active membership list, made up of people who yearly renewed their commitment to their membership vows. The report offered two approaches for ascertaining members' willingness to renew their commitments.

One is the covenant renewal approach in which all members renew their membership commitments yearly. Those not renewing their vows are dropped from membership, though such people should be visited by the pastor or deacon prior to removal from the membership role in order to ascertain the reasons for the failure to renew. A second form of discipline is the traditional yearly deacon visit. Every member of the church is visited by a deacon once a year to mutually discern and encourage faithfulness to the membership covenant. If more Brethren churches developed such a practice, it would not only lead to a stronger, more committed church body, but it would probably also lead to a renewal among the deacons and deaconesses of many churches.[6]

There has been a growing commitment among Brethren pastors to increase the bonds of fellowship and accountability among themselves as well. This commitment has been expressed through both informal and formal channels. Informally, pastors seem to be far more supportive of one another as evidenced by the large numbers of pastors involved in monthly district fellowship meetings, the yearly Pastors' Conference, and the denominational pastors' prayer chain. Formally, the Brethren elders have supported the hiring of a Director of Pastoral Ministries by ·the denomination (1980) to pastor pastors and oversee pastor-congregational relations; the establishment of a National Ordination Council (1980) to examine and approve all candidates for ordination before they are ordained by their home congregation; and the adoption of stricter guidelines (1987) for what it means to be ordained and for the discipline of pastors. Though there remain some significant issues that the church needs to address, I feel the progress made during the last decade bodes well for the future.

I would like to make a slight shift of focus here to deal with the issue of transition. I truly believe that we as Brethren, and I speak here of all Brethren, share with the church at large a most critical time. In certain ways the situation of the American church resembles the situation faced by the Brethren in the tumultuous 1870s and early 1880s. In both cases the catalytic issue was how to respond to culture. But in other ways the situation is quite different. Last century the Brethren wrestled with the question, should the Brethren remain in the Brethren sub-culture or move into the American mainstream? Today we are faced with a situation both more complex and critical. The Brethren have not changed so much as American culture has. The American culture which the Progressives and Conservatives joined in the late 1800s and early 1900s was still a culture informed by Judeo-Christian values. Today we live in a post-Christian culture that has rejected all absolutes (except the absolute that there are no absolutes) and has chosen the amoral philosophy of personal fulfillment as its guiding star. Without its traditional bearings American culture has been set adrift; it is far more at the mercy of the winds of cultural fads than ever before.

Essentially we as Brethren can choose one of four options relative to the changes occurring around us.

1) Withdrawal. We can choose to preserve our Brethren faith and heritage by separating ourselves as much as possible from the influence of American culture. It may be felt that American society has strayed so far from Biblical truths and values that it is beyond redemption. Let us seek to preserve ourselves as a holy remnant. The Old Order Brethren have argued along these lines as have those Brethren most influenced by fundamentalism.

2) Accommodation. We may argue that the place of Christians is to be in the world. We will not influence the world if we draw dividing lines between

ourselves and the rest of society. We must be seen as part of culture. Our task is to translate what we feel to be the essence of Christianity into modern thought forms and images. Of all approaches, this is the most problematic. Proponents of this view run the risk of becoming so at home in the world that they forget or misconstrue the mission of the church. They may likewise lose the distinctiveness of the gospel, playing down its radical, other-worldly, world-challenging nature.

3) Business-as-usual. We as Brethren may just continue the status quo, oblivious to the changes going on around us. We may do things the way we always have, whether in worship, church programs, or church organization. If people want to join us, fine, but we must guard against new people getting too much authority and changing things. Frankly, this approach poses a danger in many Brethren churches, both the Brethren Church and the Church of the Brethren. A revolution is going on around us, and we are content to live in a cultural backwater. If we do not take the time to understand our culture and engage it on its own turf, an ever-widening distance will separate our churches from the world. With this approach the church will become increasingly irrelevant for the majority of Americans. Christians also may be even more tempted to lead a two-faced life: the life of the respectable church-goer on Sunday and the life of the amoral secularist the rest of the week.

4) Critical engagement. The final approach is a dialectical one that recognizes the need for both separation from and involvement in the world. Our identity must derive from our relationship to Jesus Christ and commitment to His Word. This very identity will lead to a spiritual, moral, and philosophical separation from the values and behaviors of our culture. But we also recognize that the Lord we follow calls us into the midst of the world, a calling which He Himself accepted in coming to earth. This calling impels us not only to understand the world better than it understands itself, but also to engage the world with the Word of God and confront it with its need to discover true life in the living Word, Jesus Christ.

This approach mirrors the one taken by the Conservatives and, to a lesser extent, the Progressives in the 1880s. It adopts the conservative-progressive dialectic that guided the conservatives through the turmoil of the 1880s. The conservative nature of the Brethren faith derives from our faithful commitment to God's unchanging Word. This element provides the absolute standard of truth beyond which we are not willing to go. The progressive nature of the Brethren faith derives from our desire to speak the Word in the midst of whatever culture we find ourselves. We must be willing to modify our means of conveying God's unchanging truth in ways that will most effectively confront our culture with that truth. Every congregation needs to be sensitive to the Holy Spirit's leading to be able to discern the means that will speak most powerfully and clearly to its community. (Note that a conservative-progressive dialectic also includes a Word-Spirit dialectic.) This conservative-progressive dialectic can be distorted when we become conservative regarding the elements we should be progressive about and progressive on the elements we should conserve. Thus, we must beware of becoming overly conservative about the particular forms we use for expressing the faith or overly progressive about the way we understand God's Word and adapt it to modern thought forms.

One of the reasons I have spent the last eleven years of my life in a church planting effort in Columbus, Ohio, was to see whether the Brethren faith and lifestyle could be taught and caught by people who were non-traditional Brethren both in heritage and in location. My congregation indeed is non-traditionally Brethren in some of the programs and styles of worship we use, but we are more Brethren than most of the oldest churches in our denomination in terms of knowing and living out those values and commitments that have been essential trademarks of the Brethren: life-changing belief in and discipleship to Jesus Christ, living as well as believing the Word of God, a loving and caring fellowship of believers, a strong sense of accountability for each other and a willingness to give and receive counsel, a commitment to involvement in some ministry, concern for our neighbors in the world, and striving for consensus and unity in mind and spirit.

It is my belief that the Brethren faith and life is a transferable concept into any culture. It is not specific to any one external form of expression, though I know there will be those who disagree. My vision for The Brethren Church is that through emphasis on education, church growth, and home missions, we might truly disseminate the Brethren faith and life more widely throughout our culture. We as Brethren have much to offer our culture; in fact we have a lifestyle that speaks to some of the greatest felt needs of our society: loneliness, a lack of meaning and purpose, the desire to be loved and accepted, and the need for family. But we need to take seriously the challenge of conveying our faith and life in Christ in ways that will effectively engage our culture. The Brethren have a past that is worthy of emulation, but if we are to have a future, we must be willing to find ways to pass it on through contemporary forms that faithfully present God's Word in its purity and power.

[1] George Barna, <u>The Frog in the Kettle: What Christians Need to Know about Life in the Year 2000</u> (Ventura, CA: Regal Books, 1990), 32.

[2] John R. W. Stott, <u>Christian Counter-Culture: The Message of the Sermon on the Mount</u> (Downers Grove, IL: InterVarsity Press, 1978), 63.

[3] Dale R. Stoffer, "Background and Development of Brethren Doctrines, 1650-1987" (Philadelphia, PA: <u>Brethren Encyclopedia</u>, Inc., 1989), 240-241.

[4] <u>General Conference Annual, 1986</u> (Ashland, OH: The Brethren Church, 1986), 6.

[5] <u>General Conference Annual, 1988</u> (Ashland, OH: The Brethren Church, 1988), 16.

[6] Ibid., 15.

7
Recent Trends
Among Mennonites

by James C. Juhnke

A historian, Juhnke examines patterns of change and adaptation among moderate and progressive Mennonites. While cultural and social accommodation have taken place, he shows also that loss of heritage has been resisted in creative and effective ways. While some degree of compromise and acquiescence is inevitable, Mennonites have responded actively in the creation of new institutions, in the recovery and continued reformulation of the Anabaptist vision, in ecumenical involvement, and in periodic revitalization of the pacifist stance. These responses have contributed to a continuing vitality within Mennonite groups. There is reason to rejoice in a significant measure of faithfulness to a distinctive tradition.

In the 1970s and 1980s, between the Vietnam War and the Persian Gulf War, Mennonites in America struggled to maintain their identity and extend their witness in the face of rapid change. Historically, Mennonites were sectarians on the margins of society. In America they became a legitimate denomination which accommodated to American ways. The pace of Mennonite change varied widely among the different groups. The past twenty years have seen remarkable institutional vitality, combined with fears that the distinctive Mennonite religious and cultural heritage has been slipping away.

In North America, Mennonites generally have not won many members from beyond their ethnic boundaries. Early in this century Mennonite and Amish numbers grew substantially because of a high birth rate and immigration, but the growth rates in recent years have leveled off or, in some cases, declined. Mennonites are a graying church, with smaller families than in the past. One surprise has been continuing vitality and growth among the conservative Old Orders, once considered declining remnants of culture lag.[1] Another surprise has been the relative success of Mennonite mission churches overseas, which, if current trends continue, will soon outnumber Mennonites of European origin.[2] Mennonite World Conference gatherings, held every five or six years, have become huge multi-cultural celebrations.

Mennonite Double Polarity

Two polarities are basic to the American Mennonite experience.[3] On one hand there is the difference between Mennonites (and Amish) of Swiss and South German origin and those of Dutch, Prussian, and Russian origin. On the other hand there is the difference between traditionalist Old Order groups which have vigilantly maintained their boundaries against the broader society and the more progressive groups which have been more open to social change. Paul Toews, Mennonite historian at Pacific College, has suggested that traditionalists and progressives have sought renewal in fundamentally contrasting ways. The traditionalists seek renewal through boundary maintenance. The progressives seek renewal through the revitalization of the organizing centers—the nuclei—of church and community life.[4]

Progressive Mennonites, according to Toews, have fashioned a new identity in three successive overlapping ways: They have created new institutions in the manner of American denominations. They conceived new ideological or doctrinal syntheses, most notably the so-called "Anabaptist Vision." They cooperate ecumenically in inter-Mennonite voluntary associations for work in the world. An assessment of recent trends among Mennonites (and Amish) might well proceed by asking whether the Old Order traditionalists have succeeded in sustaining vitality through maintaining boundaries, and whether the progressives have sustained vitality at their centers through institutional, ideological, and ecumenical activity. This paper will focus primarily on the moderates or progressives.

Sociological Data

In 1972 and again in 1989, Mennonite sociologists conducted extensive scientific surveys of attitudes and behavior of Mennonites in congregations across North America.[5] Each survey included a sample of more than 3,500 Mennonites from carefully selected congregations. These church member surveys made it possible to compare five groups with each other (Brethren in Christ, Mennonite Brethren, General Conference Mennonite, Mennonite Church, and Evangelical Mennonite Church), to compare Mennonites with North American Protestants, to chart changes over time, and to assess which Mennonite traits were the most significant predictors of other traits.

The authors of the sociological study concluded that Mennonite identity remained strong and vital and was likely to remain so in the face of modernization. In their words,

> . . . we conclude that Mennonite [sacred] canopies are still firmly held in place by strong theological, community, family and institutional stakes, so that Mennonite

peoplehood and consciousness of kind persist, while adaptations and adjustments to the broader society occur.[6]

The most dramatic change was Mennonite urbanization. From 1972 to 1989 the numbers of Mennonites living in towns of 2,500 or larger grew from about one-third (35%) to about one-half (48%). The number who had been to college increased in similar proportions. In 1972 the numbers of Mennonite men in farming and the professions was about equal. Seventeen years later the numbers of professionals more than doubled that of farmers. The number of females in professions doubled from ten percent to twenty-one percent.[7]

The study showed that urbanization and professionalization have not resulted in significant loosening of moral attitudes. In fact, the 1989 results showed increased opposition to extramarital sexual intercourse, smoking marijuana, homosexual acts, and smoking tobacco. Meanwhile the results showed greater acceptance of gambling, social drinking, social dancing, divorce, and remarriage. The percentage of church members who were divorced was up from one percent in 1972 to four percent in 1989—far below the national average but still reflective of American cultural trends.[8] In 1989 nearly all Mennonites in this survey had television sets, but seventy-five percent of them said television had a more negative than a positive impact.[9]

Mennonite political involvements have increased significantly in recent years while the traditional dualism in church-state attitudes has eroded. Those who say they vote in elections most or all of the time rose from forty-six percent to sixty-five percent, an increase of nearly twenty points. While the numbers of Mennonites actually holding political office remain negligible, seventy-six percent say that Christians should communicate their concerns directly to government (up from sixty-one percent in 1972).[10]

Mennonites scored very high compared to American Protestants on a scale of belief in orthodox Christian doctrines relating to God, Christ, miracles, and life after death. From 1972 to 1989 these beliefs did not shift significantly, nor did Mennonite commitment to distinctive Anabaptist beliefs such as infant baptism and church discipline. The percentage of those saying Christians should not take part in war went down somewhat, while the percentage of those who said it is against God's will to swear an oath went up. Mennonites scored high on tests of Bible knowledge, with no significant erosion from 1972 to 1989. However, average weekly church attendance dropped from 70% to 65%, and weekly Sunday school attendance declined from 69% to 59%. Participation in family devotions also declined significantly.[11]

The vast amount of data from the 1972 and 1989 surveys and the extensive analyses by the professional sociologists are not conducive to brief summation. But it is clear that these scholars have not found convincing evidence for impending Mennonite crisis or demise. They rather portray a mixed picture of insistent change and creative adaptation. Some Mennonite communities have disintegrated and some congregations disbanded, especially in rural areas. But more broadly, Mennonite communal life has remained strong, religious beliefs have been kept intact, and new networks of social interaction and service activities have emerged to sustain and renew Mennonite life in the transition from farm to city.

Old and New Institutions

In the late nineteenth and early twentieth centuries, and again in the years after World War II, Mennonites created an array of denominational institutions which transformed the character of their presence in the world. Mennonite mission boards, schools, hospitals, mutual aid associations, mental health centers, publication agencies and the like became channels for aggressive activity for development of peoplehood identity and for service to the world. Not all these agencies survived or maintained their church connection. The Mennonite deaconess movement, for example, withered away and Mennonite hospitals came under wider public control. But in general the denominational institutions continued to thrive through the 1980s. Mennonite liberal arts colleges retained strong church connections and continued to raise up new church leaders nourished in fertile mating grounds of faith and culture.

Progressive Mennonites today are more preoccupied with sustaining old institutions than with creating new ones. Indeed, more than one person has observed that Mennonites have long since passed their saturation point in institution founding. Nevertheless, the past several decades have seen the emergence and flourishing of para-church agencies and new institutions which often powerfully support American Mennonite identity and witness. Among the examples are the "Mennonite Your Way" network, Mennonite Disaster Service (MDS), Mennonite relief sales, and the Mennonite self-help/thrift shops. Such agencies usually emerge spontaneously outside of the established denominational structures but go on to adopt regional and national organizational systems for sustained and efficient functioning.

The thousands of Mennonites who participate each year in MDS, relief sales, and self-help/thrift shops engage in ethnic-religious rituals which foster and secure Mennonite identity. Women sewing quilts for sale, teenagers picking up trash after a tornado, and volunteers sorting through piles of recycled clothing—all celebrate their peoplehood while engaging in popular benevolence projects which make a good name for Mennonites. The scale of these programs could hardly have been imagined several decades ago. In 1990 the Self-Help Crafts project, for example, purchased $5,652,000 of craft items overseas, providing employment for 14,000 people in lesser developed countries.[12] Most of these items are sold by volunteers in the more than seventy stores, most of which are a creative combination of sophisticated gift shops and recycling centers for used goods. Since our recently founded innovative charitable institutions also help to celebrate ethnic identity, we may expect similar new institutions to emerge in the future.

One significant institutional trend of recent years has been the growth of Mennonite Central Committee and the extension of its constituency among Mennonites. The growing MCC budgets and increasing loyalty to MCC of the substantial corps of MCC alumni in Mennonite congregations have led to some concern that it is gradually displacing the role of separate denominational agencies. During the 1980s MCC itself remained at a generally stable number of total personnel (ca. 950 to 1,000) as overseas ministries became more specialized and qualified workers difficult to recruit. Mennonite institutions remain strong, but recent trends suggest that the explosive growth of earlier decades will not be repeated.

Ideology

In the 1950s and 1960s Mennonite identity was focused upon an "Anabaptist Vision" articulated by Harold S. Bender and Guy F. Hershberger of Goshen College. This vision inspired a generation of scholars to pursue Anabaptist studies and a generation of church leaders to view themselves in an honorable and distinctive Reformation tradition. In the 1970s and 1980s a new group of scholars found greater complexity and relativity in the Anabaptist movement. It became less clear that any one definition of Anabaptist could be normative for modern Mennonitism.[13] The numbers of Mennonite scholars of Anabaptism declined while interest in more recent history increased. In the 1980s a new generation of social historians produced a four-volume history of "The Mennonite Experience in America," which located Mennonites in their American social, economic, and intellectual context more thoroughly than had been done earlier.[14] This new history, however, did not carry a central vision which promised to inspire church renewal. The charmed role of history for Mennonites, while perhaps still stronger than for comparable groups, began to decline. A new generation of sociologists competed with historians as definers of the tradition.[15] And a surge of Mennonite literary expression, primarily from the pens of Canadian Mennonite writers, has enriched and astonished Mennonite readers.[16]

In recent years Mennonite scholars have begun to overcome the tradition's longstanding mistrust of the discipline of theology. Mennonite theological dialogue has become more sophisticated, with the <u>Conrad Grebel Review</u> providing a significant forum. Two creative Mennonite theologians, Gordon Kaufman of Harvard University and John Howard Yoder of Notre Dame, have significantly influenced Mennonites as well as many in the wider Christian community. Marlin Miller, President of Associated Mennonite Biblical Seminaries in Elkhart, Indiana, recently identified three comprehensive theological efforts informed by an Anabaptist perspective which are currently under way: C. Norman Krause, <u>Jesus Christ Our Lord</u> (1987); Thomas N. Finger, <u>Christian Theology, An Eschatological Approach</u> (1985); and James

William McClendon, Systematic Theology, Ethics (1986).[17] Recent theological discussions often have focused upon issues of Christology.[18]

Inter-Mennonite Ecumenism

Mennonite identity in America has long been shaped by relationships between the numerous groups in the Mennonite and Amish mosaic. Several decades of common experiences, preeminently in World War II Civilian Public Service and in Mennonite Central Committee service, have paved the way for greater ecumenical cooperation. The two largest Mennonite bodies, the Mennonite Church (formerly known as "Old" Mennonite) and the General Conference Mennonite Church are presently exploring the possibility of merger. Whether or not these two bodies actually become one, the cooperative endeavors will proceed apace. A new Mennonite statement of faith for these two groups is well on its way. Mennonites already have their equivalent of a national anthem in a rousing doxology, "Praise God from Whom all Blessings Flow," #606 from the Mennonite Hymnal.

Recent years have seen vigorous discussions and shifting relationships among Mennonites across the United States-Canada border. The Canadians, mostly of the Dutch-Russian origin, have sought greater autonomy after decades of following the lead of United States-based denominational agencies. Inter-Mennonite ecumenicity is growing in Canada, although it has somewhat different structural forms than in the United States. The major Mennonite denominational groups (Mennonite Church, General Conference, Mennonite Brethren) continue to be binational bodies, even as they have made adjustments of organization. Not many Protestant bodies have worked as diligently at binational organization and identity in recent years as have the General Conference Mennonite Church and the Mennonite Brethren Church.

War and Peace

For all Mennonites, matters of war and peace lie close to religious identity. Mennonites refuse participation in war, a refusal which is not unanimous but which has remained an official and a powerful norm. Wars are good for Mennonites in that each military conflict which makes demands upon citizens forces Mennonites to consider the roots of Christian pacifist faith. War-prompted Mennonite benevolence becomes a moral equivalent for war. The Vietnam War (1965-73) and its accompanying cultural revolution in the United States affected Mennonites in profound ways which have not yet been examined and interpreted. The Persian Gulf War (1991), a short but massive technological war which sought popular acquiescence but made no direct claims upon citizens for service or money, presented a new challenge. What did the gospel of peace mean in a nation which played out a domestically popular role as world police power without making overt sacrificial demands upon all citizens?"[19]

Conclusion

Mennonite scholars do not agree in their assessments of recent trends in their denomination. Ted Koontz, ethics and peace studies teacher at Associated Mennonite Biblical Seminaries, recently suggested that "the current flowering of Mennonite institutions and activities is not a sign of health, but the dying beauty of a cut flower, one severed from its roots and incapable of prolonged vitality."[20] Other scholars look at the same scene and judge Mennonites to be adapting to modernity with vigor and creativity.[21] The evidence is sufficiently ambiguous to encourage both prophets and priests. Mennonites exhibit signs of vitality and faithfulness to a distinctive tradition, as well as signs of yielding to the seductions of modern American culture.

[1] Donald B. Kraybill, The Riddle of Amish Culture (Baltimore: The Johns Hopkins University Press, 1989), 14-15.

[2] Dieter Goetz Lichdi, ed., Mennonite World Handbook, Mennonites in Global Witness (Carol Stream: Mennonite World Conference, 1990), 326-7.

[3] See James C. Juhnke, "Mennonite History and Self Understanding: North American Mennonitism as a Bipolar Mosaic," in Mennonite Identity, Historical and Contemporary Perspectives, ed. by Calvin Wall Redekop and Samuel J. Steiner (Lanham, Md: University Press of America, 1988), 83-99.

[4] Paul Toews, "Dissolving the Boundaries and Strengthening the Nuclei," Christian Leader (July 27, 1982), 6-8. Also published with slightly different titles in Gospel Herald (January 25, 1983), 49-52, and The Mennonite (July 5, 1983), 316-8.

[5] The results of the 1972 survey were published in J. Howard Kauffman and Leland Harder, Anabaptists Four Centuries Later: A Profile of Five Mennonite and Brethren in Christ Denominations (Scottdale: Herald Press, 1975). The results of the 1989 survey are scheduled for publication in late 1991. The manuscript is J. Howard Kauffman and Leo Driedger, "The Mennonite Mosaic: Identity and Modernization." Summaries of some information were published in Mennonite Weekly Review as follows: John Bender, "Survey Reveals 17-Year Trends" (Jan 25, 1990), 1; Leo Driedger, "Mennonites Moving to the Cities" (June 21, 1990), 1-2; J. Howard Kauffman, "Some Ethical Beliefs Changing" (June 28, 1990), 1-2; J. Howard Kauffman, "Abortion Opposition Rises, Views on Peace Surveyed" (July 5, 1990); Leland Harder, "Mennonites Becoming More Active Politically" (July 12, 1990, 1-2; and Abram G. Konrad, "Members' Church Attendance Drops; Few Beliefs Change" (July 26, 1990), 1-2. For much the same information see the Gospel Herald issues of July 24, July 31, and August 7, 1990.

[6] Kauffman and Driedger, "The Mennonite Mosaic," 354.

[7] Driedger, "Mennonites Moving," 1.

[8] J. Howard Kauffman, "Some Ethical," 1.

[9] Kauffman and Driedger, "The Mennonite Mosaic," 377.

[10] Leland Harder, "Mennonites Becoming," 1.

[11] Konrad, "Members' Church," 1-2.

[12] 1990 Mennonite Central Committee Workbook (Akron: Mennonite Central Committee, 1990), 2, 153.

[13] The literature on the demise of normative Anabaptism is extensive. For an recent discussion of the issues, see J. Denny Weaver, "Is the Anabaptist Vision Still Relevant," Pennsylvania Mennonite Heritage (January 1991), 2-12.

[14] The first three volumes in the Mennonite Experience in America series are: Richard K. MacMaster, Land, Piety, Peoplehood: The Establishment of Mennonite Communities in America 1683-1790 (Scottdale: Herald Press, 1985); Theron F. Schlabach, Peace, Faith, Nation: Mennonites and Amish in Nineteenth-Century America (Scottdale: Herald Press, 1988); and James C. Juhnke, Vision, Doctrine, War: Mennonite Identity and Organization in America 1890-1930 (Scottdale: Herald Press, 1989). The fourth volume by Paul Toews is forthcoming.

[15] See, for example, the essays by Donald B. Kraybill, Calvin Redekop, and Alan B. Anderson in "The Sociology of Mennonite Self-Understanding," Part IV in Mennonite Identity: Historical and Contemporary Perspectives (University Press of America, 1988), 153-201. See also the sociological essays in Anabaptist-Mennonite Identities in Ferment, Leo Driedger and Leland Harder, eds. (Elkhart: Institute of Mennonite Studies, 1990).

[16] Al Reimer, "Mennonite Literary Voices Past and Present," Menno Simons Lectures at Bethel College, 1991. To be published in C. H. Wedel Series.

[17] Marlin E. Miller, "Theology," in The Mennonite Encyclopedia (Scottdale: Herald Press, 1990), Vol. 5, 884.

[18] Erland Waltner, ed., <u>Jesus Christ and the Mission of the Church: Contemporary Anabaptist Perspectives</u> (Newton: Faith and Life Press, 1990).

[19] James C. Juhnke, "Limited War in a Century of Total War," 53-60, in <u>Weathering the Storm, Christian Pacifist Responses to War</u>, Susan E. Janzen, ed. (Newton: Faith and Life Press, 1991).

[20] Ted Koontz, "Mennonites and 'Postmodernity'," <u>Mennonite Quarterly Review</u> (October 1989), 417.

[21] Kauffman and Driedger, "The Mennonite Mosaic," 354.

8

Separation, Discipline, and Nineteenth Century Quakers

by Thomas D. Hamm

In a summary both concise and comprehensive, Hamm sketches the massive changes which to took place among the orthodox Quakers in America beginning in the early part of the nineteenth century. The events which radically transformed Quaker belief and practice occurred considerably earlier than those which revolutionized the Brethren. Changes in the economy played a significant role, but Hamm's analysis is enriched by a careful explanation of how other religious movements in American Protestantism contributed to modification of the Quaker faith. The religious ferment engendered by evangelical revivalism was especially potent in spreading doctrinal innovations among Quakers. This in turn brought about internal dissension and fragmentation. Reactions to these issues caused the formation of conservative, moderate, and progressive branches. By 1900, however, Quakerism had already become a microcosm of American Protestantism at large.

About 1910 James Baldwin, author of textbooks and purveyor of useful and moral knowledge to a generation of American schoolchildren, set out to re-create for his family the Quaker world into which he had been born in the backwoods of Indiana in 1842. Many of Baldwin's memories were of the material changes wrought by the technological forces of the nineteenth century—the railroad, the steam engine, the mass circulation newspaper—in the "New Settlement" of Friends around Westfield, Indiana. When Baldwin brought his memoir to a close, however, he dwelt not on the material but the spiritual, the transformation of the Quaker faith that had shaped his youth.[1]

The Westfield of the 1840s and 1850s had been a place of women in drab plain bonnets and men in broad-brimmed hats and shadbelly coats. They spoke of "thee" and "thine" in phrases reminiscent of seventeenth-century England. They worshiped in an utterly plain, barn-like building that they called a meetinghouse, the men and women being seated separately with the "weighty" Friends facing them at the front, the waiting silence broken only by an occasional impromptu discourse believed to be uttered under the direct guidance of the Holy Spirit. "Testimonies" ruled their lives—testimonies against slavery, fighting, "light and profane literature," music, "worldly diversions," "hireling ministry"—in sum, against "the world." Their lives were proscribed by "the Discipline," a "thin, dreary volume" that regulated every aspect of a good Friend's life, from the words of the marriage ceremony to the height of the tombstone. Three overseers enforced every regulation, "holy bigots" whom Baldwin recalled as a strange cross between medieval inquisitors and modern detectives.[2]

The Friends that Baldwin found when he returned to Westfield in 1910 left the gentle publisher bewildered. They worshiped not in a meetinghouse but in a steepled church that, his Babbitt-like guide informed him, for "style and comfort" rivaled any in the state. An organ for music and a pulpit filled by a sleek and elegant pastor had replaced the grim old denizens of the facing benches. The plain language was a memory associated with long-dead forebears; gone too were shadbelly coats and plain bonnets. No one saw "the use of such any longer." The Quakers of Westfield were no longer separate from the world—they had become part of it.[3]

James Baldwin's experience was not unique; it was one that thousands of American Quakers in the second half of the nineteenth century shared. Once a sect, self-consciously set apart from the rest of American Protestantism by a peculiar lifestyle and distinctive theology, by 1900 they had become a denomination, with members outwardly indistinguishable from the rest of the world, and theology that by their own testimony differed in no important particular from that of other evangelicals. Although, if pressed, some Friends would still have claimed to be "a peculiar people," that self-conception was no longer central to Quaker identify.

This change was the result of a combination of social and intellectual forces that influenced American Friends during the nineteenth century. In 1800, although differences were emerging over such questions as the Atonement, the nature of Christ, and the authority of Scripture, all American Friends shared a commitment to a plain lifestyle and a self-conception of peculiarity as vital to the achievement of salvation. Theological controversy, however, resulted in subtle redefinition of these ideas between 1830 and 1860, at the same time that social forces were drawing Friends into a national market economy and culture. Thus the stage was set for a revolution in the 1870s and 1880s that would cast off the plain life as a positive evil, a stumbling block in the way of salvation, and make the Discipline a collection of doctrinal statements and manual of business procedures, rather than a framework for a way of life.[4]

These divisions meant that by the 1870s American Quakerism was flowing in three streams. The larger group to emerge from the great separation of 1828 was Orthodox Friends, perhaps two-thirds of all American Quakers. They will be the focus of this paper. Between 1830 and 1860 the Orthodox themselves split into two groups. A minority of uncompromising primitivists became known as Wilburites. The overwhelming majority of the Orthodox, which moved increasingly closer to the larger American culture, were known as Gurneyites. Not surprisingly, it would be the Wilburites who would hold unflinchingly to the Discipline, while the Gurneyites would ultimately cast it aside. In order to understand these divisions, we must first understand the Discipline and what it meant in the lives of Quakers before 1850, then look at the theological and social forces that made first for division and ultimately for revolutionary change.

I

The Discipline first appeared in seventeenth-century England as a series of advices and precedents collected and issued by the highest authority among Friends, the yearly meeting for business held in London. By the eighteenth century, it had assumed some of the features of a legal code, a written compilation of the rules that defined the bounds of a Quaker life. By the first quarter of the nineteenth century the various yearly meetings of Friends in America (by 1800 there were six, each independent of the others but bound together by intricate ties and traditions) were printing Disciplines. These were not static. Yearly meetings revised them from time to time and published new editions for almost every new generation of Friends.[5]

Reading these Disciplines, one is struck by the lack of variation among the yearly meetings, or even between Hicksite and Orthodox. Many of the strictures in them, moreover, were not peculiar to Quakers. Prohibitions against violations of the Ten Commandments were a given in the ecclesiastical discipline of all denominations. Other of the Quaker strictures, such as those against dancing, gambling, attending the theater, wearing jewelry, taking a fellow member to law, reading novels, or joining secret societies, were shared by many Protestants. Quakers followed other groups in their testimonies about alcohol. Before 1800, Friends had simply condemned drunkenness. By 1830, they were banning distilling, brewing, and vending. By the 1850s they were committing themselves to total abstinence.[6]

Friends, however, as everyone knew, were not like other people, and many of their peculiarities were enjoined by the Discipline. The bases of Quaker worship were dictated by the Discipline—to patronize any place that involved a "hireling" minister, or to undergo water baptism or partake of physical communion, would bring down the overseers to reclaim the erring member. The best-known Quaker distinctive, the peace testimony, was prominent in the Discipline. Not only military service, but aid to military activities in any way, such as providing supplies, or even paying commutation fees, was forbidden. The Discipline also set out the Quaker attitude toward law. Friends took literally the biblical injunction, "Swear not at all," and thus refused to take any oath. And many of the ways of the Quaker plain life were set forth in the provisions of the Discipline. One was the plain language, which forbade the use of you to a single person (accounting for the use of _thee_ and thy), or the use of titles of any kind: "Mr.," "General," or "Your Honor," would never pass the lips of a conscientious Friend. Friends totally prohibited music of any kind as a dangerous diversion. Henry Hoover, an Indiana Friend born in 1788, remembered that his father, an influential elder, thought it an unfortunate oversight that God had created birds to sing. Friends also applied the plain language to dates; they eschewed the "pagan" names of the days of the week and months of the year, making January "First Month," Sunday "First Day," etc. Marriage had to be within the group, according to the unique Quaker marriage ceremony that maximized group participation and oversight. And peculiarity and plainness affected Friends even after death. The Discipline banned mourning costumes, and for a century Friends struggled to keep their burying grounds and graveyards free of tombstones, which they considered an unnecessary vanity. When, in the 1820s, some yearly meetings finally made some concessions, they mandated that grave markers be "plain," their height and width regulated and their inscriptions limited only to the name and necessary dates.[7]

Some peculiarities were a matter of custom rather than ecclesiastical legislation. Most notable among these was the plain dress. Perhaps nothing is so readily identified with Friends, or so responsible for identifying them with other "plain" groups. Yet the Discipline was vague on the subject. Instead, the plain dress was largely a matter of tradition. Quaker plain dress was not a matter of colors; our accounts suggest that in their choices Friends were not terribly different from their neighbors. Plainness was a matter of cut and style. A male Friend was set apart from his neighbors by the cut of his "shadbelly" coat, with its lack of cuffs and collars and narrow lapels, and by his broad brimmed hat, the lower the crown and broader the brim the better. A plain bonnet set off the female Friend. Again, color was not the decisive factor, although most were black or gray. Instead, style was paramount: a bonnet that was square in the back was worldly and fashionable, while round was plain.[8]

Friends justified these peculiarities in a variety of ways. Some, like pacifism, they saw as clear commands of Scripture. Others, like dress, served as a constant reminder to the world that there was a better way. Friends were to be a "city on a hill," and the plain life was a visible manifestation of that commitment.[9]

Perhaps most of all, however, the plain life served as a "hedge" against the world. In 1859, Richard Carpenter, a minister from New York, noted that some were criticizing the plain life as a "husk." But a husk was necessary, he responded, to protect the tender growth inside. And growth was the dominant metaphor in the Quaker conception of religious life. Friends did not see salvation as the result of a single, decisive, instantaneous experience of conversion or being "born again," so central to evangelicalism. Rather Friends saw the pursuit of salvation as a gradual experience, involving many "baptisms" of tribulation and suffering that purged away the dross from the soul. Central to this experience was separation from the world, so that the "still, small voice," the Inward Light of Christ, could guide the believer toward salvation.[10]

To implement these regulations, Friends created an elaborate disciplinary machinery. Each congregation had overseers, those strange crosses between Torquemada and Philip Marlowe, charged with reporting offenses to the monthly meeting for business and discipline. The monthly meeting would then appoint a committee to visit the offender and labor to bring him or her to a sense of repentance and to condemn his or her misconduct. If successful, the offender would appear before the monthly meeting and read an apology. If he or she proved obdurate, then would come being "read out of meeting," or disowned, the Quaker equivalent of excommunication. This was a ban only from participating in the affairs of "Our Society," however; disowned Friends were not shunned and were indeed encouraged to continue attending meetings for worship, in the hope that they would eventually repent.[11]

II

Friends took the Discipline and its requirements very seriously. Between 1755 and 1775, Friends in Philadelphia Yearly Meeting disowned over three thousand members, about 20 percent of their total membership. My own work in the records of Whitewater Monthly Meeting in Indiana shows that it kept up such a record—between 1809 and 1850 it disowned 659 members.[12]

The first source of erosion of this way of life came in the 1820s, with the first great split among American Friends, the Hicksite separation. Suffice it to say that Hicksite Friends, led by the Long Island minister Elias Hicks, saw themselves as defending traditional Quakerism against innovations creeping in from the larger evangelical culture. Their opponents, the Orthodox, saw in "hicksism" a perversion of Quaker tradition, founded on deism and infidelity. The result was a split that has endured to the present day.[13]

Opposition to the Hicksites, however, did not make for permanent unity among the Orthodox. They agreed that they had failed in not moving more quickly against the Hicksite heresy: thus their inclination, for the next generation, to move ruthlessly to discipline dissenters. But the Orthodox were of two minds otherwise. One group, the overwhelming majority, came to believe that the Hicksite heresy was the result of inadequate devotion to evangelical truth. They found their leader in the English Quaker minister Joseph John Gurney. The smaller group was convinced that the society's problems were the result of a drift away from the views of the early Friends. They became known as Wilburites, after their best-known minister, the New England Friend John Wilbur. The result was another series of separations in the 1840s and 1850s, complete with lawsuits, pamphlet wars, and anathemas hurled by both sides.[14]

The Wilburites committed themselves to uncompromising primitivism, and became the most strife-prone of the various Quaker factions. The New York Wilburites split over printing one section in the journal of a deceased minister; the Ohio Wilburites divided into three groups over the question of their relations with the other groups. The Ohio group that survived went on using the 1819 Discipline, without significant revision, until 1922. The few Friends still adhering to the plain life today are descendants of the Wilburites, and those in eastern Ohio will tell you that they are the only true Quakers left in the world.[15]

The Gurneyites, in contrast, gradually moved closer to the larger evangelical culture of the United States. Gurney's influence was critical on certain matters of doctrine, particularly in separating justification and sanctification. Before Gurney, Friends had seen the two as inseparable—one became justified by being sanctified. And the plain life was an aid in that gradual process of growth into the holiness that brought salvation. But, under Gurney's influence, the Friends who became known as "Gurneyites" came to think in terms of an instantaneous conversion experience, similar to those of evangelicals, with sanctification following as a gradual experience. Thus the theological basis of the plain life was undermined.[16]

Other factors also drew Gurneyite Friends into the larger evangelical culture of the United States. Quakers had long been noteworthy for their involvement in humanitarian reforms, and Gurneyites formed links with evangelicals in the antislavery movement, in which Friends, of course, had been the pioneers. In the 1840s Friends also became involved in interdenominational work for Sunday schools, temperance, tract societies, and Indian rights. Friends also threw themselves into the politics of the Second Party System; they were nearly all Whigs, and, after 1854, Republicans to a man, with a few exceptions among Friends in the slave states.[17]

Friends were also being affected by the social transformation of the United States between 1840 and 1860. William Tallack, an English Friend who traveled through North America visiting Quaker communities in 1859 and 1860, painted a picture of idyllic rural Quakers, particularly in the West. Living in simple plenty, wearing plain clothes of their own making, eating the fruits of their own labor with enough left over to trade for the few necessities they could not produce, they seemed to Tallack to inhabit an almost perfect world. This world, however, was changing. The railroad, the telegraph, and the printing revolution, combined with a market economy, were making for "assimilation and consolidation" into the larger society. "In their most secluded homes," Tallack wrote, "there is a growing fondness for the refinements of literature and science." Addison Coffin, an Indiana Friend, agreed. In the late 1850s, "there was great unrest in every part of social, political, religious, and domestic life. New thoughts seemed suddenly to come into the minds of every one."[18]

This ferment produced changes in the plain life and the Discipline. Much of this was the work of a new generation of young Gurneyite leaders who wanted to reform the society, purging it of anachronisms while retaining its distinctive principles. They continued the interest in social reform. They tried to change Quaker preaching, emphasizing fluent and articulate speech over the "sing-song" style that had been the norm. They proposed softening the administration of the Discipline, particularly the marriage regulations, emphasizing reclaiming, rather than disowning, offenders. The result would be a new Society of Friends, one that preserved the distinctives of unprogrammed worship, pacifism, plainness, and the equality of women, while paring away the outdated practices that obscured vital Quaker beliefs like pacifism, the spirituality of the ordinances, and unprogrammed worship.[19]

This movement, however, never came to fruition. Beginning in the late 1860s, it was swept away by a wave of evangelical revivalism among Gurneyite Friends that had its origins in the post-Civil War interdenominational holiness movement. This movement, within twenty-five years, revolutionized American Quakerism. A group of young Quaker ministers, mostly from Indiana, Ohio, and Iowa, led it, all converts to second-experience holiness views. They used the doctrines and tactics of holiness to introduce into Gurneyite meetings all of the techniques of revivalism. Thus scenes like these became common in meeting houses from New England to Kansas:

- Spiceland, Indiana, 1873: There were a number engaged in exhortation and vocal supplication, besides many others singing, while others were down at the mourners' benches, and the most of the rest on their feet, who had arisen at the call of the preacher, all going on at the same time. Meanwhile children, and even young women, evidently wild with fright, were crying, women hastening through among the men, and men among the women.

- Bear Creek, Iowa, 1877: Benjamin B. Hiatt, leading a revival, called on all who wished to lead a new life to come to the front seats. About twenty people scrambled forward, some climbing over the benches. Friends who remained at their seats were visited there by others and had prayer groups form around them. Some prayed aloud, some wept, some broke out in anguished testimonies, some sang snatches of hymns. Horrified, conservative Friends began to move toward the doors of the meetinghouse. As they did, one elderly woman climbed upon a bench and spoke in meeting for the first and only time in her life: "The Society of Friends is dead. This has killed it."[20]

This revolution was in part a culmination of the religious acculturation that Friends had undergone over the past generation. But it was also founded in a brilliant use of traditional Quaker language and ideas. Traveling ministry was one of Quakerism's most venerable traditions; revivalists were simply traveling ministers with a new message. Friends had emphasized unstructured worship; the revivalists made effective use of that. Most of all, they exploited the centrality of holiness and sanctification in Quaker thought. Much of the revivalists' success can be traced to their showing a way that brought the experience without the humiliations of peculiarity and the exactions of the plain life. Instead of silence, excitement; instead of grimness, ecstatic joy; and all in the name of a higher, more Scriptural faith.[21]

When it ceased to serve a spiritual function, the plain life faded away among all save the Wilburites and a few elderly Friends; plain speech was an ingrained habit rather than a requirement. Silent meetings disappeared, as Friends took up music and adopted a pastoral system of ministry. The old ways of marriage were discontinued as well, as Friends came to define their community not as "Our Society" but as the community of evangelical Christians. And as Friends began to proselytize, literally thousands of new members came in through revivals, and little was done to educate them in Quaker beliefs and traditions. Thus commitments to pacifism, women's ministry, and racial equality faded.[22]

Not even all Gurneyites accepted these changes. In Indiana, Ohio, Iowa, Kansas, and North Carolina, there was another round of separations by Friends opposed to revivalism and holiness innovation. Eventually they joined forces with the Wilburites. And in most of the yearly meetings there remained forces of moderation that acquiesced in most of the changes that the revival brought but sought to soften their impact.[23]

And so, by 1900, Quakerism had become a microcosm of American Protestantism. The Hicksite Friends, perhaps twenty thousand in number, were still traditional in many ways, but acculturated in others, in a process we have yet to explore. The four thousand or so Wilburites and Conservative Friends, disproportionately aged and dwindling in number, remained committed to the old ways. The hundred thousand Gurneyite Friends had become part of the larger Protestant world. Within a decade they would come to experience its new tensions, setting the stage for battles between fundamentalists and modernists that still divide them today.[24]

[1] [James Baldwin], In My Youth: From the Posthumous Papers of Robert Dudley (Indianapolis: Bobbs-Merrill 1914); Donald E. Thompson, comp., Indiana Authors and Their Books (3 vols., Crawfordsville, Ind.: Wabash College, 1966-1981), I, 14.

[2] [Baldwin], In My Youth, 12-42, 86-111, 187-209.

[3] Ibid., 488-93.

[4] I have delineated these changes in detail in my The Transformation of American Quakerism: Orthodox Friends, 1800-1907 (Bloomington, Ind.: Indiana University Press, 1988).

[5] Elbert Russell, The History of Quakerism (New York: Macmillan, 1942), 73-78, 215-28.

[6] This paragraph is based on comparing the following:

Discipline of the Yearly Meeting of Friends Held in New-York for the State of New-York and Parts Adjacent as Revised and Adopted in the Sixth Month, 1810 (New York: Mahlon Day, 1836); The Discipline of the Society of Friends of Ohio Yearly Meeting (Mt. Pleasant, Ohio: Elisha Bates, 1819); Rules of Discipline of the Yearly Meeting of Friends Held in Philadelphia (Philadelphia: J. Mortimer, 1828); The Discipline of the Society of Friends of Indiana Yearly Meeting (Cincinnati: Achilles Pugh, 1839); Rules of Discipline of the Yearly Meeting of Friends, Held in Philadelphia (Philadelphia, 1856); and Discipline of the Society of Friends of Indiana Yearly Meeting (Milton, Ind.: Jesse Kendall, 1850). The last two are Hicksite

[7] See Indiana Discipline (1839), 19, 35, 37-39, 60-65, 70-74, 91-93; Henry Hoover, Sketches and Incidents, Embracing a Period of Fifty Years, ed. Willard C. Heiss (Indianapolis: John Woolman Press, 1962), 7; Bernhard Knollenberg, Pioneer Sketches of the Upper Whitewater Valley: Quaker Stronghold of the West (Indianapolis: Indiana Historical Society, 1945), 30. An especially detailed account for the debate over "artificial grave stones" appears in the Deep River Monthly Meeting Men's Minutes, 2nd Mo. 3, 1831 (North Carolina Yearly Meeting Archives, Friends Historical Collection, Guilford College, Greensboro, N.C.).

[8] [Baldwin], In My Youth, 91; William Tallack, Friendly Sketches in America (London: A.W. Bennett, 1861), 18-23; Mary Pickett to Mary Branson, 7th Mo. 24, 1833, Box 1, Isaac W. and Benjamin B. Beeson Collection (Indiana Division, Indiana State Library, Indianapolis).

[9] J. H. Dillingham, "Testimony of the Friends Dress," Friends' Review, (3rd Mo. 5, 1870), 433-36; Editorial, ibid., (6th Mo. 3, 1850), 728.

[10] Journal of the Life of Joseph Hoag, an Eminent Minister of the Gospel in the Society of Friends (Auburn, N.Y.: Knapp and Peck, 1861), 243-44; George A. Schooley, ed., The Journal of Dr. William Schooley: Pioneer Physician, Quaker Minister, Abolitionist, Philosopher, and Scholar, 1794-1860, Somerton, Belmont County, Ohio (Zanesville, Ohio, 1977), 18-19; Carpenter quoted in Horace J. Edgerton, "Peculiarities of Friends," Friendsville (N.C.) Current, (12th Mo. 1926), 4. For the centrality of growth in Quaker religious thought, see Hamm, Transformation of American Quakerism, 2-5.

[11] [Baldwin], In My Youth, 100. This procedure was uniform. See, for example, Indiana Discipline (1839), 84-86.

[12] Hamm, Transformation of American Quakerism, 53-55; Jack D. Marietta, The Reformation of American Quakerism, 1748-1783 (Philadelphia: University of Pennsylvania Press, 1984), 55.

[13] Hugh Barbour and J. William Frost, The Quakers (Westport, Conn.: Greenwood, 1988), 169-82; H. Larry Ingle, Quakers in Conflict: The Hicksite Reformation, (Knoxville: University of Tennessee Press, 1986).

[14] Hamm, Transformation of American Quakerism, 28-34.

[15] A. Day Bradley, "New York Yearly Meeting at Poplar Ridge and the Primitive Friends," Quaker History 68 (Autumn 1979), 75-82; William P. Taber, Jr., The Eye of Faith: A History of Ohio Yearly Meeting, Conservative (Barnesville, Ohio: Ohio Yearly Meeting, 1985), 95-98; Charles P. Morlan, A Brief History of Ohio Yearly Meeting of the Religious Society of Friends (Conservative) (Barnesville, Ohio, 1959), 54. The most complete account of the Wilburites, written by an extreme conservative, is William Hodgson, The Society of Friends in the Nineteenth Century: A Historical View of the Successive Convulsions and Schisms Therein during That Period (2 vols., Philadelphia, 1875-1876), II, 167-344.

[16] Hamm, Transformation of American Quakerism, 20-28.

[17] Ibid., 20-28, 61-62.

[18] Tallack, Friendly Sketches, 27-29, 31-32; Addison Coffin, Life and Travels of Addison Coffin (Cleveland: William G. Hubbard, 1897), 115.

[19] For a general discussion, see Hamm, Transformation of American Quakerism, 42-73. There is no single authoritative statement of the views of these reformers. Some excellent examples of their thought include Address by Dr. Dougan Clark (n.p., 1858); B.A. Marshall, "In Essentials, Unity; In Non-Essentials, Liberty; In All Things, Charity," Friends' Review, (5th Mo. 29, 1858), 593; "The Marriage Question," ibid., (1st Mo. 16, 1864), 312-13; "Plainness of Apparel," ibid., (6th Mo. 8, 1867), pp. 648-49; "Tones and Gestures in Preaching," ibid., (6th Mo. 7, 1856), 616-17; and Francis W. Thomas, An Address to the Society of Friends (Richmond, Ind.: Central Book and Tract Committee, 1863).

[20] Walter Edgerton, Modern Quakerism Examined and Contrasted with That of the Ancient Type (Indianapolis: Printing and Publishing House, 1876), 7; D. H. P., "Spiceland General Meeting," Christian Worker, (2nd Mo. 5, 1874), 60; Darius B. Cook, History of Quaker Divide (Dexter, Iowa: Dexter Sentinel, 1914), 70-72; Hamm, Transformation of American Quakerism, 74-97.

[21] Hamm, Transformation of American Quakerism, 88.

[22] Ibid., 85-88, 102-11. I explored some of these changes more fully in my Western Yearly Meeting Quaker Lecture, Where We Are and How We Got Here, (Plainfield, Ind., 1990).

[23] Hamm, Transformation of American Quakerism, 102, 111-20.

[24] Ibid., 144-73, 175. There is no general history of Hicksite Friends after the separation of 1827-1828. A suggestive work is Philip S. Benjamin, The Philadelphia Quakers in the Industrial Age, 1865-1920, (Philadelphia: Temple University Press, 1976). For statements of the modernist Quaker outlook, see Rufus M. Jones, The Trail of Life in the Middle Years, (New York: Macmillan, 1934); and Elbert Russell, Quaker: An Autobiography, (Jacksonville, Tenn.: Friendly Press, 1956). The fundamentalist view of Quakerism is set forth in Edward Mott, The Friends Church in the Light of Its Recent History, (Portland, Ore.: Loomis, n. d.).

A Response:
Patterns of Cultural Transformation
in Four Denominations

by Donald B. Kraybill

Introduction

How does one sort out trends in other denominations? The denominations described in the four preceding papers are first cousins of the Church of the Brethren. Two of them share common roots with the Church of the Brethren, and the other two (Friends and Mennonites) have shared many similar concerns over the years and have worked cooperatively with the Church of the Brethren on numerous projects, especially ones related to peacemaking.

At first flush the four papers appear as diverse descriptions of four different religious traditions struggling with social change in various times and settings. Hamm's work charts the story of the Friends in the last quarter of the nineteenth century. Changes experienced by the Brethren Church in the twentieth century and particularly after 1960 are assessed by Stoffer. Juhnke describes several groups of Mennonites with a primary focus on progressive Mennonite groups since 1970. The paper by Benedict discusses current transitions among the Old German Baptist Brethren. What do these four religious groups in different times and geographical settings have in common, if anything?

In many ways the four traditions array themselves across a rough continuum of assimilation into mainstream culture. The Quakers drifted into the cultural mainstream first and, according to Hamm, had become part of the world by 1910. After parting ways with other Brethren groups in the early 1880s, the "progressive" Brethren Church began to embrace more fully the ways of modernity. The Mennonite groups described by Juhnke assimilated at different times and rates. The two major Mennonite groups (Mennonite Church and General Conference Mennonite Church) experienced assimilation in the middle of the twentieth century. Among the four traditions, the Old German Baptist Brethren have resisted the tide of acculturation the longest and the most effectively. Thus, both in terms of the time and scope of cultural assimilation, the groups described in the preceding chapters can be arrayed in the following order, from most assimilated to least: Friends, The Brethren Church, The Mennonites and the Old German Baptist Brethren.

The intriguing analytical question however is why a particular group assimilates at a particular juncture of history. What are the socio-cultural catalysts that precipitate the flow into the cultural mainstream. Why did the Gurneyite Friends drop their sectarian distinctives in the 1870s and 1880s and not the Mennonites? Moreover, why do some groups assimilate somewhat easily while others seem to stubbornly thwart the sweep of history? What circumstances have enabled the Old German Baptist Brethren to resist assimilation so effectively? These are the sort of questions that bubble to the surface when the historical experiences of these four traditions are laid out along side each other.

Similarities in the Four Traditions

Despite their ostensible variety, the four religious traditions surveyed in the preceding pages do share a number of common themes. These shared features are particularly pronounced if the groups are contrasted prior to their turn toward modern ways. The authors identify separation from the world as a common theme that circumscribes the experience of all four groups. In this sense all of the traditions have sectarian roots. They viewed the larger culture as a threatening and hostile force from which they sought to remain nonconformed. Moreover the groups emphasized internal unity—a major theme at communion and love feast celebrations. The unity was enhanced by a common *Ordnung* or Discipline that outlined expected behavior.

Hierarchical forms of traditional authority were also shared by the four streams of religious heritage. A bishop or presiding elder exercised considerable influence over the community, interpreting and enforcing the normative expectations. The expectations for membership involved individual accountability. Members were expected to submit to the collective understandings of the community about religious belief and practice. Self examination services as well as visits by elders or deacons deterred excessive individuation. When the moral boundaries of the community were seriously transgressed, individuals were expected to make public confessions of their wrongdoing and promise to heed the counsel of the elders. Recalcitrant members who refused to confess their errors were excommunicated from the community of faith by all four religious traditions.

The four groups also had a free ministry system that selected members of the congregation for leadership without formal training or salary. Male members of the congregation were expected to serve in ministerial roles if called upon by their fellow believers. Prior to the turn of the twentieth century the four groups supported few centralized institutions. Their collective life was embodied in informal exchanges with minimal organizational development.

The "old" Mennonite Church, for instance, did not form a national, general conference until 1898. Although some of the other groups had a national meeting much earlier, they still had relatively few large organizations—at least not bureaucratic ones—beyond the local congregation.

All four groups rejected the use of force in human relations. This was a key mark of internal self consciousness as well as public identity for all the groups including the Church of the Brethren. Whether they called it nonresistance or their peace testimony, rejecting the use of force meant that they not only refused to participate in warfare but also eschewed litigation and political office-holding because these activities also involved the use of force. Finally the four traditions emphasized an ethic of service. They sought to extend compassion—to give the cup of cold water to the needy, the hungry and the refugee. These traits were shared by all four of the groups in the nineteenth century, prior to their embrace of modern ways. Many of the features in various states of flux continue to characterize the groups.

Transformations in the Four Groups

Against this backdrop of common cultural contours, the authors describe four major transformations among the respective groups. The extent and breadth of these changes varies of course by a group's niche on the continuum of assimilation. The most fundamental shift described by all the authors is the transformation from a sectarian stance of separation to an accommodation to the structures and values of the larger culture. This transformation is most pronounced among the Friends and least experienced by the Old German Baptist Brethren who respectively occupy opposite poles on the continuum of assimilation. Although the Old Orders most successfully maintain lines of separation, as Benedict's paper notes, their boundaries of nonconformity are also eroding. In Benedict's words, the two primary questions which the Old Orders currently and the other groups in the past have struggled with focus on separation and unity: "How much separation shall we maintain from the general society and how much unity and agreement among us is necessary?" Although their degree of cultural separation varies, all four of the groups have experienced a shift in their posture toward the dominant society—a turn toward greater accommodation and less separatism.

A second transformation not described in detail by any of the authors yet lurking in the background of all four case studies entails a migration from the farm to the factory. At different times and places the four communities experienced a shift off the farm—a shift which in many ways precipitated some of the other changes. This occupational transformation leads to a third restructuring which the four authors trace, again in varying degrees—a move from what was formerly a homogeneous group to one with wide ranging diversity. From beliefs and occupations to dress and ethnic origin the four religious traditions have all drifted in the direction of diversity. The Old Orders have certainly experienced less of this. Finally, the groups have seen the emergence of formal and somewhat bureaucratized institutions to accomplish many of their major collective goals. The informal, spontaneous networks and social ties of the past have given way to more formal and rational forms of organizational life: mission boards, publishing houses and schools, to name but a few. Once again this development is least pronounced among the Old German Baptist Brethren.

Despite their different geographical settings and religious roots the four traditions did share key traits in common before they encountered the forces of modernity, and they have experienced, in differing degrees, at least four major social transformations. Each of the authors in his/her own way provides a descriptive narrative of each group's journey, but they do not propose an explanatory model that identifies the factors that propel or impede the assimilation process. That task is perhaps most appropriately relegated to a comparative analysis.

Tracing the Factors of Change

Rather than critiquing the individual papers, I will identify some of the salient factors that shape the rate and nature of a group's accommodation to the larger society. Why did the groups modernize at different times and in different ways? What were the factors that nudged them toward or away from the social mainstream? Although space considerations prevent an analysis of each community, it may be helpful to sketch the skeleton of a more general model that points to some of the key variables operating in the modernizing context.

In a somewhat simple fashion significant sources of change can be sorted into external and internal influences. Exposure and contact with the following external forces will surely shape the nature of a groups response to modernity: industrialization, urbanization, education, mobility, mass media, significant political events, and other religious groups and movements. All of these macro social factors shape the crucible of the social context which forges a communities response to the modern world. The rate of cultural assimilation will surely be retarded among groups that cling to an agrarian way of life, shun urbanization, devalue higher education, and reject mass media. Groups which welcome or at least are open to these influences will likely be propelled more rapidly into the cultural fray of modern life.

Although it would be tempting to entirely lean on such macro socio-economic factors to account for the rate and nature of assimilation, it would neglect a host of historical and theological factors which surely play a role as well. Several internal factors may partially account for the different patterns of acculturation identified by the respective scholars in these four groups.

First, a particular theological ethos in the legacy of a group may shape its response to engagement with the larger culture. The Friends' notion of the inner light within each individual and the Brethren emphasis on a noncreedal faith as well the historic influence of pietism on Brethren theology may make both of the Quakers and the Brethren more prone to welcome individualism. Although they are technically noncreedal, the Mennonites have placed more emphasis on "statements of faith" which provide a sort of doctrinal drag on social change which may retard the assimilation process. The particular theological ethos of each of the four traditions would need to be explored in detail in order to discover the ways in which each one has steered their interactions with modernity.

Second, the concrete social experiences of a group will also shape its behavior at the intersection with the larger social world. The severe persecution of Anabaptists in the sixteenth century profoundly filtered the Mennonite experience over the centuries. The <u>Martyrs Mirror</u> provided a reservoir of martyr stories that shaped the consciousness of succeeding generations even up to the present. The legacy of persecution harbored a deeper sectarian stance among Mennonites than that found among those groups which experienced only minimal conflict with the larger social order. Does the social fact that the Friends were largely of British origin and spoke English account for their earlier social intercourse with modern ways? This is in contrast to the slower assimilation of the three other religious groups all of whom spoke German. The German language and identity may have stifled the drift of the Brethren, Mennonites, and Old Order German Baptists toward the dominant culture which was encapsulated by English language.

Third, the ethnic composition of a group—influenced by evangelism and intermarriage—also plays a role in a community's openness to outside influence. Mono-ethnic communities of faith are more likely to respond in a common fashion to outside threats and will also be more concerned about articulating their unique historical identity. Members of such groups may more likely feel a direct line of psychological association back to founding members of the movement. The demographic balance of old timers and new-comers and their religious and ethnic origins certainly shape a group's clarity of identity and vulnerability to other streams of thinking.

A fourth factor involves a religious community's organizational structure: its polity. Institutional patterns may facilitate or deter social change. Strong centralized control mechanisms allow a group to respond to outside pressures quickly and with a single voice. The level of ecclesiastical authority—congregational, district, or national—as well as its legitimacy will surely play a significant role in a groups negotiations with modernity. A centralized authority structure may welcome acculturation and thus accelerate the process beyond the desires of local congregations. The same structure could serve the opposite function as well. Nevertheless polity patterns do make a difference in how a tradition responds to change.

Finally, the particular political mix—the conglomeration of actors, forces, interest groups, and electoral processes—often shape the outcome of events in significant ways. Powerful or weak leaders functioning in specific historical contexts steer or impede the course of events in peculiar ways.

Thus, attempts to understand why a particular group drifted with the tide or bucked it at a certain moment in history must take into account the spectrum of both external and internal forces, all interacting together in a dynamic and unpredictable fashion. The actual outcomes are contingent, of course, on the particular mix of factors interacting at a specified juncture of history.

Reconstructing a Religious Heritage

Despite the dynamic interaction of these variables in the crucible of time, a religious community may pursue at least five different strategies as it seeks to negotiate its way through the whirlpools of modernity. One option is to accent the primacy of heritage over the exigencies of the social context. Compared to the other three traditions, the Old German Baptist Brethren have focused more of their energies on italicizing their traditional ways rather than flowing with the common tide. At the other extreme, a community may reject its past by engaging in a sort of collective adolescent rebellion. The faculty of a college associated with one of the historic peace churches considered the establishment of a peace club for students in the early 1970s as too sectarian, something beneath the dignity of thoughtful and tolerant cosmopolitans.

More likely responses than these opposite reactions may involve some form of reconstructing and reappropriating of a group's tradition. The reconstruction can be done with distortion or with integrity. A distorted reconstruction entails the use of key words or ideas from the groups legacy but in ways that misconstrues the original meaning. Key concepts and terminology, in essence, are taken and turned on their head and used to argue the opposite of their initial intent. Carl Bowman in an early chapter of this book contends that the Church of the Brethren, for example, began using the phrase, "no force in religion," in new ways in the twentieth century. A phrase that originally referred to the state's noninterference with the life of the church was reconstructed in the context of the growing American individualism to mean that the church could not interfere in the life of its members even with such central issues as participation in warfare.

To reconstruct a tradition with integrity means that the images, words, and meaning floating in the reservoir of a group's legacy are reappropriated for new times and places. But a reconstruction characterized by integrity means that the original intent of the ideas and concepts is safeguarded in the process.

PART IV

SPECIAL TOPICS OF CHANGE:
TWO CASE STUDIES

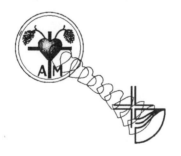

9

The Organizational Imperative
And its Implications:
The West Marva Example

Emmert F. Bittinger

This paper examines the transition of the denomination from a simple to a highly complex organization. The primary focus is on the effects of organizational change itself rather than on policy, polity, or the performance of specific leaders. While this area has received little scholarly attention, the implications for the denomination are significant and worthy of examination. The impact upon the definition of mission, the ideological gap between leaders and laity, the decline of church discipline with the passing of the authority of the Elders, changes in leadership styles, and changes in denominational world view are matters especially stressed. These transitions have contributed in subtle ways to modification of the denomination's self-understanding, to its perception of its mission, and to a distancing of itself from the older vision of its founders. The author concludes with the question, "How may organization best be used to enable the church to be faithful to the best from its Pietist and Anabaptist heritage?"

I

Recently increasing attention has been focused upon the developments which have marked the Church of the Brethren in the past one hundred fifty years. Scholarly study of these changes is long overdue in light of the fact that several indicators appear to reveal 1) a decline in the membership of the denomination, and 2) a weakening of loyalty and commitment to the denomination and its programs.[1]

One of the most pervasive and revolutionary changes in the denomination has been its organizational transformation. While most lay persons are aware of the ubiquity of church organization, indeed sometimes complaining about its heavy demands on their time at the local church level, few may have a long-range view of how these changes have affected the life of the denomination. Furthermore, few Brethren scholars have subjected this aspect of denominational change to rigorous analysis either from the historical or sociological standpoint.[2] In the absence of a developed background of scholarly studies pertaining to this phenomenon in the Church of the Brethren, the present paper should be regarded as a tentative excursion into a largely unexplored area of Brethren history and culture.

The present paper is informed by a study of the history of organization in the West Marva District.[3] Documentation for much of this paper is found in that study. Changes parallel to and accompanying the evolution of church structures in West Marva District were noted in that study. Some of those changes were significant and far reaching, having to do not only with the organizational processes themselves, but also the allocation of resources, redefinition of mission, the transformation in leadership styles, and the way in which the church expresses its corporate existence.

Church Structure Around 1850

At the middle of the last century, the Brethren had a minimal amount of formal church structure. What existed at the time was based on the New Testament model: the ministry (with three different degrees and specified functions for each), deacons in the local congregation, an institutionalized pattern of annual meetings in which decisions were made on the principle of consensus and to which local congregations were represented usually through their ministers, and local congregations holding councils under the authority of an elder.

At this time, no bureaucracy, church headquarters, publishing interests, or standardized system of written communication or record keeping existed as a part of church structure. To the knowledge of the writer, the denomination did not have a single employed minister or officer in 1850. Annual Meeting exercised central authority and would appoint committees to visit local congregations in order to settle differences or explore conditions needing outside help.

This is in marked contrast with the present time. Today the denomination is highly complex in its structures at the national, district, and local levels, being organized into specialized branches which carry on diverse activities in practically every part of the globe.[4] Structures are highly integrated within themselves and within the General Board. Vertical integration exists from the central to the congregational levels with effective lines of communication in continuous operation. Full time specialized officials function as heads of the major divisions and branches at different levels. The quasi-democratic principle is preserved in representation both at the level of Annual Conference and the various levels of the bureaucracy.

Indeed, periodic restructuring, maintenance, and operation of the bureaucracy are major aspects of church life at the end of the twentieth century. The work and life of the church today are set almost totally in the context of organized structures. The changes from 1850 to the present are so far reaching and pervasive that it has literally revolutionized church life and the concepts relating to it. The church had a non-professional, "free" ministry in 1850, and hierarchical levels were minimized. Ministers and Elders, drawn from the local membership, were closely associated with the life of the people.

The Beginnings of the Organizational Revolution

Early initiatives pertaining to the formation of district structures and their use came from the Virginia elders led by John Kline. After carefully formulating their proposal in a special council in February, 1856, they presented it to Yearly Meeting that year. It is important to note that this early initiative arose out of a strong home mission impulse. The Virginia elders believed that districts could provide the structure by which the propagation of the gospel could be financed and accomplished.[5]

Annual Meeting, however, was not yet ready to recommend districts be formed as a general pattern. Nor was it ready to provide a method of financing home mission work.[6] Out of respect to the strength of the proposal and the influence of the Virginia elders, the Annual Meeting did concede to local congregations the privilege of forming districts (Articles 22, 23) only for the purpose, however, of "settling difficulties, etc., and thus lessening the business of our general Yearly Meeting."

This decision in 1856, obviously, did not sanction the mission plan proposed by the Virginia elders. The minute allowing congregations to join in "forming of districts" effectively obscures the importance of the mission impulse which was the sub-stratum of the entire discussion. Thus, the formation of districts has come to be thought of by most historians as primarily concerned with taking the burden of local matters off the agenda of Yearly Meetings.

The leading elders of Virginia and western Pennsylvania, however, thought differently. They continued to push for organized home mission work through the use of a district plan, and they brought the matter up repeatedly. By 1866, the push for "districting" had become so strong that Yearly Meeting found it necessary to permit the formation of districts generally. During that year and shortly thereafter, districting took place throughout the nation. Undoubtedly the primary impulse for districting was the pragmatic need to relieve the heavy work load of Yearly Meeting, but the mission impetus was certainly a part of the picture, too.

Districts And The Mission Impulse

The forming of districts was a major event in the growth of organization in the denomination. Districts provided distant and multiple settings for the consideration of church problems and local issues. They provided local forums for the ministers of each district to develop their talents and to promote the cause of the church. Mission boards, within the district setting after 1880, were among the first structures to be launched locally. Mission had priority. Sunday Schools, rare until the 1880s, soon began to spread. The elders meetings, an ancient structure, continued to play a major role.

Immediately following the formation of the West Virginia District in 1866, a strong home mission program was launched, especially in the western part of the state. This effort was built upon the earlier labors of Elders Samuel Arnold (died, 1831) of Beaver Run Congregation, James Quinter of Georges Creek Congregation, John Wise of Ten Mile Congregation in western Pennsylvania, James Kelso of Maryland, and John Kline of Virginia. Prior to 1890, these home mission efforts were guided by the Elders Body and the District Conference. In effect, the West Virginia and western Pennsylvania territories became a "proving ground" for the "missionary program" which had been so strongly promoted in the Yearly Meetings between 1852 and 1866 by John Kline and his Virginia and western Pennsylvania supporters. Local successors to these leaders carried the burden of the extensive program.

Financial Support

The beginnings of a system of financial support for district sponsored mission programs can be observed in the years following the formation of the district of West Virginia.[7] By 1877, Beaver Run, and later other congregations, had established methods of raising money.[8] The procedure used was that the elders of the church obtained an estimate of the real wealth of the members upon which a "church tax" was assessed and paid to one of the elders or deacons. At first, the members were asked to inform the elders of their real worth. Apparently many of the families "neglected" to share this information. Consequently, in a few years (1890) the elders were obtaining this information directly from the county tax office for the families in their membership.[9] In addition, a per capita assessment was laid on each adult member, thus capturing those who did not own real estate. Some of these funds were forwarded to the District Treasurer to be used to underwrite the expenses of missionary travels and projects.

Beaver Run also had provided a structure by which moneys could be collected on a volunteer basis in support of foreign missions, and these were forwarded to the denominational office. Other congregations, likely at the behest of District Meeting, soon followed this plan also.

It is interesting to note that these moneys before the 1890s had to be raised without taking offerings in church. Such offerings were forbidden by the Yearly Meeting. Funds had to be turned over to the elders and deacons on week days only, for Sundays were not to be desecrated by making monetary transactions. Perhaps a good amount of the church taxes were turned over at the time of the deacon visit.[10]

Formation of Mission Boards

Meanwhile, Yearly Meeting formed a Foreign and Domestic Mission Board in 1880. Very soon, similar boards were being formed in the districts. First and Second Districts of West Virginia formed Mission Boards in 1892 and 1893. Prior to that from 1866, an extremely active home mission program had been carried out in West Virginia and western Pennsylvania. It operated under the supervision of the Elders Body and the District Meeting. Following 1893, the Mission Boards were immediately very active in sponsoring the mission effort.

In the 1890s and the first decade of 1900, the West Virginia districts experimented with the idea of choosing and supporting persons who would function as specialists. They were called "district missionaries" or "district evangelists," depending on the district. This plan was not unequivocally successful due to a variety of problems, including lack of skills, doctrinal deviations, and lack of time to do the work.[11]

The period of greatest activity of the Home Mission boards extended into the middle 1920s followed by a gradual decline in the mission impulse and in the work beginning in the late 1920s and extending into the 1930s and 1940s. During the peak period the missionary impulse may be described as a prior and consumate cause for several of the missionary minded ministers with respect to the attention and commitment which it engendered. The program to start and support new churches comprised a major part of the agenda of District Meeting and apparently served as a principal justification for the meetings themselves. Mission reports were highly anticipated, and those ministers involved in successful activities were duly rewarded in receiving informal recognition and great respect.

The Minister-Missionary Role

This public recognition of the mission cause provided high motivation for a very difficult labor. District Conference provided a means for rewarding success in the missionary role. It provided a means for rewarding ministers who possessed certain kinds of traits, such as good interpersonal skills, powerful preaching ability, an authoritarian and charismatic style capable of inspiring strong support and almost worshipful regard. In other words, the ministers whose accomplishments were attracting highest regard were those who were most successful in persuasive preaching and building large congregations with many preaching points. This personality pattern and reward system may be presumed to have acted as a selective device and an incentive for calling and entering the ministry. Thus, a certain type of leader and ministerial role came to the fore during this period of most active district-sponsored home mission activity in West Virginia, 1866 to around 1930.

Prior to 1920, a total of thirty mission points and churches had been established west of the Cheat River and in Randolph County, West Virginia. A total of sixty-four ministers served or were called in the work of the churches in the Second District where the bulk of the home mission work took place.

Sunday Schools

In addition to the mission activity, a parallel development was taking place, having begun around 1880. This was the Sunday School movement. Sunday Schools represented an early but controversial extension of the concept of mission. Consequently, they were not immediately integrated into the congregational authority structure.

It is worth noting that the mission impulse strongly penetrated the Sunday School rationale in the West Virginia districts. The reports to district conference stressed the number of persons attending, the number of new schools organized, the ones which were "evergreen," (meeting year around) and the number of conversions.[12] It is clear that the sense of mission permeated the movement, yet the mission of the church appears to have been rather simply conceived. It was thought of primarily as the building up of the church, the "propagation of the gospel," or the founding of new "arms".

New Departures in Mission & Structure, 1900-1945

During the decade of 1910 and afterward, however, the concept of the mission of the church underwent remarkable expansion and diversification. Organizational expansion facilitated and accompanied this tremendous widening in the concept of mission.[13] The success of the Mission Board and Sunday School organizations provided both an example and a motivation to form a new structure for every new cause deemed to fit into the rapidly expanding and generalizing concept of "mission."[14] It was easy enough, once the idea became acceptable, to form committees, boards, or appoint directors.

Temperance, peace issues, needs of children and youth, religious education, women's work, church camps, and international catastrophes all came into the more broadly defined area of "mission" as the denomination entered the period of the 1910s and 1920s. A few of the structures are listed below. Although incomplete, the list is illustrative.

- Temperance Boards and the temperance motif, 1914.
- The peace cause and peace committees, 1914.
- Child Rescue and the Maple Grove Home, 1918.
- District Ministerial Board, 1917/1918.
- Sisters Aid Societies, 1919.
- Vacation Church Schools, 1919.
- Board of Religious Education, 1926.
- District "Field Man", 1928.
- BYPD (youth), 1931.
- Men's Organizations, 1932.
- Church Camps, 1934.
- Children's Directors, 1939.
- Council of Boards, 1939.

The formulation and reformulation of new structures continued, of course, beyond 1940. During this latter period, Brethren continued to come to grips with new concerns and issues at the Annual and District Conference levels. In 1946, the Annual Conference adopted the proposal to form a General Brotherhood Board structure, an attempt to preserve the representative function as well as promote a greater degree of centralization and coordination. The pattern of developing new program and structure continues to the present. The trend is held in abeyance perhaps only by a strong counterbalancing need to consolidate programs and structures and to economize in the light of financial limitations and personnel shortages. Thus, in recent decades, consolidation, realignment, restructuring, and the combining of programs within a single office or structure have all been strongly manifested.

Organizational Refinements: Joint Field Programs, District Realignments, and Consolidation

In West Marva territory, the movement to coordinate, unify, and bring under closer control the various more or less independent structures which had accumulated over the years since 1910 received a strong impetus in the formation of the Council of Boards in 1940.[15] At church headquarters, the Council of Boards unification effort had begun in 1927. This initial effort arose more from a need for integration and coordination than from financial desperation. This new board brought an additional layer of "officials" into a supervisory capacity at both the national and district levels, thus adding new strata to the bureaucracy.

Meanwhile, the movement toward the employment of District Field Men, later called executives, was being implemented in various parts of the Brotherhood. The program was being encouraged from national headquarters. The beginnings of a field secretary program in First District of West Virginia go back to 1939 when it was a part time position with remuneration coming from the Mission Board treasury.

The need for a full time executive was soon recognized, and this was initiated on a trial basis in 1954. Due to costs, the program was a joint tri-district effort involving First and Second West Virginia and Western Maryland.

During this time, long term studies of district boundaries had been undertaken. This effort at first sought to rationalize boundaries in order to more efficiently serve certain areas and churches. As this effort continued, it gradually became merged with an effort to unify and consolidate the three districts into one unit. Considerable opposition and no little inertia delayed the consolidation effort, but it was completed by 1965, and the West Marva District was formed. At present, the district office is located at Oakland, Maryland, and employs a full time executive and secretary.[16]

Summary of Organizational Patterns and Trends

Some of the more subtle bureaucratic patterns, trends, and counter trends as they developed in West Marva territory will now be examined.

Rational Coordination

Rational coordination, a goal seldom fully realized, is a prominent feature of bureaucracies. It involves the desire and need to maximize efficiency and improve quantity and quality of output. Among others, this includes specialization of roles, establishment of agencies and offices for the processing of information and implementation of activities, and the efficient management of these through the setting of policy procedures throughout the various levels of the bureaucracy. Rational coordination also includes any tendencies to reformulate or modify existing structures in order to achieve greater efficiency and consistency.

All of these processes are readily apparent upon examination of the West Marva District and the national organizational structures. Efforts at specialization of roles can be seen as early as the 1890s in the appointment of district missionaries and district evangelists. Efforts to combine and coordinate scattered, formerly unrelated structures can be seen in the attempts to bring various scattered programs under the new "religious education" board in the 1920s. More thoroughgoing efforts at management and coordination are identified with the Council of Boards movement which began at national headquarters and spread to the district levels in the late 1930s and 1940s. Each of these levels added a new bureaucratic layer, new officials, and an additional distancing of top officials from the grass roots. The formation of "higher offices" also involves the creation of some degree of authority and control over "lower offices."[17]

The controversial movement in the 1950s and 1960s to eliminate the office of elder also may be seen as an aspect of rational coordination. The office of elder was a part of the older, pre-bureaucratic period, and as such it was seen as excess baggage. The issue of the Elders Body was further complicated by the rapid transition between 1920 and 1940 to the professional ministry.[18] By authorizing the cessation in 1967 of the ordination of elders, the Annual Conference cut off entrance to the highest degree of the ministry and effectively assured a "safe future" for professional pastors by removing a chief source of competition, interference, and conservatism. The authority of the Elders Body was further diluted when non-elders and lay persons were permitted membership and service in the group. Part of the desire to reduce and eliminate the eldership also apparently had its roots in the cognitive need for a "neat" and uncluttered system in which structures and offices perceived to be irrelevant, unneeded, or "dysfunctional" could be eliminated.

The Issue of Organizational Authority and Discipline

The Elders Body also had a significant disciplinary function. As such, it was out of step with much of modern psychological theory and the contemporary ethos which was playing down the need for discipline, punishment, and control. Thus, with the decline of the Elders Body, the transfer of disciplinary functions to the organizational structure was tentative, incomplete, and muted. This had far reaching consequences with respect to a commitment to discipline within the congregations, districts and brotherhood. The use and effectiveness of discipline under the organizational system needs research and study.

The commitment to church discipline under the new system remains muted and exceedingly controversial. Within a permissive society, the membership is divided on the issue. A very different moral climate exists today. Some are comfortable with a religious environment in which church discipline is regarded as unnecessary because the love ethic teaches them to be inclusive and accepting of those who "suffer" from various "problems" and "difficulties."[19] The concern instead becomes: how can the church help such individuals to bear up or recover?

The older view assumed the need for discipline and even exclusion of those who refuse to repent from "sinful" and "evil" patterns of behavior. Adherents of this view believed more traditionally that sin is destructive to both the individual and to the fellowship of believers. They believed that confession, repentance, and forgiveness were necessary aspects of the healing process. The now widely disseminated theory of moral relativity had not yet destroyed the belief in the need for discipline to hold up standards of moral behavior within the denomination and local church.

A contemporary view, strongly reinforced by the secular culture, would resist church efforts at discipline as an infringement on "personal freedom" in a society of freedom-loving individualists. According to this widely held view, each individual has the right to determine his own definition of right and wrong. Persons holding such radically individualistic views would deny even the church, or any religious authority, the right to proclaim moral right or wrong for the individual.

In the general cultural climate of the latter half of the twentieth century, the whole cloth commitment to the dominant values of freedom and individualism held by most members appears to have effectively brought an end to the church imposing any significant amount of discipline of its members.

Vertical Integration

Vertical integration refers to the formation of various lines of communication and authority within the system from the top offices at the center down to grass roots. It would include any efforts at standardizing the names and functions of the offices at the various levels such as the naming and re-naming of commissions at the national,[20] district, and local church levels and the establishing of linkages among the levels.

An early example of efforts at vertical integration may be seen in the initiative launched by J. W. Lear, the Director of the Denominational Council of Boards in 1928. Bro. Lear sought to have the First District of West Virginia appoint its first "field man," suggesting that Bro. Ezra Fike, Secretary of the District Mission Board, might be a suitable person.[21] This new office, which constituted an additional level of organization, would serve to transmit information and promote the raising of funds for the various programs authorized by Annual Conference. In reality, the office became a link between the organizational center and the district organizations.

Consolidation and Centralization

The period from 1910 to 1925 saw the formation of numerous new structures, committees, and boards, usually created to pursue some new cause or concern. At first, there was little coordination or connection between these disparate groups. These structures handled concerns ranging from temperance, Sunday Schools, Children's Work, Men's Work, Women's Work, youth work, camping, Child Rescue, ministerial supervision, and others.

The need for consolidation and centralization soon was felt at the national and local levels. Thus, many of the above were unified under the Board of Religious Education, creating an additional level of structure. Likewise, major categories of concern, such as education, ministry, missions, and service, came to be centralized under the Council of Boards movement which began locally in the late 1930s. Additional waves of consolidation occurred in the 1940s, the 1960s, and approximately every fifteen years following that.

Other patterns of consolidation include the combining of districts to enlarge territories and increase the numbers of churches for the purposes of unifying program and supporting increasingly expensive district-level structure and personnel. Consolidation of program under smaller numbers of commissions or agencies has also continued to occur at the national level.

Concerns for efficiency, coordination, and financial costs have served at various times to fuel significant trends toward consolidation, centralization, and restructuring.

II

Effects of Organizational Change on Church Life

The following summary of suggests some effects of organizational development on Brethren life. These should be thought of as hypotheses which are as yet insufficiently established by research. Some evidence pertaining to them is found in the study of the West Marva District. The burden of this paper is to raise these issues, encourage research, and give some suggestions regarding possibly significant direct and indirect effects of the organizational transformation. The reader is again reminded that changes in denominational life are exceedingly complex. Numerous other causal influences are active and interactive in affecting the trends to be discussed below.

The presumed effects will be illustrated as trends or directions of change on a time line running from 1850 and extending to 1990. Since these movements have not been measured, the time line is meant to suggest merely the passage of time and progression (including possible periods of regression) for each trend. The time line is not meant to suggest that change has progressed to an extreme or far right degree. Rates of change were variable, uneven, even stop and go, or different in each area. These particular trends chosen for discussion were selected because they seem to be most obvious from a careful study of Brethren organizational life. This approach is not to be confused with "ideal types" or a simplistic image of change as automatic, driven, or moving from one opposite pole to another.

Trends Associated With Organizational Growth I		
INFORMAL --------- *PROCEDURES* --------- FORMAL		
1850 ————————1900————————1950————————1990		
more reliance on custom, tradition		follow set, written rules
fit decisions to individual need		categorical decision making

In the absence of written or formalized rules and procedures, the church tended to follow custom and tradition. Formal organizations follow procedures which are determined by previous written prescriptions as in a constitution or rule book or job prescription. It becomes incumbent to "follow the written rule," regardless of how well or how poorly the rule fits the case.

One of the principal complaints against bureaucratic systems is lack of response to the unique problems associated with particular individuals or situations. This stems from the need of the bureaucracy to respond to large numbers of cases by means of forming policies to handle them in categories of so-called "similar" types.

Trends Associated With Organizational Growth II	
SIMPLE ------- *ORGANIZATION* ------- COMPLEX	
1850 ——————1900——————1950——————1990	
few levels of hierarchy	many levels, center at top
little need for integration	vertical integration
little need for specialization	high level of specialization
tasks done, problems solved as needed	rational coordination
low focus of attention on structure	high focus of attention
resource allocation: low focus and amounts	high focus and amounts
resource allocation: "free" personnel	many employed personnel

The Leaders-Laity Gap

Levels of hierarchy imply social and cultural (including "philosophical") distance or insulation of leaders from the life of the people. Communication in a typical bureaucracy would be up and down the line. Distance would be revealed if leaders lacked understanding of and sensitivity to the problems, needs, and viewpoints of smaller, marginal, and rural congregations and of untrained ministers with whom they seldom or never interact.

Cultural distance is also increased when upper leaders and officials have advanced educations, different work environments with their own mutually reinforcing sub-cultures, different life styles, and more liberal outlooks whereas grass roots members and leaders would tend toward less education and more conservatism as a general rule. The problem would be aggravated if there is little contact of officials with the grass roots of the numerous churches of average or smaller than average size. Ill effects of this discontinuity could include declining morale, low levels of commitment, and loss of loyalty to officialdom, even alienation.

A related problem exists if ego-centered or power hungry leaders occupy higher offices. A love of prestige and power can corrupt the self-concept and enter into human relations. Even church bureaucrats can act arbitrarily, manipulate people, and take advantage of their office. Ego rationalizations sometimes make it possible for such leaders to feel that their achievements give them a kind of personal superiority. Perhaps even more serious harm results when such leaders attempt to impose what they believe to be their own "superior" conceptions and "philosophies" upon the denomination. A worst case scenario could be imagined if officials at the peak of power seek to impose their own personal agendas and try to displace or undermine the goals and agendas of the church at large or of some influential segment of the church, such as traditionalists or progressives. Such persons may cross the indefinite line between "servant of the church" and self-appointed savior of the church.

Social and cultural distance may also be increased by geographic distance. The Elgin center is quite distant from the demographic center of the denomination. Eighty percent of the membership lives east of a north south line running with the eastern boundary of Illinois.[22] An example of cultural distance in the 1850s was the "Far Western Brethren" whose doctrines and practices gradually became differentiated from the those of the brotherhood.

Vertical integration, the second trend in the time scale above, is sought because of the need to communicate information and resources up or down "the line" and to permit the needed personnel or offices to give and receive directives. This also implies a power structure, but this varies with the type of church government. It also implies the possibility of alienation of grass roots from top leaders and offices due to a feeling of "powerlessness" and sense of being manipulated, a situation which also varies with type of church government.

Specialization of tasks and occupations, the third trend in the time scale above, is a general condition in American society. In 1850, the great majority of Brethren, including ministers, were farmers, and this singularity of occupation helped to provide a ground for social and ideological solidarity. In contemporary society, specialization of tasks, geographic mobility, and occupational and educational differences can work to undermine solidarity by producing diversity of life styles, tasks, education, outlook, goal orientation, attitude, and even world view.

Rational coordination, the fourth trend in the time scale, implies the tendency to rearrange, modify, and reformulate structures, personnel, and procedures. These kinds of rapid changes can undermine traditions, loyalty, continuity, and support. A sense of insecurity, manipulation, and alienation can arise among personnel and members.

Rational coordination, however, is a necessity in order to maximize efficiency, enhance production, conserve costs, etc. It relates to "the design of the structure" which in turn relates to "quality and quantity of output." Careful planning along with sensitivity may minimize harmful effects on personnel.

The fifth trend in the time scale is the need to focus attention on structure in order to achieve efficiency and to monitor production. This trend of change relates to the amounts of energy, time, and personnel that are needed to run, plan, manage, coordinate, and periodically reformulate the system. In recent times, comparatively large investments of time and concern have been needed to plan, develop, and resolve problems of structure and restructuring. They are costly also in financial resources and morale.

It must be kept in mind, however, that organization is necessary in the modern world. It is not to be considered undesirable; some of its accompanying disadvantages can be minimized. Organization is able to facilitate a vast amount of goal oriented activity (mission) which otherwise could not take place.

The sixth trend relates to money resource allocation. In the 1850s, the denomination operated mostly on a non-monetary basis with the free ministry. Today, money is needed not only to pay a relatively large staff but to underwrite a variety of programs sponsored by the denomination. The monetary system allows much wider participation of the laity in supporting the various missions of the church.

On the other hand, considerable effort and focus must be placed on fund raising both at the local and national levels for the program to succeed, and nearly the entire program operates within the monetary system. Yet if great distance in philosophy and aim—or even alienation—separates the membership from its upper level officials, commitment will be endangered and monetary income will level off or decline.

The seventh trend relates to personnel resource allocation. In 1850, the denomination did not have a single employed person. Ministers, deacons, and committees did the work on a voluntary basis. Today, employed personnel (both lay and clergy) at all levels are deeply involved in the work of the church. This trend greatly increased output through work of full time, specialized personnel. Work done by volunteers has also undoubtedly grown. It also produced power and prestige shifts from deacons, elders, and free ministers to full time pastors, executives, commissions, etc. Many other changes accompanied the transition from free ministers to the professional ministry some of which have been addressed in this paper.

Definition of Mission

Organizations usually have a reason for being: a goal, aim, or "mission." The mission assigned to organization may also passively change with the times. Furthermore, the definition of mission itself may actively evolve within the organization as a result of internal interactive influences and of creative thought on the part of executives and commissions. If a large degree of social and ideological distance[23] exists between the leaders and the membership, and if leaders are assuming different definitions of the church and its mission, such leaders may tend to lose the commitment of the membership.

While selection of commission members is ostensibly democratic and representative, it often tends to be more selective of local leaders who are known for ideas compatible with commission stances and who are a "known quantity" as team players. Such team players are not apt to criticize proposals, raise too many questions about program, or throw doubt upon plans of action. When national commissions and higher officials surround themselves with "yes" people, cultural continuity between officials and laity may be endangered. To the extent that the selection process excludes diverse, even critical, viewpoints, ideological distance and alienation of support may ensue as programs evolve beyond the range of the membership.

In addition, a subtle process of selection goes on. Those aspects of mission get emphasized which lie within the area of what an organization as such is best able to accomplish. Aspects of mission not easily amenable to implementation by means of existing organizational machinery and channels tend to remain undefined and neglected. One may wonder whether evangelism might not be one of these more difficult, neglected areas of mission under our present organizational setup.

Views of Mission	
1850 ——————1900——————1950——————1990	
relatively simple, singular	complex, numerous "missions"
to draw people <u>out of</u> the world	to engage world, improve society
consensus regarding mission	lack of consensus; many missions

The heart of bureaucratic expansion is the formation of specialized agencies, offices, and branches to fulfill new or sub-divided goals. In 1850, the mission of the church is believed to have been relatively simply defined as maintenance of the fellowship, "propagation of the gospel," and winning people to Christ. In the period after 1900, many new expressions of mission appeared, usually being given a structural niche (branch, office, or committee) for promotion purposes—a new structure for each new cause. The nature of organization easily permits the expansion of mission into new areas.

When multiple missions and foci prevail, priorities must be set and constantly monitored if those designated as basic are to be assured of success. Those aspects of mission which are essential are those that have to do with the survival and growth of the organization. They are the maintenance and nurture of the members and the winning of new members, priorities which the older Brethren seem to have kept clearly before them. Thus multiple missions tend to detract attention and resources from those parts of mission having to do with survival: maintenance, nurture, and winning new members. They also tend to attract special constituencies and encourage the formation of special interest groups, each seeking to promote their own ends, sometimes endangering overall denominational solidarity and well-being. On the other hand, multiple missions attract special constituencies and allow a wider range of service and activity.

The second trend in the time scale relates to how Brethren define their relationship to the world. The old Brethren did not conceive of changing the world (society) but desired to be separate from it and to remain untainted by it. They did not dream of modifying the systems of the world. They regarded the world, but not the people in it, as alien and unredeemable. For example, they never would have thought of applying pacifist principals to international relations (an endless pastime of modern pacifists). They regarded wars as an inevitable part of worldly conditions from which Brethren must be separate.

Modern Brethren, under the influence of the social gospel and its successors, believe in a prophetic mission to call the society to account, modify social conditions, and engage its members in those social issues involving moral values. This view, now widespread among denominations whose membership resides in the mainstream of American society, is optimistic. It seeks to make the gospel relevant to the contemporary social setting. It is characteristic of those denominations which define themselves as part of society and its culture and seek to direct their ministry toward it.

At the same time, this particular position or attitude is fraught with danger for Brethren. Being in the world rather than set apart from it means Brethren need to attempt to clarify the guidelines between "right and wrong," moral and immoral behavior, and godly and ungodly life styles. Without this important effort, our behavior as Christians will tend to change in the direction of becoming indistinguishable from that of non-Christians. This danger may suggest the need for strong prophetic preaching to our own members (as well as to society). It may also point to the need for a kind of church discipline which can be justified, defended, and tolerated in a radically individualistic, freedom-loving society.

The third trend in the time scale relates to the degree of consensus in the church regarding mission. In 1850, Brethren may have had a relatively strong consensus and commitment to a more limited concept of mission.[24] Today, the desire to extend the mission of the church to the realm of social issues brings along with it much controversy. Because the social issues have penetrated the membership and affect behavior, it would appear that the church *must* address these issues. Some degree of alienation, disenchantment, and membership loss, however, may be a part of the price that must be paid. Danger ensues, however, when especially disruptive issues are "pushed" by progressive leaders, special interest groups, or organs of the church. It is worthy of note that the early church did not attack at one time all the social issues of its day! The church must also maintain sufficient cohesion, loyalty, and support to remain a viable organization. Thus the church must balance this pragmatic but essential principle with its call to engage in prophetic ministry.

Social-Ideological Distance Between Ministers and Congregations

Social distance refers to differences in social status, income, prestige, power, cohesion, and degree of identification of minister and people. Ideological distance refers to differences in goals, theology, world view, and understandings of reality. Here the discussion will refer to how such cultural discontinuity has increased between ministers and congregations. This relates to organization in that members and pastors represent different levels and statuses within the organization. In addition, college and theological training may create different world views and understandings of reality, particularly of "theological reality." Thus cultural continuity between minister and congregation is endangered.[25] Studies are needed to attempt to measure this subtle element. It may play a larger role than is currently thought in the relations of pastors and people. It seems possible that this is a major factor in shortening of pastorates and of young ministers leaving the ministry entirely.

In 1850, most congregations obtained their ministers (free) from among themselves. Chosen because they exemplified and embodied basic Brethren beliefs and practices, they were unified with the people. Most likely, people and minister were of the same occupation, farming, thus increasing their sense of mutuality. In addition, the old Brethren consciously played down the status differences of ministers and people by not allowing pulpits and platforms for ministers. This further emphasized that ministers and people were unified in standing on the same level before God and among the people.

Today, social and ideological discontinuities of pastor and people are magnified in various ways. Ministers are often set apart by specialized occupational training including counseling, theology, philosophy, methods, etc., all of which help to produce an outlook and understanding (world view) which is different from most members. This can occur despite the fact that many or most members are highly educated, because by virtue of specialized training, they, too, are distanced.

Perhaps the most crucial source of the philosophical and world view differences between pastor and congregation is derived from the influence of higher education in college and seminary. In these educational settings, youth are necessarily exposed to the developmental view of history and life and the influence of the "higher criticism" approach to the study of the Bible. While these aspects of higher education are essential to the training of ministers in today's world, it may be a serious error to fail to anticipate and relate to the consequences of such world views to ministers and congregations. Failure to address the problems which this conflict of assumptions and world views can create may weaken the motivations of young ministers to continue in the pastorate.

Likewise, the implications for the relations between ministers and congregations needs to be assessed.

Social-ideological discontinuities are most destructive to congregations when, because of the shortage of ministers, the smaller churches decide to call ministers of non-Brethren origin. Such ministers often lack even rudimentary knowledge of Brethren faith and practice. They certainly do not share the Brethren "cultural base." Examples include three of the older congregations of West Marva District. Even though they had undergone the usual training courses, these ministers of non-Brethren origin soon repudiated their vows of faithfulness to the denomination, withdrew support of the Brotherhood, went independent, and split their congregations. When they were unsuccessful in obtaining title to the church property, they built new churches nearby or found places of meeting and tried to draw off Brethren followers.

Ministers/Leaders: Ideal Style and Role Pattern	
1850 ——————1900——————1950——————1990	
charismatic; deep convictions	balance of complex roles; strong administrative component
authoritarian-paternal	democratic, managerial

This trend relates to changes in the ministers role model which is most highly rewarded with success. This is important because it provides the model for the leader to emulate and an incentive toward achieving it.

Likely the most successful ministerial role a hundred fifty years ago was that of an older, somewhat charismatic, fatherly-authoritarian elder with deeply held loyalty to Brethren faith and practice. His role was especially strengthened by an ability to "discern the sense of the meeting" and to express the ideals of unity and commitment to Brethren faith and practice. The ability to do this arose out of the minister's closeness to and identity with the congregation. The specific aim was to persuade the listener that Dunker faith and practice was more correct compared with other ways. If charismatic, this added more to the power to persuade. Persons of this sort became very successful evangelists during the period from 1890 to 1940.

Today, the professional pastor is the dominant model. He or she has a variety of role skills. Talent in administration is becoming a strong need as larger congregations move into varied programs and multiple staffing. He or she is held responsible, as is any CEO, for the way a complex program runs and how the staff get along. The pastor may keep somewhat distant and aloof from his or her flock.

It appears that the role pattern and professional image of the Brethren leader and official today has shifted closer to (but is still far from identical with) what has been described as the "bureaucratic personality." Certainly it is very distant from the charismatic[26] and paternal role type of a hundred years ago in which the minister tended to be more ideologically unified with his people. The impact that this shift might be having on the maintenance and evangelistic mission of the church remains unassessed.[27]

It is obvious that there is a wide divergence in the role patterns of the two periods. The ultimate significance of this may reside in the changed basis for obtaining new members. For the earlier period, persuasive preaching by a somewhat charismatic minister was crucial, especially during evangelistic meetings. For the modern period, gaining new members becomes an *administrative challenge* in which the problem is tackled by balancing several programs including membership classes, pastoral visiting, and involving the congregation in the practice of effective procedures and methods. Coordination of all approaches, *an administrative model*, is believed to provide success.

Other issues center on the importance of a sense of urgency regarding salvation, the call to discipleship, the usefulness or need for utilizing Brethren belief and practice and other doctrinal contents as a part of the evangelistic effort. Should theologically vacuous methods and procedures be used in a diverse society? Should the denomination continue quietly to drift away from the older religious world view which emphasized sin, confession, repentance, faith, redemption, and a New Testament based life style which stands against a morally decadent culture? Should the church continue to stress the new psychologistic, personalistic, therapy-centered theology combined with a socially oriented mission? Are the Brethren pioneering a "new approach" or jumping off the gang plank?

Preaching Focus	
1850 ——————1900——————1950——————1990	
New Testament centered	personal needs, contemporary
defense, justification of Brethren faith/practice	topical, variety
keep members loyal to the faith/practice	keep members attending and giving

Few sermons have been preserved from 150 years ago. This makes comparison by means of "content analysis" impossible. Periodical literature, doctrinal debate publications, tracts and pamphlets, sermon outlines, etc., do exist, however, and some of the dominant themes or foci of preaching during the nineteenth century are revealed.

A striking change appears to be the loss of emphasis upon maintenance and conservation of Brethren belief and practice and upon the use of that theme as the basis for winning new members. How can the Brethren keep significant aspects of their unique mission and calling alive if they neglect to preach it and apply it in a morally and intellectually relevant way in its contemporary social and cultural settings?

Changes in Lifestyle			
1850 ——————————1900————————————1950————————————1990			
non-conformity to world uniformity		merged into American mainstream diversity, little difference from other churches	

Here the issue becomes to what degree should the Brethren faith and practice be recognized as distinct thereby becoming a witness to the world of a Christian lifestyle. In what specific ways should the Brethren lifestyle, on a religious and moral basis, differ from the American lifestyle? How should such essential differences be promoted and established? How can Brethren construct a New Testament lifestyle of moral and intellectual integrity in today's increasingly sophisticated and educated society? These are crucial issues to the Brethren who once stressed a radical New Testament lifestyle.

Basis of Congregational Solidarity			
1850 ——————————1900————————————1950————————————1990			
kinship and family ties strong sense of community		participation in one or more organizational niches	

Rural families were large and bound together not only through common religious loyalties but also by need for economic cooperation in farm work. These influences tended to build strong, tightly bound local communities having intense commitment. Changed conditions today force the church to rely on different means of building community. Thus a function of local organization is to tie members in by giving them a responsibility and obligation at definite niches within the structure, and loyalty tends to center around the local church.

Religious World View			
1850 ——————————1900————————————1950————————————1990			
being separate, untainted by the world sectarian views; "Brethrenism" rejection of many views of other faiths		being in world as leaven ecumenical; inclusive; open openness to beliefs of other religions	

The shift in world view is significant in understanding the contemporary Brethren self-image. The implications of this major shift are extensive and center on crucial aspects of how Brethren see themselves today. The transition is so drastic that the question may be asked: are the Brethren still the Brethren? Is an extreme form of openness to all belief systems the way we wish to go? It is unlikely that the Brethren will ever again conceive of themselves as being separate from the world. The question then becomes, how shall we define ourselves in the world? How can we be faithful to the best within our Anabaptist and Pietist traditions? And how can the church be faithful to its ancient calling and at the same time answer God's calling to serve the present age?

Conclusion

This discussion has presented a picture of a relatively informal and simply organized religious body in 1850 undergoing transformation into a highly organized and formally structured denomination in 1990. These changes have occurred very gradually. Consequently, there has been little awareness of the transition and of its impact on the denomination.

Although numerous variables have been involved in bringing about the trends of change which have marked the church in the past 140 years, the impact of organizational development itself appears to have been significant. These changes have had far reaching effect upon the church at every level from congregational life and human relations to conceptual patterns including theology and world view.

Organization is imperative. There is no turning back to simpler times in this age of complex structures. This paper is not a harangue against organization as some kind of unfortunate compromise with evil. The life of the church today is expressed and fulfilled through organization. It is seen as a means by which the church's mission is accomplished. What *is called for* is to examine the negative or problematic side of organization. The older informal patterns also had their problematic side! By becoming aware of the problems inherent in organization, and by planning and neutralizing the tendencies normally associated with organization, some harmful effects may be reduced. By remaining unconcerned or by refusing to come to terms by means of intelligent response, the church runs the risk of languishing somewhere on the vague border between outright decline and vigorous growth.

Perhaps most significant for the well-being and future vigor of the denomination are the issues of social, cultural, and ideological discontinuity between the membership and the "higher levels" of the organization as per the Elgin bureaucracy, the Seminary, and the Colleges.[28] The question of distance or discontinuity in ideology and world view is very critical, for this problem may contribute to a rather large part of the loss of support and commitment which characterizes a considerable proportion of the membership today.

Also crucial is the issue of mission and how it is defined and directed. Certainly the church is called to a strong, prophetic mission relating to serious social issues facing society. Yet in so doing, does it face the danger of undermining lay commitment and alienating significant support from the membership? Certainly the church does not operate on the secular norm of exploiting social issues in the mistaken notion that by so doing it is increasing interest, support, or readership.

Multiplicity of "missions" implies the need to prioritize. It is suggested that at times in the past the old missions of maintenance of the fellowship and winning new members may have been set back as urgent new "missions" came to the fore.

Furthermore, subtle changes in world view and theology have taken place. This trend, a part of the cultural discontinuity issue, was also impacted by changes in American culture and the influence of higher education, especially the wide dissemination of psychologistic and personalistic views of human behavior, the developmental view of history, and higher criticism. Within some circles, this world view appears to be supplanting the older theology of sin, confession, repentance, and redemption. The issue here is the increasing gap between leaders and the membership at large.

Major changes in the role of ministers has occurred. In addition, the work of the church is shared today by many officials and associated personnel whose role patterns are quite different from that of 140 years ago. It is suggested that little knowledge exists regarding the effect of these modifications on the maintenance of membership morale and growth.

The aim of this discussion is to raise these issues to the level of awareness, to bring about discussion, and to stimulate research. Should the Brethren today make a special effort to decide what they wish to retain or reinterpret out of their rich Anabaptist-Pietist heritage? Should they attempt to identify the "essence" without which they are no longer Brethren? Beyond that, should Brethren purposefully attempt to recover, reformulate, and propagate the useful and morally relevant aspects of their belief and practice as a basic part of their mission in the world today? And finally, how can the power and versatility of organization as a tool be used to fulfill these ends?

The old Brethren, as a gathered body in Christ's name, carefully and laboriously "discerned the truth" from the New Testament under the guidance of the Holy Spirit. Is not this a route that Brethren could follow in discerning their particular truth? The answer to this question may be exceedingly crucial to our contribution as a unique part of the religious scene in America as we approach the beginning of the twenty-first century!

¹ See Carl F. Bowman, A Profile of the Church of the Brethren (Elgin: Brethren Press, 1987). This booklet summarizes Dr. Bowman's findings regarding contemporary Brethren belief and practice. The Brethren Profile Study was conducted in 1985 in connection with research for the doctoral degree at the University of Virginia. See also Dr. Bowman's chapter in Donald F. Durnbaugh, Church of the Brethren: Yesterday and Today (Elgin: Brethren Press, 1986).

² A body of literature does exist pertaining to the polity of the church. This mostly relates to the pattern of church governance and how it functions. It does not usually focus upon the subtle and long-term impact of organization itself on church life. For an analysis of polity issues, see Brethren Encyclopedia, "Polity;" Donald F. Durnbaugh, ed., The Church of the Brethren: Past and Present (Elgin: Brethren Press, 1971); Donald F. Durnbaugh, ed., The Church of the Brethren: Yesterday and Today (Elgin: Brethren Press, 1986). Both of these volumes contain chapters on polity as well as fairly complete bibliographies on the topic. See also Roger Sappington, The Brethren in Industrial America: 1865-1915 (Elgin: Brethren Press: 1985) which contains a chapter on polity and organization, and S. Loren Bowman, Power and Polity Among the Brethren' (Elgin: Brethren Press, 1987). A recent autobiography by Raymond Peters, Foothills to Mountaintops: My Pilgrimage to Wholeness (Elgin: Brethren Press, 1990), a long term executive of the Church of the Brethren, now retired, contains interesting insights on how his position at the peak of the bureaucracy impacted his attitudes and self-concept and on how the different offices and branches of the bureaucracy inter-related with each other. The doctoral dissertation by Carl F. Bowman, "Beyond Plainness: Cultural Transformation Among the Brethren from 1850 to the Present," Ph. D. diss., Univ. of Virginia, 1989, contains a section which examines church organization.

³ West Marva District consists of the northern half of West Virginia and the western part of Maryland. The present district was formed when First and Second West Virginia and Western Maryland united in 1965. The history of these districts, from their founding to the present is discussed in Emmert F. Bittinger, Allegheny Passage (Camden, Maine: Penobscot Press, 1990), chapters 20, 21, and 22.

⁴ In addition, a number of more or less independent age group service organizations exist with only symbolic connections with the denomination. These include the colleges, seminary, homes and villages for the aging, the Brethren Benefit Trust, Inc., and so on.

⁵ Historians have usually attributed the desire to form districts to the need to lessen the heavy work agenda of Yearly Meetings. It was believed that district meetings could relieve Yearly Meetings by handling many of the more local problems, or propose solutions to Yearly Meeting, thus lessening the burden. A careful study of the proposal shows, however, that the Virginia and western Pennsylvania ministers saw the cause of missions as a crucial part of the rationale for creating districts. These elders sought with great effort to persuade Yearly Meeting to allow district structures for the purpose of facilitating home mission work. (See Allegheny Passage pages 718-722 and D. H. Zigler, History of the Brethren in Virginia, (Elgin: Brethren Publishing House, 1914), pages 63-72)). Thus the initiative to form districts was two-fold, both pragmatic and idealistic.

⁶ The proposals of Kline and the Virginia elders were exceedingly controversial, because the plan included the raising of funds within the proposed districts. These funds would underwrite the expenses of traveling teams of missionary ministers. This proposal casts Kline and the Virginia elders as "progressives." Conservative elders strongly fought against any payments to ministers, and were opposed to districts which they feared would be divisive or challenge the authority of Annual Meeting.

⁷ The financing plan was undoubtedly initiated through District Meeting. Minutes of early meetings, however, are lost. Consequently, the elements of the district plan must be inferred from the way the plan operated at the congregational level.

[8] This financing method was similarly adopted in several congregations and was obviously promoted and recommended by District Meeting. Yearly Meeting had approved this procedure in 1865 including the interpretation that members were obligated to pay their assessment or they would "fall under the judgment of the church."

[9] Bittinger, 272-275. Notable is the fact that the Beaver Run Congregation kept lists for a number of years, several of which are extant. These listed the members by head of family and gave the worth of their real estate in dollars.

[10] If this assumption is true, the financial function of the deacon visit would have been considerably weakened when the Yearly Meeting allowed the collecting of Sunday church offerings in 1895 (Minutes, Article 9). In addition, church offerings provided a certain anonymity in giving. This would have undermined the system of church taxes, for records could no longer be kept of each individual's financial contributions. In any case, church "offerings" placed the members' financial support more clearly in the category of "voluntary" as over against the category of "obligatory" as in taxation. The conceptualization of church giving as voluntary and private has continued to strengthen during the past century.

[11] These evangelists had to support themselves by their own occupational activities, with the exception of Elder David Miller of Second District who received district support. He also sold his business and proceeded to raise his own support through his meetings.

[12] See Bittinger, p. 763. This high stress on the missionary function of Sunday Schools must not be confused with "child evangelism." The Brethren as anabaptists opposed infant baptism and regarded child evangelism as inappropriate. Those being baptized were youthful members of the Sunday Schools who had requested baptism or had been converted during the congregational evangelistic meetings. The role of Sunday Schools in bringing about the gradual decline in the age of applicants for Brethren baptism has yet to be assessed, but it may be hypothesized to have been an important factor.

[13] The rapid increase and diversification in the conceptual content of the idea of "the mission of the church" appears to be inextricably intertwined with the growth of organization. Indeed one wonders if this fact is not associated with the well known tendency for bureaucratic structures to grow and expand.

[14] These can only be mentioned in brief. The interested reader may examine the history of their formation in Allegheny Passage, chapter 21. This chapter also attempts to explain why and how the mission of the church could at this time undergo rapid redefinition and reformulation. These developments are linked not only to events internal to the denomination, such as the partial resolution of the dress controversy, but to national events such as World War I, the Prohibition Movement, the national women's movement, etc.

[15] Bittinger, 790-91.

[16] The presentation of these complex developments in West Marva District is necessarily extremely shortened. The fuller discussion together with documentation may be examined in Bittinger, Allegheny Passage, chapters 20, 21, 22.

[17] The creation and use of such bureaucratic power, however, is considerably muted in those religious organizations which are based upon democratic or congregational principles.

[18] Bittinger, 766-67.

[19] Partly as a result of the pervasiveness of the therapeutic and counseling varieties of psychological theory, those church leaders tending to this view define the problem more as one where the individual needs help, self-understanding, and self-esteem. The old theology of sin, confession, repentance, and redemption became outmoded within this therapeutic or psychological framework. Concern no longer lies with a perceived need to preserve the group by means of strengthening religious norms of behavior or to keep the church "unsullied from the world." Rather, the individualism so pervasively expressed in the culture of modern America has been substituted, and the church becomes more interested in counseling or ministering to the suffering of individuals. Little concern is given to the impact of the individual's moral deviations on the normative climate of the congregation as a whole.

[20] Modification of the commission pattern has occurred in recent years at the center, and some functions have been transferred to the district level.

[21] See Bittinger, p. 788.

[22] See The Brethren Encyclopedia, vol. 3, p 1468.

[23] Obviously, such a great gap or degree of cultural discontinuity endangers the morale and commitment of the members as they observe directions, decision-making, plans, and programs which to them appear to be inconsistent with their own ideological commitments.

[24] The alleged consensus regarding mission did not endure long past 1850, because the progressives soon began to suggest that Brethren should become involved in foreign missions, a trend which the conservative members resisted.

[25] Of course, leadership implies some degree of cultural discontinuity and difference of understanding else leadership becomes meaningless. The minister needs to be "ahead" of his people. On the other hand, when that distance is "too great," weakening of commitment or even alienation can occur. An extensive study of the decline of the Disciples denomination in recent times has pointed to the importance of the "gulf [which] exists between the theological and moral views of Disciples ministers and active members of Disciples congregations." See D. Newell Williams, A Case Study of Mainstream Protestantism: the Disciples' Relation to American Culture, 1880-1989 (Eerdmans Publishing Co.: Grand Rapids, 1991), pp. 13, 14, 23.

[26] Although not a dominant influence today, charismatic ministers can still arise and make a significant contribution to the church. This is a stronger possibility if they are able to attach to or formulate an organizational base. An example would be M. R. Ziegler and his work with the World Council of Churches and with Brethren Service. Although charismatic leaders are not always compatible with organizational settings, when they are they can comprise an especially powerful combination.

[27] The author is not suggesting that leaders today must return to an impossible and outdated role pattern. Nor is it being suggested that no changes should take place. Perhaps most needed on the part of officials and pastors is a better understanding of and deep empathy with the life of the members at the grass roots level. For officials and educators, this calls for less insulation from the church at the congregational level, especially with the large number of churches which are struggling merely to survive.

[28] The educational organizations are a special case, most being relatively independent of the denomination and serving large non-Brethren constituencies. Nevertheless, they have had a massive impact upon the theology and world views of the leadership. While much of this ideological change can be defended as necessary adaptation, the problems which attend this part of our cultural discontinuity may need to be thoughtfully addressed in order to maintain our denominational unity.

10

Congregational Transformation:
A Case Study of
the Lititz Church[1]

by Donald R. Fitzkee

Donald Fitzkee's richly detailed paper describes key changes in the life of the Lititz congregation, thus portraying a vivid image of Brethren transition at the local level. Breadth is thereby added to the previous descriptions of change at the district and denominational levels. Especially useful is the opportunity to examine how developments at the denominational level impacted a strong congregation located in a traditional Brethren environment. The effects of Annual Conference decisions, the employment of professionally trained "outside" ministers , and the decline in the role of the "free" ministers and deacons are illuminated in the happenings at Lititz. Although the church is situated in the heart of conservative Lancaster County, Pennsylvania, the record reveals the presence of strong influences leading toward change as well as powerful restraints. In spite of the potential for conflict, remarkable transformations quite similar to those within the denomination, did occur. They revolutionizied the life of this strong congregation.

Introduction

During this century the Church of the Brethren has undergone a radical transformation. One by one the peculiar pillars on which the church's past was built have crumbled and been replaced by a more modern foundation. While helpful studies have examined these larger trends in the Church of the Brethren, a congregational case study is an equally fruitful method of grasping the scope of change. After all, to speak of changes in the Church of the Brethren ultimately is to speak of changes that either found their genesis in or later affected congregations.

Therefore, this paper focuses on key changes in the life of a congregation, that of Lititz, Pennsylvania, during the first seventy-five years of its existence

(1914-1989). Among these are changes in leadership and organizational patterns; music, worship, and buildings; and attitudes toward the world, non-Brethren church bodies, and congregational discipline.

The danger of drawing assumptions about the larger church from the study of an individual congregation is that the pace of change in Church of the Brethren congregations has been uneven. Many congregations have been selective in their appropriation of new ideas and practices. The uniqueness of the Lititz story lies in its relative lack of selectivity in the face of change. Despite its beginnings as a traditional Brethren congregation in conservative Eastern Pennsylvania District, the Lititz church was quick to adopt most of the twentieth-century innovations that swept through the Church of the Brethren. Thus, Lititz provides an excellent catalog of twentieth-century change.

Background

The borough of Lititz was founded by Moravians in the mid-eighteenth century. Until 1855 a lease system prevented non-Moravians from owning land in Lititz. The abolishing of the lease system opened the community to the Brethren and others. With the founding of the West Conestoga congregation in 1864, the Brethren in Lititz became members of that congregation. This affiliation occurred because Brethren congregations at this time had distinct geographical boundaries.

By 1887 enough Brethren lived in Lititz to warrant construction of a meetinghouse. So a small frame house, forty by fifty feet, with adjacent horse sheds, was built at the eastern end of town on Willow Street.

The West Conestoga congregation granted the Lititz Brethren permission in 1913 to organize a separate congregation. During the Christmas season of 1913, elder J.G. Royer, president of Mt. Morris (Ill.) College, held revival services in the Lititz house and stayed on to help organize the new congregation. The Lititz Church of the Brethren was officially organized January 10, 1914, with 119 charter members.

Membership grew steadily up until the late 1920s, when a leadership vacuum created by the death of the congregation's two primary leaders evidently contributed to numerical decline. The most rapid period of growth came in the latter half of the 1930s, following the hiring of the congregation's first salaried pastor. Membership continued to grow steadily through the 1970s. By 1989 membership had leveled near the eight hundred mark.[2]

Ministers and Deacons

In 1914 few congregations in Eastern Pennsylvania District employed salaried pastors. The free ministry, a system of leadership in which nonsalaried ministers and deacons were elected from within the congregation's ranks, was the norm. Together ministers and deacons formed the "Official Board," which prepared the Council Meeting agenda, cared for congregational discipline, and spearheaded the spiritual nurture ministries of the church. The congregation's elder-in-charge presided over the board, moderated council meetings, and coordinated the ministry of the church.

When the Lititz congregation was organized in 1914, J. W. G. Hershey was the sole minister. The congregation elected I. W. Taylor, an elder in a neighboring congregation, to be elder-in-charge. In September 1914 the congregation held elections for an additional minister and two deacons. The open election for a minister resulted in a tie between Harvey Eberly and Henry R. Gibbel, so both were called to serve. Two deacons were called in a similar election and "all four, along with their wives, were installed that same evening."[3] In January 1919 J. W. G. Hershey was elected elder-in-charge and Henry R. Gibbel became church clerk. Together they provided primary leadership for the next decade.

Both Hershey and Gibbel were well-known in the community, the district, and beyond. Both were school teachers in the Lititz area before forming an insurance partnership in 1890 and managing the Lititz Agricultural Mutual Fire Insurance Company. Both were advocates of higher education and served on the boards of Brethren educational institutions.[4]

The late 1920s were turbulent and transitional. In 1926 the congregation moved from its simple frame meetinghouse to a more adequate, modern brick building on Center Street. Also by this time, Council Meeting minutes reveal that more and more members were violating congregational standards on issues of nonconformity. By March 1927 violations seemed to be widespread. The Council Meeting minutes report that, "The elder plead with the members sympathetically not to cause any offence to the Church and her Lord." With firm leadership never more necessary, in 1927 Henry R. Gibbel died. The following year Elder Hershey asked to be relieved as elder-in-charge because he no longer felt the congregation's support. The congregation refused to grant his request and voiced support for his leadership. He continued as elder-in-charge until his death in 1929.

Thus within a two-year period the congregation lost its two primary leaders. Rather than looking within the congregation, Lititz Brethren turned to the outside. Nathan Martin, of Lebanon, was elected elder-in-charge, and oddly, no new ministers were called from within the congregation to replace Hershey and Gibbel. One longtime member suggests that no one in the congregation stood out as a candidate for ministry, and the remaining ministers lacked the necessary skills to assume central leadership roles.[5] At least, it seemed no one in the congregation could provide the caliber of leadership that Hershey and Gibbel had provided.

Less than a year after Hershey's death in March 1930, the congregation for the first time broached the question of hiring a pastor, but the matter was deferred indefinitely. At the following March Council Meeting several ministry-related concerns were heard. There were requests for a part- or full-time pastor, more "spirit-filled sermons," and more visiting of the sick by ministers. One member stated bluntly, "We need the help of a pastor or a younger minister." The pastor question was raised again in March 1932, but no action was reported. Finally, in July 1932 the congregation voted to hire a part-time pastor. The following month A.C. Baugher, academic dean at Elizabethtown College, was called to preach once a month at Lititz as their part-time pastor. Baugher was elected elder-in-charge the following spring.[6]

The part-time pastor arrangement sufficed until 1935, when requests for a full-time pastor came to Council Meeting and a search committee was appointed. In May 1935 the congregation approved a $6,000 budget—its first—and called by a plurality vote James M. Moore as pastor with a starting salary of $1,800.

Moore, a graduate of Mt. Morris Academy and Bethany Biblical Seminary, had served on the Bethany board of directors, taught Old and New Testament at the seminary, and in 1930 was Annual Conference moderator. During his ten years as pastor at Lititz membership grew from 301 in 1935 to 418 in 1945.

Organizational Development

In the midst of the pastoral debate in the early 1930s the congregation was taking steps toward getting more organized. Around 1930 the congregation began to prepare an annual schedule of events. In 1934 the first congregational directory was published and a new Board of Christian Education was formed. Prior to 1934 the Official Board and the Sunday school organization, both reportable to Council Meeting, were the main organizational entities. The new Board of Christian Education was given broad responsibilities, overseeing the entire Christian education program and other areas not directly linked to Christian education, such as appointing choristers for revival meetings and lining up special music. While the Official Board was open only to men, Florence Gibbel, wife of Henry R., was elected "chairman" of the new board.

Although additional committees were added to the church's organization during the 1930s and 1940s, the Official Board, composed of ministers and deacons, remained at the heart of the organization. From the congregation's beginning, power was centered in the ministers and deacons who served for life. Thus in addition to their responsibilities for spiritual nurture, the deacons and ministers were the primary administrative unit of the church. All that changed in 1955, when the congregation adopted a new plan of organization, replacing the Official Board with a Board of Administration.

The new board was divided into seven five-member commissions: Christian Education, Ministry and Evangelism, Missions and Service, Music and Worship, Properties and Finance, Fellowship and Recreation, and Spiritual

Nurture. Ministers and deacons comprised the Spiritual Nurture Commission. In addition, the elder-in-charge position was replaced with the moderator, a position open to the laity. The office of deacon was downgraded from a lifetime calling to a three-year term. Term deacons were elected for the first time in 1958.

Feelings in the congregation toward these changes, which had been recommended by Annual Conference, were mixed. E. Floyd McDowell, who became pastor of the congregation in April 1955 and gave impetus to the organizational change, saw it as a positive way to transfer responsibility from deacons and ministers to the rest of the congregation. Before the change the Official Board apparently had a reputation for being conservative and perhaps was not moving fast enough for the rest of the congregation on some matters.

"You had entrenched power," said McDowell. "I think the church recognized that. Even the deacons recognized that. Some were reluctant to admit it, I suppose, but they recognized that it would be good to get other people involved."[7] Those reluctant deacons saw that the new pattern would virtually overnight strip them of the authority they had exercised. The downgrading of the deacon from a life term to a three-year term could only have added insult to injury. Qualifications for the deaconship were again changed in 1986 when a new organizational plan altered the Board of Administration and opened the office of deacon to single and divorced members.

By the same token, the new organization left little room for ordained ministers other than the pastor to exercise meaningful leadership. Responsibilities once held by deacons and ministers were assumed by the laity, and the responsibilities of the elder-in-charge were divided among the pastor, the moderator, and the church board chair. "The sharing of power was the very key to what happened in the church during the next four or five years."[8]

The move was clearly a step away from centralized, authoritative leadership toward broad-based decision making by the laity with implementation carried out by salaried staff. But as laity became more involved in the board, interest in Council Meeting waned, perhaps because members felt the bulk of the major decisions were made by the board anyway. Thus, a move designed to open decision making to the laity, it could be argued, in fact relegated decision making to a smaller number of lay people than before. In 1961 the congregation approved measures to shore up Council Meeting attendance, but they proved ineffective. When attendance dipped to forty-one at a meeting in May 1964, concern was raised that the necessary ten percent quorum of members was not present. At the September 1964 Council Meeting the congregation voted to waive the ten percent quorum requirement from the constitution.

By the early 1960s it was evident that one salaried pastor could not meet the growing congregation's needs. D. Howard Keiper was hired as part-time minister of visitation in 1964, and in June 1969 a full-time associate pastor was added. In 1989 the congregation was served by three pastors, two full-time and one half-time, and by paid music staff.

Discipline: the Church, the World, and Worldly Churches

The early Lititz Brethren took seriously scriptural instructions to remain separate from the world. By enforcing exacting dress requirements and prohibiting participation in activities considered "worldly," the congregation drew clear lines between themselves and the sinful world. To join the church was "to come out from among them and be separate."

In the early days women were required to wear prayer coverings, bonnets, and plain dresses. Men were discouraged from wearing neckties, flashy watches, and the like, and were encouraged to wear plain coats without lapels. Frequently Council Meetings concluded with "wise admonitions" from the elder, such as reported by the March 1921 Council Meeting minutes: "After an admonition by the elder against stylish dressing and foolish wearing of the hair, the meeting was adjourned."

Members were prohibited from attending carnivals, picnics, the theater; playing baseball on Sundays; and more. Congregational requirements were enforced with rigorous discipline. Serious infractions required confessions before the congregation or resulted in disowning. In November 1914, less than a year after it was founded, the congregation disowned a woman for fornication. Other behaviors for which members were disowned in the early years were drunkenness, disorderly conduct, and marrying while a previous spouse was still living.[9]

By the mid-1920s, however, the congregational consensus on plainness and separation was beginning to break down. Deacons visited every member each winter and asked for concerns regarding the church. The number of complaints raised by members during the Annual Deacon Visit increased steadily. These concerns were then aired at the spring quarterly Council Meeting in March. During the late 1920s and early 1930s complaints were registered about women who wore hats and jewelry, used "powder and paint," curled their hair, and who refused to wear the covering seven days a week. Other concerns were raised for more modesty, longer dresses, and the like. In 1933 one member called sisters to wear their prayer coverings "when in society as well as in services." Another member asked the congregation to "take the Bible for our guide, not the world. Where will the church be in ten years from now if we don't turn back and start over?"

As it turned out, ten years later the church had taken quite a different stance. Concerns regarding dress, with the exception of an occasional plea for the prayer covering, had disappeared from the minutes by 1943. Actually, most women in the congregation continued to wear prayer coverings on Sunday mornings until the 1960s. By the early 1970s, however, the covering virtually disappeared. In 1989 about one percent of the women in the congregation wore a prayer covering to church on Sunday morning. A few more donned coverings for Lovefeast.

The March 1936 Council Meeting, the first spring Council Meeting after Pastor Moore's arrival, seems to have been a turning point. The deacons, returning from the Annual Visit, brought twenty-one suggestions and two requests dealing with the rising tide of worldliness in the congregation. No action was taken on any of these matters, not even an admonition from the elder.[10]

Congregational discipline also was on its way out by then. One by one, the congregational mechanisms that insured some accountability from members were dismantled. Members were disowned into the mid-1930s, but the congregation's appetite for dramatic confessions was apparently decreasing. In 1937 the congregation authorized the Official Board to handle sensitive discipline cases, thus ending the council meeting confessions. The board continued to deal with some discipline cases into the late 1940s but apparently no longer recommended disowning.

A case handled at the September 1937 Council Meeting demonstrated how much the congregation's attitude toward discipline had changed. At that meeting the congregation voted to retain as a member a man who divorced and remarried while his former wife was still living. Pastor James Moore served on the two-member committee that drafted the recommendation approved by Council Meeting:

> We, the committee appointed by the Official Board on August 16 to investigate matters regarding Bro. _____, have carefully and prayerfully considered the whole matter, and recommend the following action: 1. We reaffirm our acceptance of the Scripture teaching on the sanctity of the marriage contract, that what 'God hath joined together, let no man put asunder.' 2. In light of the Scripture and Annual Conference decisions, we cannot sanction or approve of a marriage while a former companion is living. 3. In the case of Bro. _____ we have taken into consideration all the circumstances as we know them, including [his] attitude and his expressed desire to remain with the church, as well as Conference decisions and the attitude of the Brotherhood in general and also of the Lititz congregation. We recommend as follows: (a) That the responsibility of this union be left between Bro. _____ and God. (b) That the church bear with the situation, and permit him to remain and work with the church in the laity. (c) That [he] be urged to a continual growth in consecration to God and the fullest possible harmony with the doctrines and practices of the church.

The story of Mayno Hershey further illustrates the congregation's shift away from strict requirements and discipline during the 1930s. Hershey came to Lititz in 1929 from a Brethren congregation in Ohio, where she was a member in good standing. Lititz would not accept her as a member. They objected to her bobbed hair, her gold ring, and her card playing. In addition she wore a hat and refused to dress plainly or wear a prayer covering all the time. Hershey refused to modify her behavior and continued to attend the church. In 1937 she was accepted as a member. During the eight-year interim, she had not modified her behavior, but the congregation had relaxed its standards.[11]

About the same time the Annual Deacon Visit came to an end. Each year deacons had visited every member and asked several questions aimed at assessing their commitment to Christ and the church. The visit persisted until 1939. In January 1940 someone questioned whether the visit should be continued. By a strong vote of 33-3 the congregation voted to continue the visit. But at the March 1940 Council Meeting, when deacons typically would report the results of their visits, they instead reported that they were "unable" to make the visit. Deacons were instructed to "reconsider their report and fulfill their duty," but they elected not to, and the Annual Visit came to an end.[12]

One long time deacon suggests that the deacons had grown discouraged because people "weren't exactly telling the truth. Some of the folks would say, 'Yes, we're in the faith,' but the deacons knew that they weren't anyhow. It was a little shady there."[13] Also, in 1935 and thereafter, with the beginning of the full-time pastoral program, the pastor assumed visiting responsibilities.

Thus, during the decade of the 1930s the congregation virtually rewrote the rule book on separation from the world and congregational discipline. According to the new rules it was the individual, not the congregation, who made decisions about appropriate Brethren behavior. The barrier between the church and the world was disappearing.

Still to be removed was the barrier between the Brethren and other Christians. The congregation began chipping away at that wall in 1935, when less than a month after Pastor Moore's arrival the congregation voted to cooperate with "other churches in the town of Lititz" for a Thanksgiving service. The following year Pastor Moore participated in a community pulpit exchange. He preached in the Lutheran church, while a United Brethren minister preached at Lititz.[14]

Other barriers to ecumenical cooperation persisted. Members of other Christian denominations could not commune with the Lititz Brethren, and the congregation would not transfer memberships to other denominations. Those who wished to unite with other denominations were unceremoniously dropped from the Lititz membership roll.

The board discussed the question of transferring memberships to non-Brethren denominations in 1945, and at the March 1946 Council Meeting "The church voted to grant a letter to Richard Myer, who wished to join the Lutheran Church of Brickerville." Open communion was approved five years later, when in September 1951 the congregation voted 42-12 to adopt open communion. All Christians could now participate.[15]

Ecumenical involvement at the local level continued to grow. The congregation eventually joined the Warwick Association of Churches and the Lancaster County Council of Churches. In 1979 Lititz Brethren worked alongside other Christians to support the Leighton-Ford Crusade in their area.

In 1989 a Lititz member served as president of the Lancaster County Council of Churches.

While the issue of cooperating with other denominations was resolved with little apparent controversy, the basis for accepting non-Brethren into the fellowship was far more divisive.

From their beginning, the Lititz Brethren rejected all forms of baptism other than trine immersion. So when members of other denominations wished to join the Brethren, they had to be rebaptized by trine immersion. Over time, Lititz members frequently married members of other churches. By the time Pastor McDowell arrived in 1955 the church had a number of couples where one partner was a member and the other was not. These non-member spouses were active in the church, even holding offices in some cases, but were not members because they refused rebaptism.

In 1956 a "Resolution on the Question of Rebaptism" was debated by the congregation for an hour and a half. The resolution stated:

> Whereas the local church through the years has sustained serious membership losses due to our own members joining the denomination of the spouse, and,
> Whereas the local church has failed frequently to add prospective members because of the requirement of re-baptism,
> Whereas the requirement of re-baptism represents a denial of the validity and religious experience of other groups, and,
> Whereas in the Church of the Brethren nationally over half of its churches no longer require re-baptism, be it resolved:
> 1. That the local church continue to teach and practice Trine Immersion as the historic initiatory rite of entrance into the church.
> 2. That in receiving into membership those from other evangelical bodies, if they are satisfied with the method of their previous baptism and if their manner of life indicates genuine religious experience, we accept such persons on their confession of faith.

The resolution was brought to a vote in October 1956, with sixty-four percent of the congregation, just shy of the required two thirds, voting in favor. Not until October 1958, after the Annual Conference had sanctioned receiving new members on affirmation of faith, was the issue resolved by a vote of 61-16.[16] Sunday school superintendent Melvin Brubaker, a Mennonite, was the first member to be admitted under the new policy.

While in years past the Lititz congregation focused on separation from the world and other churches, in more recent years, the congregation opened its facilities to a wide variety of groups, such as Meals on Wheels, Scouts, time-release religious education, even aerobics classes, as a way of reaching out into the community.

Buildings, Music, and Worship

The music and worship practices and the buildings in which the Lititz Brethren worshiped evolved along with the congregation's attitudes toward the outside world. Gradually, the Lititz Brethren's move into the cultural mainstream was reflected in their church buildings and worship practices.

Built in 1887, the congregation's first building was a simple, rectangular structure, designed for the single purpose of worship. The worship was equally simple, consisting of Scripture reading, kneeling prayer, unaccompanied congregational singing, and preaching. The Lititz Brethren initially knelt for all prayers and closed each prayer with the Lord's prayer. Singing was in German and English, and in the early days the entire service would periodically be in Pennsylvania Dutch dialect. Frequently, following the sermon, which was the focal point of the worship, one or more deacons would rise to bear testimony to what the minister of the day had said.[17]

Beginning in the 1920s the congregation began to tamper with its time-tested order of worship. A request came to a Council Meeting in 1921 to limit the use of the Lord's Prayer to one time per service. The request was granted, but the action was rescinded a short time later. The congregation approved the addition of "special singing" to their worship in March 1926, and a men's chorus and mixed chorus were formed around that time.

By the early 1920s it was evident that the congregation was outgrowing its facilities, both numerically and socially. By 1924 membership had more than doubled to 247 members. A thriving Sunday school was limited by lack of facilities. All classes met in the meetinghouse's one large room at the same time. A locating committee in 1922 was authorized to purchase a site on Center Street, and after four years of debate and controversy the new Center Street church was dedicated November 25-28, 1926.

The new building, while still relatively simple in design, was certainly not plain. The old frame meetinghouse was replaced by a more respectable brick church house with nicely rounded windows. Inside, the central pulpit was perched atop a raised platform, and an area to the left of the pulpit was clear to accommodate the choir. Chandeliers hung from the ceiling. Situated in their new, more modern facility the Lititz Brethren were facing toward the future.

Worship practices continued to change slowly. A committee was appointed in January 1939 to study the "special music question." Several requests for more congregational singing had come to Council Meetings. Perhaps this indicated that some thought special music had begun to play too prominent a role in the congregation's worship at the expense of congregational singing. At the March 1939 Council Meeting the music committee's report was adopted, setting up a permanent five-member music committee to administer the church's special music program. The report also set forth goals and purposes of special music and called for the establishment of a church music fund.

At the same meeting the church approved the use of the first musical instrument in the Lititz church—a harp—at a wedding. The congregation voted to grant the request for the harp "with the understanding that the granting of the request applies in this case only." In December 1940 the congregation granted a request for an "organ or similar instrument" to be used at a wedding. Again it was emphasized that the ruling applied in this case only. Finally, in March 1943, the church gave blanket approval for musical instruments at weddings and other special occasions, under supervision of the music committee.[18]

Not until the arrival of new pastor Jacob Dick in October 1945 did the piano complete its long journey toward permanent placement in the sanctuary. In January 1946 the congregation approved use of a piano in the "auditorium" for a choir cantata. A year later a Sunday school class gave the church a piano as a gift. The new piano was used mostly for choir rehearsal and was not housed in the auditorium. As the choir began to occasionally sing accompanied pieces, the piano was moved into the auditorium as needed. Eventually the janitor grew weary of moving the piano in and out of the auditorium and said "we should either leave the piano in or out. So we left it in."[19]

In 1945 the church hired its first full-time music director, Albert Ebbert. He was a member of the Lutheran Church. In 1946 a member donated $100 to start an organ fund, and the congregation purchased a Mohler pipe organ in 1951 at a cost of $5,131. An organ prelude was added to the order of worship. The purchase of choir gowns was approved that same year.[20] Thus, by the early 1950s the congregation's informal choruses had been replaced by a respectably clad choir led by a salaried music director.

Other moves toward respectability were made following the congregation's move into its new building. Around 1928 the congregation began baptizing some new members in the baptismal pool at the Lancaster Church of the Brethren rather than in muddy streams. The church installed its own baptismal pool in 1940 after a member proposed it and agreed to pick up the tab. By 1950 the congregation no longer knelt regularly for prayer. With the arrival of new pastor Earl Bowman in August 1952, the congregation for the first time was served by a pastor who wore a robe in the pulpit.

In sum, by the early 1950s the congregation's worship practices and facilities had become much like those of other Protestant groups. The congregation had clearly paddled out of the Brethren backwaters into the Protestant mainstream. But their journey was not yet complete.

By the mid-1940s, just twenty years after moving into the new building, the congregation was showing signs of outgrowing the Center Street church. After close to ten years of discussion of the merits of relocating or building an addition to the present building, the congregation was nowhere near consensus. With the arrival of pastor Floyd McDowell and the reorganization of the board, the plans started to move ahead.

After some fifteen years of discussion and planning, the Council Meeting in November 1957 heard the board bring a comprehensive proposal recommending: 1) the purchase of new land; 2) a new building as proposed by architect George Savage; 3) the appointment of a sixteen-member building committee; 4) the adoption of a unified budget and planned giving program;

and 5) employment of professional financial consultants to spearhead the financial drive. The proposal passed by a narrow 89-80 margin and building began in 1961.

The spacious new Lititz church was dedicated June 14-17, 1962, at a cost of $406,349.52. Included in the original plans were a gymnasium and chapel. These were added in 1969.

In a 1964 Council Meeting report Pastor Olden Mitchell noted that "our denominational church building counselor has described our building as possibly the most adequate total church plant in the Brotherhood." He reported that more than fifty churches had sent representatives of their building committees to examine the Lititz "plant."

While the little meetinghouse on Willow Street was notable only for its austerity, the size and expense of the new "church plant" on Orange Street attracted the attention of many. The new building, located on a growing edge of Lititz, featured a prominent steeple illuminated by strategically stationed spotlights. During the day natural light filtered into the stately sanctuary through stained glass windows. The front of the sanctuary featured a divided chancel with a communion table in the middle.

On Maundy Thursday 1962 the communion table was pressed into service as the congregation observed for the first time bread and cup communion without the full Lovefeast.[21] In 1964 a second bread and cup communion was added to the bi-annual Lovefeasts. While the move toward bread and cup communion generated little controversy, some concerns were expressed that attendance at Lovefeast would decline.[22] Over time statistics confirmed that there was good reason for concern. Lovefeast attendance peaked at 426 in 1962, the year bread and cup communion was introduced. By 1988 Lovefeast attendance had declined to 294, while membership had grown to 776.

Influences Promoting Change

The transformation that has taken place in the life of the Lititz congregation has been near total. Like a tadpole that has grown into a frog, the congregation is clearly the same creature, yet one must strain to see the points of continuity between the old and the new.

While it is difficult to explain how a congregation could undergo so radical a transformation in a relatively short period of time, a few observations can be made about the factors that facilitated change at Lititz.

First, like most congregations, Lititz has been open to the influences of the community in which the congregation is located. In the early years the congregation shielded itself from these influences. Later, as dress and other marks of distinctiveness were abandoned, the ethos of the community penetrated more deeply into the congregation. Lititz, though located in conservative Lancaster County, was different from surrounding communities because of its Moravian heritage. The town had two exclusive private schools and generally seemed to value "culture" and education. These values have been evident in the Lititz congregation as well.

A second key factor was leadership. Early leaders J.W.G. Hershey and Henry R. Gibbel were champions of higher education at a time when most Brethren of Lancaster County were suspicious of too much "book learning." Beginning with the Hershey and Gibbel families the congregation over the years has seen a steady stream of young people go off to college and return with new ideas about what the church should be.

Pastors also facilitated change. Congregational discipline began to wane and ecumenical involvement began shortly after the arrival of the congregation's first pastor in 1935. A new pastor in 1955 was followed by a radical reorganization of the congregation's structure and the waiving of the rebaptism requirement for new members coming from other churches. Bread and cup communion was instituted shortly after the arrival of another pastor in 1962. While all these changes may have taken place without the impetus of new pastors, each pastor clearly left his mark on the congregation.

New buildings also seem to have been associated with key changes. The down playing of discipline and nonconformity picked up steam when the congregation abandoned the plain Willow Street meetinghouse for a more modern church on Center Street. While it is an oversimplification to say that a new building specifically brings about changes, buildings are intricately intertwined with congregational life. It has been said that a congregation shapes its building, and the building in turn shapes the congregation. This dynamic may have been at work in the Lititz congregation.

A final factor promoting change was the Annual Conference. The congregation seems to have had high respect for Brethren institutions in general. In most instances the Lititz Brethren were reluctant to move ahead of Annual Conference but were quick to follow. Thus, when the congregation broached the issue of open membership in 1956, the votes for change came up short. Two years later, after Annual Conference had spoken at Des Moines, open membership was adopted. The new plan of organization adopted in 1955 also came at the recommendation of Annual Conference, as did several other key changes in the life of the congregation.

Conclusion

The Lititz Church of the Brethren is an instructive case study for Brethren seeking to understand recent trends in the church and their implications for the future. What is clear is that the Lititz church is not what it used to be. What is less clear is which Lititz Church of the Brethren—the old or the new—has been more faithful to New Testament principles and the historic Brethren vision of the church.

APPENDIX A

Membership			
Year	Membership	Year	Membership
1914	119	1954	496
1919	165	1959	568
1924	247	1964	612
1929	226	1969	675
1934	267	1974	716
1939	368	1979	767
1945*	418	1984	784
1949	468	1989	784

Average Attendance			
Year	Attendance	Year	Attendance
1947**	247	1969	355
1949	274	1974	274
1954	274	1979	356
1959	318	1984	372
1964	380	1989	368

*Data not available for 1944
**Average attendance data not available before 1947
Sources: Congregational directories and Council Meeting minutes

APPENDIX B

Ministers and Moderators in the Lititz Congregation

Free Ministers, 1914-1932

John W. Myer Sr.	Harvey M. Eberly
J.W.G. Hershey	John W. Hevener
Henry R. Gibbel	John I. Byler Sr.

Pastors, 1932-1989

1932-1935	A.C. Baugher (part-time)
1935-1945	James M. Moore
1945-1952	Jacob T. Dick
1952-1955	Earl M. Bowman
1955-1959	E. Floyd McDowell
1959-1966	Olden D. Mitchell
1964-1973	D. Howard Keiper, Minister of Visitation (part-time)
1966-1982	W. Clemens Rosenberger
1969-1978	Arlin G. Claassen, Associate Pastor
1978-1979	Robert L. Life, Interim Associate
1980-	Ralph Z. Moyer, Pastor for Special Ministries
1982-1983	Howard W. Bernhard, Minister of Visitation (part-time)
1983-	Jimmy R. Ross
1989-	Henry L. Renn, Pastor for Christian Nurture (half-time)

Ordained Ministers Within the Congregation, 1932-1989

Harvey M. Eberly	Carlos Ziegler
John W. Hevener	Henry G. Bucher
John G. Hershey	Glen Crago
John I. Byler Sr.	Herman B. Heisey
John T. Byler	Nevin H. Zuck
Amos P. Geib	Harold M. Kenepp
Franklin K. Cassel	Robert D. Kettering
Nathan Heffley	Curtis W. Dubble

Elders-in-Charge and Moderators

1914-1919	Isaac W. Taylor	1960-1966 Henry G. Bucher
1919-1929	J.W.G. Hershey	1966-1972 John G. Hershey
1929-1932	Nathan Martin	1972-1978 Elwood H. Gibble
1932-1933	John I. Byle	1979-1981 Harry H. Badorf
1933-1936	A.C. Baugher	1982-1984 Henry G. Bucher
1936-1945	James M. Moore	1985-1987 Larry D. Sauder
1945-1961	Norman K. Musser	1988- Jefferson D. Crosby

Sources: Council Meeting minutes and congregational directories, and The Brethren Encyclopedia, Vol. 3.

APPENDIX C

Key Events in the Lititz Church of the Brethren
1887 .... The West Conestoga congregation (now Middle Creek) erected a meetinghouse in Lititz.
April 1903 ...... West Conestoga approved the organization of a Sunday school at the Lititz meetinghouse.
March 1913 .... Lititz received permission to organize as a congregation separate from West Conestoga.
January 1914 ... Lititz congregation organized.
December 1914 . Congregation baptized its first new members.
March 1922 .... First Vacation Bible School approved.
March 1926 .... New church erected on Center Street.
July 1932 .... Congregation voted to employ a part-time pastor
July 1934 .... First congregational directory printed.
May 1935 .... Congregation called first full-time pastor, approved first budget and every member solicitation campaign.
October 1935 ... Voted to participate in community Thanksgiving service.
September 1938 . Approved the use of individual communion cups.
March 1939 .... Permission granted to have the first musical instrument in the church—a harp used at a wedding.
August 1939 .... Voted to build first church parsonage.
February 1940 .. Voted to install first baptismal pool in the Center Street church.
March 1940 .... Annual deacon visit is discontinued.
September 1951 Congregation approved "open communion."
April 1951 ...... Organ in sanctuary is dedicated.
August 1955 .... Adopted new plan of organization: Board of Administration replaced Official Board.
May 1957 .... Approved employment of part-time church secretary.
November 1957 . Congregation adopted first unified budget.
April 1958 ...... Elected first term deacons.
October 1958 ... Voted to accept non-Brethren as new members without rebaptizing them.
September 1961 . Approved first bread and cup communion service.
June 1962 ...... New church on Orange Street dedicated.
April 1964 ...... Voted to hire first part-time second staff.
May 1968 .... Congregation agreed to hire first full-time associate pastor
March 1969 .... New parsonage completed.
September 1969 . New fellowship hall addition and chapel dedicated.
September 1972 . Congregation received pew Bibles.
September 1986 . New organizational plan approved.

[1] This paper is adapted from Donald R. Fitzkee, The Transformation of the Lititz Church of the Brethren, 1914-1989, a 75th Anniversary History, (Lititz, Pennsylvania: published by the Lititz Church of the Brethren, 1990).

[2] For a summary of trends in membership and average attendance, see Appendix A at the end of the article.

[3] Council Minutes, 1914.

[4] For more complete biographies of J. W. G. Hershey and Henry R. Gibbel, see History of the Church of the Brethren, Eastern Pennsylvania District, 1915-1965, (Lancaster: Forry and Hacker, 1965), 280-282.

[5] Interview with Beatrice Mohler, February 1, 1989.

[6] Council Minutes, 1932

[7] Interview with Floyd McDowell, January 30, 1989.

[8] McDowell.

[9] Council Minutes, 1914.

[10] Council Minutes, 1936.

[11] Interview with Mayno Hershey and Laura Barwick, October 14, 1988.

[12] Council Meeting minutes, 1940.

[13] Interview with Landis Stehman and other Lititz members, February 9, 1989.

[14] Council Meeting minutes, 1935.

[15] Official Board and Council Meeting minutes, 1945, 1946, 1951.

[16] Council Minutes, 1958.

[17] Interviews with various members.

[18] Council Minutes, 1943.

[19] Landis Stehman interview.

[20] Council Meeting minutes, 1951.

[21] Diary of Marian Shenk.

[22] Interview with Harry Badorf and other Lititz members, February 9, 1989.

A Response to Two Case Studies

by Donald E. Miller

Don Fitzkee has given us a compelling account of change in the Lititz, Pennsylvania, Church of the Brethren congregation over a period of one hundred years. He focuses in particular upon leadership and organization; the church and the world; and buildings, worship and music. Under these topics he asks several basic questions regarding changes during the past century. Is decision-making more widespread? Are people more committed? Is worship more reflective of the New Testament? In the course of these changes has the church become more faithful? His answer to the first three questions is "No." To the last question whether the church has become less faithful Fitzkee's answer is "Yes."

The leadership of the congregation from the time it was established in 1887 was the free ministry until 1932, when a part-time pastor was employed. A board of ministers and deacons presided over the congregation until 1955, when a new organization was adopted. The new system established a moderator and a board of administration. Two years later deacons were appointed for limited terms. Fitzkee observes that in spite of the effort to be more inclusive in decision-making, in fact decision-making became more exclusive. Fewer members attended council meetings, fewer took an interest in the affairs of the congregation, and more assignments were turned over to the professional staff. During the 1960s multiple salaried staff were employed to meet increasing responsibilities. Fitzkee's point is that over the course of the years church members are taking less responsibility for the life and witness of the church than they did under a free ministry system.

With regard to the church and the world, early Lititz members drew a line of separation between themselves and the world. This separation was symbolized by a distinctive mode of dress. The consensus about the distinctive dress broke down in the 1920s and 1930s. By 1970 the wearing of a prayer covering by the sisters had virtually disappeared. By 1940 the annual visit of the deacons to each member had ceased, and at the same time church discipline ceased. By 1956 Christians of other traditions were accepted into the congregation upon confession of faith. Fitzkee concludes that the breakdown of the separation of church and world has not led to an increasing commitment on the part of members. Rather there has been a declining sense of anything distinctive related to church membership.

Services originally consisted of singing and worship within an austere, simple meeting house. Over the years these has become elaborate under professional leadership. The meeting house has been replaced by an architecturally designed building that has been a showcase of innovation. Has this led to worship that is more intentionally reflective of New Testament faith? Fitzkee's answer is "No."

Our commentator concludes that there are few signs of greater faithfulness as a result of the changes that have occurred in the Lititz congregation over the past century. Rather the congregation would seem to be less faithful. Decision-making is less widespread than earlier. People are less committed to a distinctive expression of their faith. Worship is less reflective of its New Testament roots. In a word, the congregation seems less committed to New Testament faith than it did in earlier years.

The key question in Fitzkee's account is this: what are the marks of faithfulness? Let me suggest six marks of faithfulness that have been characteristic of Brethren from the time of the Schwarzenau baptism in 1708.

Commitment to Jesus Christ as Lord and Savior leads all the rest. Brethren have understood ourselves to be committed to Jesus Christ as the one who saves us and the one who shows us the way to live. Brethren have been traditional in accepting Jesus Christ as the revelation and presence of God Almighty, as the one who atoned for our sins, and as the one to whom we owe utmost loyalty. We seek to live according to the mind of Christ, which is known according to the other marks of faith listed below.

Another mark of faith is commitment to the New Testament as our guide to living. In the New Testament we find the fullest revelation of God's will and the fullest testimony to Jesus as our Savior and Lord. Where there are differing interpretations of New Testament passages, Brethren have referred to the early Christian community to see how they interpreted the passages in question.

Faith finds its expression in an open and mature confession of faith through believer's baptism. Such confession of faith is amply referred to in the New Testament. Children are included in the community of faith as family members until such time as they make their own declaration of faith.

To be members of the body of Christ is to be willing to be guided by the community of believers through worship, prayer, Bible study, and mutual discernment of the mind of Christ for our lives. Therefore, the counsel of sisters and brothers in the faith is an integral part of New Testament faith. The will of the congregation and of the Annual Conference is similarly important. However, community opinion is always tempered by reference to God's Will, the Mind of Christ, the guidance of the Holy Spirit, the study of the New Testament, and the conscience of individual believers. The result is an openness to new understanding of faith and that resists creedal formulation.

Brethren understand the way of Christ to be a way of love rather than of violence. The testimony of Christ in the New Testament repudiates the way of violence and makes the way of peace and reconciliation an essential mark of genuine faith. As the believer h?s been reconciled to God in Jesus Christ, so believers are to be reconciled with all persons insofar as they are able. The church, therefore, testifies to and hopes to embody the way of nonviolence.

True faith is expressed simply, directly, joyfully, and wholeheartedly. Faith is not simply objective and unrelated to the believer. Rather, true faith is felt and expressed as joy, even in times of suffering. Faith is expressed simply and directly, the root of "simple living." Faith is expressed as care and service for those about us, especially for those in special need.

If these are the marks of faithfulness, then the question of whether the Lititz congregation has been faithful during the past hundred years is not as easily answered. Willingness to be guided by the community of believers in a spirit of worship allows that there may be many changes over the years. Commitment to the New Testament does not quickly bind us to an easily discerned pattern of worship. The variety of worship patterns were present already in the early church. The challenge of Fitzkee's commentary is in its implicit urge for us to consider again what it means for a congregation to be genuinely expressive of New Testament faith.

***

The subject of Emmert Bittinger's case study concerns the West Marva District from 1866 until 1990. His focus is upon the growth of organizational structure in relation to such issues of church life as definition of mission, ministerial role, leadership, allocation of resources, doctrine, and life style. Bittinger's thesis is that the organization of the denomination has changed from being simple and informal to being complex and highly structured (bureaucratic). With structural complexity has come a separation in the world-view of the membership and the structural elite. The older and simpler theology of sin and salvation is being replaced by a theology of social and psychological influence, and the concept of mission has moved from "spreading the gospel" to multiple social issues. The role of the minister has changed from informal preacher to employed professional manager and psychologist. Without saying that such changes in church life are simply a result of organizational changes, Bittinger does observe that they seem to be related to one another.

Bittinger reports that the West Virginia District was formed in 1866 primarily to develop financial support for home missions. At the same time the denomination was in the process of developing a Foreign and Domestic Mission Board (1880). By 1890 Sunday Schools were being organized in West Virginia and other districts. During the early decades of the twentieth century the mission issues expanded along with their attendant organizations. At the denominational level the many resulting boards led to a council of boards, and in 1946 to a General Brotherhood Board. The accompanying trend in the districts was to employ part time "field men," later replaced by full time district executives. Similarly the informal free ministry of the nineteenth century was replaced by employed, seminary-trained, professional pastors.

The organizational pattern related to the process just described was from simple to increasingly plural, from informal to formal. Bittinger observes that such plurality required "rational coordination" and specialization of roles. It also led to vertical integration, the formation of higher-level managers over lower-level activities. These trends were accompanied by consolidation and centralization.

The corresponding trends in church life are many. The simple understanding of mission as drawing people out of the world is replaced by multiple missions that engage people in the world and that are often highly controversial. Leadership moves from an informal, charismatic style to a formal, administrative, managerial style. Preaching changes from defense of New Testament faith to topical consideration of social and psychological issues. The closeness of the people to their informal preachers is replaced by social distance between the people and professionally trained pastors.

The focus upon unity of faith and nonconformity to the world is replaced by merging into the mainstream of church life. The sense of community gives way to loyalty and concern about church attendance. Concern for the integrity of Brethren belief is replaced by open, inclusive, ecumenical concerns. The small financial needs of an informal organization are replaced by the large financial requirements of a large bureaucracy. In summary the trend toward bureaucratization has dramatic correlates in changing church beliefs and practices.

In his analysis Bittinger makes it clear that change of denominational life and organization is inevitable. Indeed survival is impossible without change. Furthermore correlated changes do not prove a casual relationship; the relationship may be coincidental. Other factors, perhaps many other factors, may be involved. Bittinger, however, does believe that the relationship between organization and church life suggests a more considerate approach to change. He suggests that Brethren should decide what in Brethren belief and practice is essential and what is not. Brethren should be more intentional in deciding about the essence of Brethren belief. Otherwise Brethren will lose their mission and purpose as a result of undetermined cultural and organizational changes.

Bittinger's analysis is admittedly impressionistic in that his typology has not been carefully researched. Until further historical work is done it remains largely intuitive. One should not thereby quickly dismiss his observations. They are extraordinarily powerful, and they ring true to one who has been close to these processes. Yet, remember that these tendencies are not unique to Brethren. They may very well have been a part of much church life in America during the same period of time. The same trends can be seen among Mennonites and Friends whose beliefs parallel the Brethren. One would need comparative studies to bring out the uniqueness of Bittinger's observations with regard to the Brethren.

One of the limits of Bittinger's approach comes from his use of typology. Having set up a series of parallel ideal types, all things seem to move inexorably from one type to the other, e.g. from charismatic to bureaucratic. Other typologies might lead to different conclusions.

Let me cite one example. For many years observers have suggested that nineteenth century Brethren resisted the Sunday School Movement, then waffled in their decision, and finally adopted it. A typology of resistance versus adoption leads to the conclusion just stated. However a closer historical look yields a different conclusion.

The Sunday School Movement came to the United States at the turn of the nineteenth century with the establishment of the Sunday School Union in Philadelphia. Union Sunday Schools sprang up across the country until 1837, when the Union collapsed from financial difficulties. At that time denominations picked up the sponsorship of Sunday Schools. Some Brethren churches started Sunday Schools in the early 1840s. The movement declined during the Civil War and was revived by Moody, Finney and others after the war. However they organized it around the concept of local, regional, national, and world political conventions. They spoke of it as the Sunday School Army.

Early adoption and later resistance to Sunday Schools was not indecisiveness in the face of cultural influence. Rather the Sunday School Movement changed dramatically in its character. The Brethren response was quite appropriate in terms of Brethren peace beliefs. The typology of resistance, indecisiveness, and acceptance is not accurate regarding the Sunday School Movement.

I suggest an alternative approach to organization and church life is to look for times of greatness in the life of the church. The times of greatness are those in which one or another of the basic beliefs and practices are expressed with particular power. Such times are usually accompanied by charismatic leadership. In fact charisma should not be relegated to earlier, simpler times. Bureaucracy can survive only with an element of charisma. The great times in the church have occurred when charismatic leadership sprang forth with resulting organizational changes.

The great times in the church have been those in which believers have acted out their convictions with renewed energy and commitment. The origin of the Brethren in Germany was such a time. The early colonial period in America was another such time. During the colonial period the ideal of a plain style of life was created in those communities where Brethren, Friends, and Mennonites lived together. The testimony of the plain peoples was carried to the frontier in the nineteenth century. Bittinger documents the rise of home and foreign mission, which was another of the great periods of the church. So was the development of Brethren Service in the middle of the twentieth century.

Each of these events was under the influence of religious trends of the times. Each of them involved considerable strain in belief, and, indeed, several resulted in major divisions in the church. Each saw leaders come forth who were charismatic, in close touch with the people, and able to develop new organizational structures.

The typology of the great times in the life of the church does not move from a golden past to an impossibly flawed present. Rather it looks at each time in terms of its possibilities and limitations, in terms of influences and beliefs of the time. Therefore we are not called to reverse history, to recreate an impossible past. Rather we are called to plunge into the circumstances of our time, to respond to the call for greatness in this era. There were many complexities in past responses of the church as there will be many in this day. However, God calls the church to greatness in every age, and so the call comes in this time. Brethren were born not of doctrinal dispute but of an overwhelming desire to express their faith in Jesus Christ "in the manner of their living." Leadership and risk are integral to such a call. This too can be a great time in the life of the church.

PART V

SPECIAL TOPICS:
HYMNODY
AND THE
PEACE WITNESS
IN TRANSITION

11

Changes Reflected in Brethren Hymnody:
Trends And Implications

by Hedwig T. Durnbaugh

In a careful study and analysis of changes in hymnody, Durnbaugh notes the loss of essentially the entire Pietist heritage which marked the early German language hymnals used by the Brethren beginning with their first hymnal in 1720. The failure to retain this important part of their spiritual identity happened as Brethren moved from the German language into English, a process which required the publishing of new hymnals. Because of lack of awareness of, and perhaps indifference to, this treasure, the theological identity of the Brethren has undergone significant change. The author suggests the importance of comparing the vitality and value of what was lost with that which was put in its place.

Introduction

A religious group or denomination defines itself not only by its theology but also by its practice and piety. One aspect of piety is hymnody which, in the present context, refers to the body of hymns published in the hymnbooks of the Church of the Brethren. Of these hymns, only a very small percentage was written by Brethren authors. The majority comes from other sources. Although portions of this hymnody have been printed in various types of collections and for various purposes, this discussion will limit itself to a broad outline covering the chief hymnals in existence to date which reflect the hymnody of the Church of the Brethren at large. Ephemeral, supplementary (except for Die Kleine Harfe), regional (i.e., Das Christliche Gesang-Buch, 1874 and 1879), and special-purpose publications of hymns will not be considered here. This overview will cover the time from 1720 until 1951.

The Church of the Brethren is one of many denominations which, in the course of their history, changed from their original language and culture to those of an English-speaking country. One of the underlying questions of this overview, therefore, will be to what degree the people of this denomination have retained their original hymnic heritage and thus the piety which it represents.

In looking at Brethren hymnody, it will become evident that in this particular sphere of their life the Brethren operated on two entirely separate tracks, a German and an English one. Beginning with German only, they then branched out into two lines that ran at first parallel to each other and later in divergent directions. Finally, the German track came to an end altogether and the Brethren were once again on a single track, but this time it was the English one. It is not surprising that as English increased during the two-track period, German decreased. However, unlike several other denominations in similar situations, the Brethren did not carry their German heritage of hymns into their English-language hymnody as the Moravians did; nor did they succeed, like the German Lutherans, in recovering a significant part of it after a long hiatus.

A Brief Overview of Brethren Hymnody

The First Single Track: German Hymnody

Brethren hymnody began with a German hymnal entitled Geistreiches Gesang-Buch (Spirit-filled hymn-book) which was printed in 1720 at Berleberg in the county of Wittgenstein, Germany. Apart from its historical significance, its main intrinsic interest for the Brethren lies in the fact that it contains the senior Alexander Mack's baptismal hymn, Uberschlag die Kost (Count well the cost) and one hundred texts by one of the Solingen Brethren, probably Wilhelm Knepper.[1]

In format and content, this hymnal drew in equal measure on two important hymnals of its time: the paradigmatic Pietist hymnal, Geistreiches Gesang-Buch (Spirit-filled hymn-book), compiled by Johann Anastasius Freylinghausen, son-in-law of August Hermann Francke,[2] and Davidisches Psalter-Spiel der Kinder Zions (Davidic psaltery of the children of Zion), the hymnal of the Community of True Inspiration, which was used by radical and separatist Pietist groups.[3]

The Brethren hymnal of 1720 was followed in the American colonies by Das Kleine Davidische Psalterspiel der Kinder Zions (The small Davidic psaltery of the children of Zion), printed by Christoph Sauer in 1744. Contrary to popular tradition, this was not the first Brethren hymnal, nor was it a later edition of Das Davidische Psalter-Spiel of 1718. This second hymnal of the Brethren constitutes at once a break with, as well a partial continuation of, the first. Whereas Alexander Mack's baptismal hymn is not included, fifty-five of the Knepper hymns are. After this, the hymnal of 1720 seems to have vanished from the memory of the Brethren. It was not discovered until more than two hundred years later.

Das Kleine Davidische Psalterspiel holds a special place in the German hymnody. Although it does not contain any Brethren-authored hymns other than those which were reprinted from Geistreiches Gesang-Buch (1720), it is the only German hymnal of the Brethren that makes a conscious statement of Brethren theology in the manner in which the rubrics are arranged. Although the hymnal was modelled after the German Pietist hymnals of the early eighteenth century, the person(s) responsible for its publication rearranged the traditional sequence representing the Pietist "Economy [Order] of salvation" to reflect Brethren teaching. Thus, the nine rubrics for the church year are followed by what may be called "The Brethren Order of Salvation." In the following list, the headings are translations of those in Das Kleine Davidische Psalterspiel, the ordinal numbers represent the numbering of the rubrics in the hymnal, the numbers in parentheses, the number of hymns in each rubric:

10. Of human misery and damnation (8)
11. Of the true repentance and conversion (10)
12. Of the true faith (9)
13. Of holy baptism (4)
14. Of the love for Jesus (23)
15. Of brotherly and universal love (6)
16. Of foot-washing at the love-feast (1)
17. Of the holy supper and the proclamation of the death of Jesus Christ on the cross (7)
18. Of following Jesus (7)

Rubrics 10-12 were inserted here from the Pietist Order of salvation; rubrics 13 and 17, in the Pietist hymnal follow the section on God as the means of his grace; rubrics 14, 15, and 18 are taken from the spiritual exercises or virtues required by the Pietist order; rubric 16 is an adaptation of the rubric, "Of the holy supper and love-feast of believers," in Davidisches Psalter-Spiel.[4]

The predominant type of hymn in these two German hymnals is that of classical (conservative) German Pietism; the melodies are of the genre generally referred to as German chorale, sung in unison without printed music. (In conventional church services, the hymns would have been accompanied by the organ.) These features remain characteristic for the German hymnody of the Brethren until its demise.

The Double Track: German and English Hymnody

As more and more English-speaking members joined the Brethren, the need for an English hymnal increased during the last quarter of the eighteenth century. The first English-language hymnal for the Brethren, The Christian's Duty, was published in 1791 by Peter Leibert of Germantown.[5] Immediately the nature of the two separate tracks becomes apparent. Whereas the two

German hymnals bear the stamp of German Pietism, The Christian's Duty is composed of the new hymnody of the first "hymn explosion" in the English-speaking world (in eighteenth-century England; the next such "explosion" occurred in the 1960s in most European churches). The chief exponent of this phenomenon, Isaac Watts, accounts for twenty-nine percent of all hymn texts in this first English hymnal of the Brethren.

Though intended to remedy an unsatisfactory situation by providing a hymnal for new, non-German-speaking members, the publication of this English hymnal nevertheless resulted in a two-fold loss. First, the hymns that had been significant to the German-speaking Brethren were not transmitted to the English-speaking members. Thus, either group had to enter into and accept an entirely different frame of devotional practice and experience when worshipping in the other language. This is all the more regrettable, because at the same time, in 1792, several hymn texts written by Brethren of the first two generations were published as part of a slim supplementary hymnal entitled Die Kleine Harfe (The small harp) which was usually bound with Das Kleine Davidische Psalterspiel in numerous subsequent editions. Secondly, the distinctive theological statement which the Brethren had made in Das Kleine Davidische Psalterspiel was lost.

According to the preface, The Christian's Duty contains "the most approved Hymns, of the several Books [previously in use in English services] of the most approved authors." The existence of the German hymnal is not mentioned, nor are there any references to expressions of Brethren theology or practices in this hymnal. However, considering the origin of this new English hymnody of the Brethren, this not surprising.

After the turn of the nineteenth century, a change occurred in the format of new German as well as English hymnals published for the Brethren. Heretofore all hymnals had been printed in octavo size; from now on through the remainder of the century they were printed, with one exception, in duodecimo, but still with texts only.

The first hymnals in this new format were Die Kleine Lieder Sammlung oder Auszug aus dem Psalterspiel (The small collection of hymns, or, extract from the psaltery) and A Choice Selection of Psalms, Hymns, and Spiritual Songs. These two were the hymnals which appeared both in an edition for the "Eastern" and one for the "Western" Brethren, reflecting Brethren migration to the Middle West with the later Western editions being published by Henry Kurtz. The pocket size was intended as a convenience, but the smaller format also meant that the contents had to be reduced. This which was achieved by cutting back the number of stanzas of many of the hymns. Whereas the German hymnal has a preface, the English one has none. The arrangements of the rubrics of both hymnals are a purely mechanical alphabetization of the headings.

Although later editions of these two hymnals were occasionally bound together, there exists no relation between their respective contents which, on the whole, remain unchanged throughout subsequent editions. In the German hymnal, however, a few hymns of probable Brethren authorship reflecting some Brethren teachings were added in later editions, particularly that of 1829 which contains the baptismal hymn, <u>Diesen Täufling bringen wir</u> (We bring this person to be baptized). In the English hymnal, Watts continues to dominate with twenty-seven percent of all hymns; there is no evidence of Brethren-authored texts.

By the time the first editions of these two hymnals were published—1826 and 1830, respectively—a new type of hymnic genre had come on the scene, the camp-meeting song. This is characterized by the addition of repetitive elements, such as refrains and choruses, to existing hymns which were thus adapted to the outdoor mass-revival meetings of the time.

It may well have been under the influence of the revival movement that two new rubrics were introduced into Brethren hymnody. In <u>Die Kleine Lieder Sammlung</u> they appear as "Hymns of invitation" and "[Spiritual] Awakening," the latter being the largest category in the hymnal with eighteen numbers. In <u>A Choice Selection</u> such hymns were listed under "Invitation to praise" and "Invitation to repentance." The texts of three German hymns in each of the two categories mentioned were indeed of those that had been adapted as camp-meeting songs, but judging from their appearance on the page none of them were sung in that style. However, one of these hymns of invitation, <u>Ihr jungen Helden, aufgewacht</u> (You young heroes, awake), a Knepper hymn from <u>Geistreiches Gesang-Buch</u> (1720), became one of the most popular songs of the German camp-meeting movement.[6]

The most significant event of the nineteenth century in respect to Brethren hymnody was the decision by Annual Meeting to issue an official hymnbook. In 1867 <u>A Collection of Psalms, Hymns, and Spiritual Songs,</u> popularly known as "The Brethren's Hymn Book," was published. Three years later it was followed by the German <u>Neue Sammlung von Psalmen, Lobgesängen und Geistlichen Liedern</u> (New collection of psalms, hymns, and spiritual songs). Both are still text-only hymnals. Although they, too, were frequently bound together, they hold no hymns in common.

According to Henry Kurtz's preface to the German hymnal of which he had been the compiler, it was to be "of a similar character and form so that it could be bound with [A Collection . . .] and not be entirely unworthy of its position." Whereas the German preface deals exclusively with the history of Brethren hymnody thus far, James Quinter, the English hymnal's editor, went a little beyond mere technicalities by devoting the opening paragraph to the place of praise in worship and a very brief one to stating that "The doctrinal character of the hymns has not been disregarded, and it is hoped that nothing will be found in the book that will materially conflict with the teachings of the gospel." However, Quinter makes no reference to Brethren teachings, which, again, is not surprising given the nature and availability of English hymns of his time.

The tables of contents reflect the organization of the two hymnals, and here it can be noted that the English one is far better and more logically organized than the German hymnal.

At this approximate mid-point of the double track, the shift of emphasis to English hymnody becomes obvious. Not only is <u>Neue Sammlung</u> less than half the size of <u>A Collection</u>, it also contains nine English hymns by five authors in German translations, the largest number thus far, whereas no translations of German hymns are found in <u>A Collection</u>, though they were available at the time. In addition, a change in the method of providing melody references can be noted in the German hymnal. Heretofore this had been done by giving the text incipit of a suitable well known German hymn with its own tune. Now the English method was applied of referring, not to a melody, but only to the appropriate English poetic meter, such as "C.M." (common meter), etc. This not only makes little sense in connection with German texts and their melodies, it is also inapplicable in the majority of instances.

Until this time all hymnals were printed without music. However in 1872, Benjamin Funk, son of the Mennonite singing-school teacher and music publisher Joseph Funk, collaborated with H. R. Holsinger in the publication of the first Brethren hymnbook with tunes, <u>The Brethren's Tune and Hymn Book,</u> so that, as stated in the preface, "there may be a union in song as well as in doctrine." This book was to accompany <u>A Collection</u> (1867) and thus the hymns and their sequence are identical in the two publications. The tunes are claimed to be "nearly all of those venerable airs that have stood the test of time." The union in song proved to be wishful thinking, however. Already in 1879 a new edition became necessary because "there were a number of improvements recommended by those especially interested in good church music" and the hymnal was "thoroughly revised, making use of only such tunes as would best harmonize with the sentiment of the hymns."

The chief problem with this tune book was that it did not represent what the majority of the Brethren sang during the second half of the nineteenth century but what some people in the Shenandoah Valley liked to sing. The music, which was taken to a great extent from the Mennonite <u>Harmonia Sacra</u>,[7] stood in the tradition of folk- and camp-meeting songs. The tunes and especially their three- or four-part arrangements in seven-shape notation reflected the singing style of singing-schools and social gatherings. If what and how the Brethren at large sang at that time was indeed reflected in the second edition of this first Brethren tune and hymn book, then well before the third quarter of the nineteenth century they sang very much the style of hymn one finds in the current <u>Brethren Hymnal</u> with the exception of the gospel songs, which date from a later period.

This latter genre became popular during the last quarter of the nineteenth century among the English-speaking population as the hymnody used by the urban mass-revival meetings. It is a genre in which the Brethren showed their quantitatively greatest productivity, particularly and for the first time, as composers. The next English hymnal, The Brethren Hymnal (1901), contains nineteen texts chiefly of gospel hymns written by Brethren authors (with Adaline Hohf Beery contributing the largest number, six) and the music (for four-part singing) to 119 chiefly gospel-hymn texts, with the two hymnal editors providing the majority (George B. Holsinger, fifty-eight; J. Henry Showalter, forty-five).

While the Brethren thus ushered in the twentieth century with this thoroughly Anglo-American hymnal, their German hymnody was heading for its demise. The last German hymnal, Eine Sammlung von Psalmen, Lobgesängen und geistlichen Lieder (A collection of psalms, hymns, and spiritual songs), a very slim hymnal first published in 1893, appeared for the third and last time in 1903.

As instructed by Annual Meeting, Eine Sammlung drew very heavily on the two preceding German hymnals. Despite its very modest size this last German hymn-book nevertheless is of some significance. It still contains a considerable number of hymns (381) albeit in greatly shortened form; it introduces six hymns on two new topics: missions (five) and anointing (one); and it reinstates a table of contents that reflects Brethren theology.

The Second Single Track: English Hymnody

Two hymnals belong to this last stretch of the track, namely Hymnal (1925) and The Brethren Hymnal (1951). Although each contains several German hymns in English translations, those seem to have been chosen by accident rather than by design. There is only one hymn that has been carried over from the German hymnody (if that was indeed the case), namely "O Sacred Head Now Wounded." The German original, O Haupt voll Blut und Wunden by Paul Gerhardt entered the German hymnody in a lateral edition of Das Kleine Davidische Psalterspiel in 1797, was received into some of the nineteenth-century German hymnals, entered the English hymnody in 1867, and from then on was printed in all subsequent English hymnals. Prior to Hymnal (1925), no other translations of German hymns had been added.

In addition to the above hymn by Paul Gerhardt, the Hymnal of 1925 contains six German hymns in English translations. One of these, "Give to the Wind thy Fears" (Befiehl du deine Wege), also by Paul Gerhardt, had been part of the early German hymnody of the Brethren in the first two hymnals.

The Brethren Hymnal (1951) added twenty-four German hymns in English translations but did not print again two that had been in Hymnal (1925). Altogether The Brethren Hymnal contains twenty-nine translations from the German, or a little less than five percent of the total number of hymns. Fewer than half of these (thirteen) had at one time or another been received into a German hymnal of the Brethren and three are by Brethren authors, namely "Bless, O Lord, This Church of Thine" (Jesus Christus, Gottes Sohn) by Alexander Mack, Jr.; "O How Is the Time So Urgent" (O wie ist die Zeit so

wichtig) by Jakob Stoll (not by Alexander Mack!); and "Savior of My Soul"
(Heiland meiner Seel) by Johannes Naas. None of these hymns from the
German hymnody are part either of the German or the English core hymnody
of the Brethren, that is to say, none of these appears in all of the chief hymnals.

Until its end, the German hymnody remained a completely separate
sphere, and no efforts were made at any time to carry some of that heritage over
into the English hymnody.

Conclusion and Implications

In surveying the route which Brethren hymnody has taken, one observes
not an adaptation but rather an acculturation to the Anglo-American situation.
Heritage and piety of the German hymnody faded away as English language
and English hymnody increased in importance and influence. The few
translations of German hymns that were received into the English hymnals of
the Brethren did not enter in a direct line from their German ones but were
probably selected from other contemporary hymnbooks, a customary way of
hymnal compiling. The small percentage of German hymns in English
translations does not constitute a recovery and consciousness of the German
hymnic heritage of the Brethren.

Thus, in the area of hymnody, the Brethren have lost their German heritage and, along with it, the type of piety and spirituality that the hymns reflect.
Here the question must be raised as to what, precisely, was lost in this process.

The Brethren see themselves as being, on the one hand, theologically in
the tradition of sixteenth-century Anabaptism and, on the other, in their piety
as being a product of the eighteenth-century German reform movement of
Pietism, with a strong affinity to Radical Pietism.

With respect to their German hymnody, the discrepancy between teaching
and practice, theology and piety, is immediately obvious. The greater portion
of this hymnody bears neither the stamp of Anabaptism nor of Radical Pietism
but of that style of conservative, "churchly" Pietism which is associated with the
circle around Francke and Freylinghausen at Halle.

Steffen Arndal, the leading Danish scholar of Pietism and its hymnody,
identifies three constituent aspects which are typical for all types of revival
movements and their bodies of song: the individual, the social, and the
historical aspects.[8]

Under the first, the hymnic themes deal with the changes that have
occurred in the individual and the associated problems. Under the second,
hymnic themes deal with the affirmation of unity within the group, often
expressed in opposition to their hostile or theologically alien environment.
Under the third, the themes with the prospect of a final victory in the eschaton.
In Brethren German hymnody, the first aspect is the most strongly expressed,
and the third is the least so.

Given the discrepancy between Brethren theology and piety and the Brethren emphasis on Anabaptism, the loss of German hymnody could have been a hidden gain had the gap between theory and practice been filled by English hymns that emphasize the second or social aspect. Yet this was not the case in any of the hymnals, whether published upon private or official initiative, all prefatory statements regarding Brethren teachings notwithstanding. Instead, Brethren hymnody increasingly took on the features of British Victorian and American nineteenth-century conventional hymnody, with an infusion of original but rather mainline-oriented hymnody towards the middle of the twentieth century.

Thus there was a distinct two-fold loss as German hymnody faded out of the denominational life of the Brethren. First, along with the hymns, a source for private and individual devotion, spiritual nurture, and strengthening of the faith was lost. This was all the more difficult to replace, because after the demise of German hymnal-printing for the Brethren, text-only hymnals, which had served for reading as much as for singing, were no longer published.

Thus, and secondly, along with the hymns the acknowledgement of the validity to meet the spiritual needs of the individual through hymns was forgotten over time. This loss was magnified by a negative reaction to the gospel hymnody of the late nineteenth century, a lack of understanding of hymnody, and the later emphasis of the communal aspects of Anabaptism.

Various factors contributed to this process of acculturation, some of which were beyond the Brethren's control. Sociologically and psychologically, the acculturation was favored by the fact that for much of the Brethren's more recent history in this country, assimilation was a national virtue. Furthermore, for their collective memory and traditions, they had only the first generations to draw on since there were no later waves of Brethren immigrants to this country who could have provided fresh infusions of their heritage.

Hymnologically, the acculturation was accelerated because the need for an English hymnody had arisen before English translations of German hymns became available (the first series of Catherine Winkworth's Lyra Germanica was not published until 1855) and the Brethren themselves, unlike other denominations of non-English background, had no poet-translators to speak of. Hymnology as a scholarly discipline with its own systematic research did not come into being in Europe until well into the nineteenth century, and it took additional time until it crossed over into North America. But even then, the Brethren had no hymnologists in their midst.

Other denominations of non-English origin also went through periods of hiatus but finally managed, in the twentieth century, to recover in part their heritage through translations of their traditional hymns into English. The committee for The Brethren Hymnal of 1951 had the means for reintroducing the denomination to its German hymnic heritage, but it did not do so. The main reasons seem to have been the absence of a sense of loss, the lack of familiarity with what which had been lost, and any felt need to do something about it.

Thus the hymnody of the Brethren, as it presents itself in the middle of the twentieth century, bears the stamp not of German Pietism but of Victorian England and nineteenth century America, the chief hymnic sources of the present hymnal. The acculturation is complete.

In the performance of this hymnody, i.e., in congregational singing, the influence of certain trends arising within general church circles which began in the early nineteenth century became more pronounced in the present century. This is reflected, for example, in the often radical reduction of hymn stanzas in the hymnals, in printing the music in full-score format and fitting all stanzas of a hymn between the staves regardless of the poetic structure of those texts, in the repetitive use of relatively few favorite hymns, and in the diminished role and significance of congregational singing in worship in favor of choir or other vocal/instrumental performances.

A survey of the Sunday bulletins of five selected Pennsylvania congregations reveals that during a period of five successive years during the 1980s the average annual use of the present hymnal was no more than seventeen percent of its hymns. Over the entire five-year span, the average use increased only to thirty-eight percent. Whenever the choir presented more than one number, when more than one choir performed, or when some other special feature was incorporated into the service, the number of hymns was regularly reduced to two, one, or even eliminated altogether.

In analyzing Freylinghausen's preface to Geistreiches Gesang-Buch, Arndal points out that the praise of God through the singing of hymns is the human response to God's awakening power. It was God and no other who had prepared this song of praise out of the mouths of babes and infants in the faith. Thus, the flourishing of hymn-singing by the people is in itself a sign of their having attained, through the grace of God, a new life in faith.[9] By implication, the trend which originated in German churchly Rationalism, to render the congregation into passive listeners who prefer the performance by a choir and a worshipful atmosphere to active, corporate participation, would mean rejection or denial of God's awakening power and absence of genuine praise of God.

The history of Brethren hymnody demonstrates how easily and irretrievably a significant part of a people's heritage can be lost while they are trying to serve the present age. In the case of their hymnody, this loss did not threaten the existence of the denomination and its reason for being, but it affected its particular type of piety and Christian life. This is all the more deplorable because the situation could have been rectified.

It is not difficult to identify other areas in Brethren theology and practice where a substantial departure from the original concepts has occurred with negative results. However, the ultimate question to be asked is not whether or not to restore the values of the past. It is, rather, one of honestly assessing and weighing the validity and value of what has been lost and comparing that with what has been put in its place.

[1] Donald F. Durnbaugh, ed., European Origins of the Brethren (Elgin, Ill.: Brethren Press, 1958), 250.

For background on and detailed descriptions of the German hymnals of the Brethren and individual hymns, see Hedwig T. Durnbaugh, The German Hymnody of the Brethren, 1720-1903 (Philadelphia, Pa.: The Brethren Encyclopedia, Inc., 1986). No special bibliographic references will be made to individual hymnals or hymns of the Brethren, German or English, hereafter cited as German Hymnody.

For bibliographic description of all German hymnals until 1884, see Donald Hinks, Brethren Hymn Books and Hymnals, 1720-1884 (Gettysburg, Pa.: Brethren Heritage Press, 1986).

[2] Johann Anastasii Freylinghausen [comp.], Geistreiches Gesang-Buch, den Kern alter und neuer Lieder in sich haltend . . . (Halle: Waysenhaus, 1741). This is the first edition which combines the contents of the two single parts published previously in 1704 and 1714.

[3] Davidisches Psalter-Spiel der Kinder Zions . . . (S.l.: s.n.,] 1718. This hymnal went through many editions both in Europe as well as in America.

[4] German Hymnody, 44-47, 140-141.

[5] For descriptions of the English hymnals of the Brethren, see Nevin W. Fisher, The History of Brethren Hymnbooks (Bridgewater, Va.: Beacon Publishers, 1950). For bibliographic descriptions of all English hymnbooks of the Brethren until 1884, see Hinks.

[6] Don Yoder, Pennsylvania Spirituals (Lancaster, Pa.: Pennsylvania Folklife Society, 1961).

[7] Joseph Funk and Sons, comp., The Harmonia Sacra: a compilation of genuine church music, comprising a great variety of metres, harmonized for four voices, (Verona, Va.: Trissels Mennonite Church, 1973), 23rd (sesquicentennial) ed.

[8] Steffen Arndal, "Den store hvide Flok vi see. . . ." H.A. Brorson og tysk pietistisk vækkelsessang, (Odense Universitetsforlag, 1989). This 486-page work deals with the Danish Pietist hymn writer Hans Adolph Brorson and the German Pietist revival hymnody. Hereafter cited as Arndal.

[9] Arndal, p. 35-36, passim.

12
What Has Happened
To Our
Peace Witness?

by Dale W. Brown

Dale W. Brown of Bethany Theological Seminary ponders the current state of the Brethren and their commitment to the peace stance so deeply rooted in their Anabaptist heritage. Having passionately devoted much of his writing career to the strengthening of this witness, he is saddened by its current weakening and erosion. Yet, relying on the Anabaptist concept of the faithful remnant, he communicates the hope that a faithful group of Brethren will keep it alive and be true to it as a much needed testimony in a violent and suffering world.

With little debate, the delegates at the Portland conference in 1991 adopted the most biblically based, comprehensive, radical, practical statement on peacemaking in our history.[1] In the major worship services, however, there was not one preacher who alluded to or dealt with the dynamics of the Brethren and the Gulf War. The sermons failed to minister prophetically or pastorally to many who supported the war or to those who were extremely lonely because of their nonconformity to a culture which glorified a mass slaughter of human beings.

The Portland conference may be paradigmatic of the status of our peace witness today. It commands respect because it is basic to our heritage. Yet, it need not be taken seriously because of its questionable status in many of our congregations and its incompatibility with American cultural religion. Conference cynics presumed that the peacemaking paper passed easily because it was so long that few would read or take it seriously. Nonetheless, I was encouraged because it was another time when I felt that such a consensus allows us to participate in the "we" testimony of Brethren peace advocates like M. R. Zigler. Other Christians were often envious of M. R. Zigler, because their peace stance was necessarily individualistic, lacking the support of a tradition or body of believers.

Genesis And Evolution

This testimony, a word Quakers often use for consensus decisions or as a synonym for witness, has been with us from the beginning. We find it in the response of Alexander Mack, Sr., to Gruber's fortieth question as to whether Mack expected a better outcome for his church than that of the former Anabaptists. Mack responded:

> We cannot testify for our descendants—as their faith is, so shall be their outcome. Nevertheless, we can say this, that the outcome of the former Baptists has turned out far better than that of all other religions. The Baptist seed is still far better than the seed of L[uther], C[alvin], and also that of the C[atholics]. . . . Not even with gallows and torture can they keep them, who are of one faith, from murdering one another in their homes, which happens often enough. What is more horrible, they go publicly to war, and slaughter one another by the thousands. All this is the fruit of infant baptism. No Baptist will be found in war . . . . The majority of them are inclined to peacefulness. . . . It would indeed be desirable that the whole world were full of these "deteriorated" Baptists. . . .[2]

Early Brethren writings followed Mack in espousing the discipleship and obedience theology of the Anabaptists. Eighteenth and nineteenth-century conference statements assumed that Brethren should follow the Jesus Way.[3] They took seriously the Sermon on the Mount teaching to love enemies and not resist evil. God's redemptive act in forgiving our sins on the cross was God's way of dealing with evil. And God's way is to be our way. Brethren knew that every New Testament writer called the faithful to imitate Jesus in following the way of the cross, the way of suffering love. Anabaptist oriented Brethren have often appropriated the stance of the Schleitheim Confession of 1527. This gathering of Anabaptist leaders, who soon became martyrs, granted the use of the sword in the realm outside the perfection of Christ. In unredeemed society the state may need to use coercive methods to preserve order. In the redeemed community of believers, however, Christians were to remain obedient to the nonresistant way of Jesus.[4]

Early Anabaptists could not fathom how those who condemned them to burnings, drownings and torture would ever follow the teachings of the Sermon on the Mount. It was not long, however, before Anabaptist leaders deviated from this stance. Such was the case with Menno Simons. When the fire encircled the bodies of his friends, he appealed to the rulers to act like the Christians they proclaimed to be.

Likewise, Brethren believed the Jesus way to be more possible in the redeemed community. They often concluded that Christians should not vote or participate in structures of unredeemed society devoted to killing. As Mennonites and Brethren felt more congenial to a democracy which granted religious freedom, they began to participate in activities of the state which did not compromise their stance. At the same time they had more confidence in their ability to influence society to live more peacefully with all peoples.

In addition to the conscious identification with the older Anabaptist movement, the peace stance remained a legacy of the Pietist Reformation, the milieu in which the early Brethren had been nurtured. In contrast to the violence and bigotry of the period, Spener and Francke, though not pacifists, espoused persuasive love in dealing with heretics and hoped that rulers would strive for a better and more peaceful world. Jacob Boehme, who has been regarded as the ideological father of radical Pietism, believed that Christians could not participate in the wars of Babel, the fallen powers of church and state. He believed that a powerful manifestation of the Spirit was about to usher in the seventh age of peace and unity and that Christians should begin to live out the reality of this vision.[5]

More research is needed to discern the extent of the impact of these eschatological expectations for a more peaceful world on the early Brethren. I agree with Rufus Bowman in his general assumptions that the early peace position was influenced by a general hatred of war which stemmed from terrible political, economic, and religious conditions following the horrible Thirty Years War. In this context he asserted the influence of the Pietists, the Mennonites, and the Quakers. The Brethren emigrated with Mennonites to Germantown. They were invited and welcomed by Quakers. And they remained in a Pietist milieu through the publications of Christopher Sauer, Sr. and other radical Pietist influences. We presume that the early Friends influenced the Brethren in having a more irenic attitude toward the American natives, in their scruples about slavery, and in adopting the consensus style of Annual Meeting. These early Pietist and Quaker environs may have implanted seeds which nurtured the evolution of the peace position in the twentieth century from a separatist Anabaptist posture to a more nonviolent transformationist stance. It may not be merely fortuitous that major peace leaders such as M. R. Zigler, Gladys Muir, and Dan West were greatly influenced by Quakerism. Our history has led many to define our peace position as a dialectic, a combination of ingredients which might be named Anabaptist, Pietist, Enlightenment, and Quaker. Often it has been interpreted as a tension between what many Mennonites name biblical nonresistance and Quaker or Gandhian beliefs in nonviolent resistance.

Recently I read the Autobiography and the book entitled Christian Non-Resistance by Adin Ballou.[6] I name him a fascinating evangelical restorationist because his writings are replete with biblical references and texts. He was central to nineteenth-century temperance, abolitionist, communitarian, and pacifist movements. His writings had an influence on both Gandhi and Tolstoy with whom he corresponded. He articulated a persuasive biblical Anabaptist case for non-resistance. But he defined Christian non-resistance as something more than passivity. Moral resistance to evil may justify physical force. However, we are not to respond to violence with violence. To the basic text, "resist not evil," he added his favorite text, "overcome evil with good." This synthesis was incorporated in the Annual Conference peacemaking document which was adopted at Portland, which approves Walter Wink's espousal of Jesus' third way which he defines as something other than fight or flight.[7]

In addition the oft-stated tensions which exist between Anabaptist and Pietist motifs, I like Carl Bowman's suggestion that we can also view Anabaptism and Pietism as mutually reinforcing currents. This would make it possible to be more inclusive in defining Brethren who are left to espouse some form of our peace witness. There are those with Anabaptist propensities who will maintain faithfulness to the way of the cross in spite of its alleged lack of popularity or relevance. Others, who imbibe a Pietist and Quaker hope for better times, will participate in the Spirit's empowerment and look for signs of the promised peaceable kingdom. I prefer to believe that our heritage at its best constitutes a creative union of both the legacies of Anabaptist faithfulness and the Pietist sense of expectancy that God might be able to do something with our witness.

Unfaithfulness And Acculturation

It is tempting to continue to delineate the variety of kinds of peace doctrine held by Brethren. However, we must consider the more relevant question related to the concerns of this gathering. What has happened to our peace witness that it is ignored, misunderstood, even rejected, or regarded as nice but impractical by most of our members?

It may be comforting to note that we are not the first generation to deviate from a strong peace stance. Some Brethren fought for the Union during the civil war because of the rightness of the anti-slavery position and their esteem for Abraham Lincoln. Historians have often noted that the Brethren often were unprepared for war because they failed to witness for peace between wars. Their quietism was usually overcome when their own sons were threatened with military service.

I have learned from Nigerians how our missionaries failed to share biblical peace teachings, perhaps, because of the peaceful demeanor of Nigerian society. When Nigerian Brethren began to enlist in the army during the Civil War, they were told that such was forbidden for Brethren. They felt like responding, "Now you tell us." Currently, Nigerians at Bethany are interested in our peace position in realizing that movements of reconciliation are urgently needed if Christians and Moslems are to stop killing each other.

In the sixties I had a conversation with a young Mennonite who had grown up in the Shenandoah Valley. He reported that the elders looked over the valley and cautioned: "See those Brethren. They used to be like us. Watch out or you will be like them." I wish I could do better in analyzing why we have lost our peace witness. However, I do not believe that knowledge alone would revive it again.

Sociologists name it acculturation. The old Brethren saw it as "getting worldly." Floyd Mallott interpreted the story of the Brethren with a Marxist flavor. Namely, the story line is about how a simple, peasant, people, who were committed to live by the Sermon on the Mount, adjusted to the most industrialized, wealthy, violent and powerful nation of the world. He related how the plain Brethren climbed into their Model T Fords to journey through the twentieth century. The first thing to fly out the window was the broad brim hat, next went the bonnet, then the Love Feast and our peace witness.

One can blame it on the media. Why is it that you and I know more about Elizabeth Taylor than a fascinating Christian like Dorothy Day? We can blame it on the inroads of "pop" religion which wraps the Bible and cross in an American flag. We can blame it on evangelistic emphases which translate Christianity as a mystery cult devoted to save souls from this world instead of our Hebraic heritage in which persons are saved to participate in God's redeeming activity in this world. We can blame it on our colleges. John Baker, who has endowed several peace studies programs, was influenced by a pacifist Dunker mother. She sent him to Juniata College where the peace emphasis was not mentioned in four years.

We can attribute it to our affluence. In a visit to the above mentioned valley, I was puzzled how an area which carries the memories of a John Kline and has produced ambassadors of our peace heritage like Zigler and Rufus Bowman could lose our peace witness. A wise young pastor put it this way. Our culture has done a more effective job in convincing them that the good life consists in possessions defended by the military than we have in interpreting the good news about the Jesus Way. It is for this reason that we need to be aware of both acculturation and unfaithfulness. We need to be realistic concerning the impact of culture. But this does not excuse our failure to share the treasure we have received.

In the context of a spirit of penitence we can recognize good motivations which have contributed to the demise of our peace witness. Our tradition has imbibed strong doses of the love theology and the spirit of tolerance of the early Pietists. For decades in the nineteenth and early twentieth century, candidates for baptism promised to deal with differences according to Matthew 18 and never to prepare for or go to war. These promises were a part of other implicit and explicit commitments to specific lifestyle requirements such as dress and total abstinence. Such expectations came to be regarded as self-righteous legalism.

At the same time Brethren were learning to love and respect neighbors of other faith traditions. When good people such as the spouses of their children wanted to be a part of the community of faith, the desire to be inclusive led them to greater leniency in interpreting the meaning of membership. They were convinced that by example and teaching the new Brethren would come to accept their distinctives. And such did happen in many instances. These tendencies were congenial to the spirit of revivalism which arose in the nineteenth century with its desire to convert persons for Christ and the church.

Yet it was common for those who did not accept the peace position to respect the heritage of the church. Many who did not espouse the position, nevertheless, wanted the preachers and leaders to believe and teach it. Growing numbers of Brethren still regarded the peace witness as a wonderful ideal but impractical in our kind of world. In times of war, however, patriotic fervor surfaced basic differences and threatened the unity of the church. Many congregations dealt with basic conflict by attempting to repress debate and teach respect for the views of others. The practice of Matthew 18 dwindled with the demise of the peace witness. In spite our growing knowledge of conflict resolution skills, Brethren continue to deal with differences by refusing to deal with them in a desire to keep the peace.

The spirit of tolerance and fear of conflict have often led to a relativism which is subversive of strong convictions. Many congregations have adopted what has been named vocational pacifism, a perspective which regards pacifism as a special calling for a few. It is assumed that whether one takes oath of allegiance to a totalitarian organization devoted to training people to kill is a matter of individual conscience which will be affirmed however one chooses. I have questioned whether the same Sunday School teacher would say to youth: "Prostitution is legal in some places. You will need to decide whether you enter the ranks. And whichever way your conscience leads, you will have our support and prayers."

How congregations express their adherence to our historic stance or tolerance of American militarism may reveal the extent of our acculturation or unfaithfulness. Much prevalent relativism goes beyond recent Annual Conference statements which affirm alternative service or noncooperation to be the recommended position of the church. At the same time, prayerful support, if not approval, is extended to those who reject the position of the church. Moreover, in recent years an alien spirit has penetrated the Brethren ethos. With some Brethren and congregations, I have sensed a mood of outright rejection and militancy against our peace heritage.

Despair And Hope

It is important to know what has happened to us, and to discover where we have been and who we are. But there is a more important question. As a people who do we want to be? What is our vision of living out our heritage at its best? Political scientist, Hannah Arendt, taught historians that they make a mistake if they predict what is going to happen on the basis of what has been and is. For history is full of surprises. What unexpected surprises for the Brethren are we willing to dream about and live for?

This kind of musing has influenced how I react to certain kinds of studies. Though not encouraged when I learn that only ten or at the most twenty per cent of our youth are faithful to our peace teachings in times of war, we may move too quickly to the assumption that we have lost our peace witness. It may not be wise for any tradition to judge the degree of faithfulness by what an age group struggling for identity chooses to do.

My visionary impulses have incorporated the same dismal data. Even if we have from ten to thirty per cent, that means from fifteen to forty-five thousand peacemakers. This is a sizable remnant! And when we doubt whether a small minority can change the world, we are encouraged by sociologist Margaret Mead's conclusion that this is the only way the world has ever been changed.

I have kept the word despair for the title of this concluding section so that I might speak out of my condition. As one who has attempted to define the Brethren vision, on several occasions I have been confronted by Christian scholars who have read something from Eller, Durnbaugh, and me. They identified with what was read enough that in moving to a new location they looked up Churches of the Brethren. But they failed to find connections between what they read and what they found. A recent graduate, who joined the Brethren while in seminary, has been faithful in attending the only Brethren church in an area in which he is pursuing a Ph.D. program. Because the new pastor is alien to and ignorant of our heritage, he planned a service celebrating the glorious victory of our forces in the desert war.

Our alumnus is struggling about his relationship to worship which "celebrates the identity between God and the United States." Our admissions office handed me a letter to answer from a student who had been accepted. Though a new member, who is enthusiastic about our heritage, he wrote that sadly he is not coming because he cannot see a place for his family after graduation. He did not wish to be a lonely, prophetic voice in a congregation which does not share the radical discipleship vision of the early Brethren.

For me, however, there are understandings which offer glimmers or even flashes of hope. The peace witness is alive and growing in Christendom. Biblical "peaceniks" are to be found in sizable numbers in Roman Catholic and ecumenical circles and in base Christian communities around the world. Just war advocates, speaking at public forums at Bethany last winter, granted that conventional wars as well as nuclear exchanges are such that applications of just war criteria require Christians to reject modern warfare. The Gulf War was the first in which major religious leaders of mainline denominations and Roman Catholic bishops shared a consensus that refused to pronounce as just a war of their own nation.

In colleges and universities we have experienced the birth of hundreds of peace studies programs. Growing numbers of global citizens are realizing that the only sane way to resolve difference will be modeled after nonviolent ways such as pursued in Eastern Europe and the Soviet Union. Political scientists have debated to whom and what to credit the fall of communism. Should more credit be given to the reforms of Gorbachev or the toughness of Reagan? As Christians why not give more credit to Jesus? For it was Jesus who inspired the nonviolent struggles of Gandhi and King, movements which served as a model for mass responses to communist regimes. The story of the quiet yet momentous role of the churches is yet to be fully revealed on behalf of the freedom marches of the peoples of Eastern Europe.

* * *

My unquenchable hope is that Brethren will respond to the moving of the spirit of peacemaking with justice. In Madison avenue lingo there is a market out there for what we have to offer at our best. Recently I participated in celebrating the twentieth anniversary of the Sojourners magazine and community. Large numbers of Christians, who often feel isolated in their communities, are hungry for a message and community which articulate understandings of the gospel of peace. Brethren representatives noted how large a constituency there is for much which is integral to our heritage. And we wondered why we do not incorporate this in church development. Too often it seems that our evangelistic strategy arises from an idolatrous wish to save our own institutions instead of a passion to share the gospel of peace in all its many ramifications. I believe that solid if not spectacular growth might be a fruit of greater faithfulness to our peace position. Otto Piper and others regard this witness as the major justification we have to continue to exist as a denomination.

Such understandings have nurtured my faith, my hope. For I have been able to give up my messianic compulsion to save our peace stance. Since I have faith that much of what we were called out to be by God is alive in many places and will continue to be basic to Christians as long as they live on this planet, I no longer carry the heavy burden of needing to save the church. I am not called to save the Church of the Brethren in order to save the peace witness or to save the peace witness in order to save the Church of the Brethren.

Still I not only love my heritage, I love the Brethren. My roots are deep in this community of faith. Freed from having to save our church, I am more free to call all of us as Brethren to be a part of what God is doing. God calls us to participate in redeeming and reconciling activity in the lives of persons and in the world which God loved and loves. And in so losing our lives, God's forgiving and enabling grace may save even us.

[1] "Peacemaking, The Call of God In History," in the Minutes of the 205th Recorded Conference of the Church of the Brethren held in 1991. Available from Annual Conference Office, 1451 Dundee Ave., Elgin, IL. 60120.

[2] Donald F. Durnbaugh, ed., European Origins of the Brethren (Elgin: Brethren Press, 1958), 342-43.

[3] See for example the first major pronouncement on war by the Annual Meeting of 1785. Minutes of the Annual Meetings of the Church of the Brethren 1778-1909 (Elgin, IL: Brethren Publishing House, 1909), 9-10. Quotes and analyses of minutes of Brethren conferences on questions of peace and war can also be found in Dale W. Brown, Biblical Pacifism (Elgin: Brethren Press, 1986), chapter 2. Also chapters in Rufus Bowman, The Church of the Brethren and War (Elgin, IL: Brethren Publishing House, 1944).

[4] This article of the Schleitheim Confession affirms what is named church-world dualism. It maintains that God ordains one ethic for Christians and another for society. I have given lectures which analyze this dualism. They remain unpublished because I am perplexed at how many strengths as well as weaknesses I keep discerning. The strength of the position lies in its biblical realism. The world is fallen. It is naive to expect governments to live according to the precepts of the Sermon on the Mount. It helps Christians be realistic about the cost of discipleship. And its adherents hold strongly to the priority of living peacefully in our own lives and communities. Conversely the position is criticized for splitting the will of God. Is it right to proclaim Christ as Lord of the church and not assert the biblical claim that Christ is Lord of the world? Do we not violate the unity of the Trinity when we pose that God commands something different for the world than God reveals through the perfection of Christ?

[5] Brethren authors have given excellent summaries of Boehme's thought and his influence on radical Pietists who impacted the early Brethren. Dale Stoffer, Background and Development of Brethren Doctrines (Philadelphia: Brethren Encyclopedia, Inc., 1989), 19-21. David C. Ensign, "Radical German Pietism," Unpublished doctoral dissertation (Graduate School, Boston University, 1955), 19-50.

[6] Both books have been reprinted more recently. Adin Ballou, Autobiography of Adin Ballou (Lowell, Mass.: Populi Vox Poppuli Press, 1896. Reprinted, Philadelphia: Porcupine Press, 1975), and Christian Non-Resistance (Philadelphia: J. Miller M'Kim, 1846. Reprinted, Philadelphia: Jerome Ozer, 1972).

[7] The Annual Conference decision affirms the much circulated second chapter, "Jesus' Third Way," in Walter Wink, Violence and Nonviolence in South Africa (Philadelphia: New Society Publishers, 1987). The same essay constitutes the last selection in an anthology edited by Angie O'Gorman, The Universe Bends Toward Justice, A Reader on Christian Non-Violence in the U.S. (Philadelphia: New Society Publishers, 1990).

Response To
Special Topics in Change

by Christina Bucher

What struck me most about Dale Brown's paper was the vivid description of the ambivalence I found there. On the one hand, Dale mourns the fact that we had no mention of the Gulf War and the denomination's peace position at the worship sessions of the 1991 Annual Conference in Portland. He also points to the great disparity between the writings of Brethren leaders and the preaching in Brethren pulpits. He directly poses the question, "Why have we lost our peace witness?"

On the other hand, Brown observes that at the theoretical level, the commitment of the Church of the Brethren to the peace position has been constant, although exactly how we have interpreted that peace witness has varied. Additionally, he notes that at the practical level, that is, at the level of the local congregation, this is not the first time our deed fails to reflect our word. Brown suggests that we are not at the tail end of a long, steady decline, in terms of our denomination's peace witness, but, perhaps, at a dip on the graph.

Also on a hopeful note, Brown comments that we have a "faithful remnant." Even if ten to twenty percent of our denomination is faithful to the peace witness, that faithful remnant can have great influence. Finally, he points with hopefulness to the ecumenical peace movement and to the growth in the peace studies programs on college campuses.

With regard to the decline in the peace witness of the Church of the Brethren, Brown identifies several contributing factors. He points to acculturation, the influence of the media, and the increasing affluence of the Brethren. Two factors identified—increasing tolerance and relativism—I will address later in my general remarks.

I found much less ambivalence in Hedda Durnbaugh's paper. In her tracing of the changes in hymnody as the Brethren adapted to the New World, she clearly notes that the Brethren lost an important part of their heritage. As the Brethren became acculturated to their new Anglo-American context, they exchanged the hymnody of German Pietism for that of Victorian England and nineteenth-century America. In addition to changes in hymnody, this process of acculturation spawned changes in worship practices. Choirs and special music replaced congregational singing. Worship became less a corporate experience of faithfulness and joy and more a worship event, with the congregation divided between performers and audience.

After hearing Durnbaugh's paper, I am left with several questions. First, I wonder if the new hymnal will continue the trend identified or if the hymnal committee has attempted to bring back at least part of our German Pietist heritage. Second, it seems that our denomination faces this issue in a new way as more and more persons of non-German descent join the Church of the Brethren. What impact will African-American, Korean, and Hispanic Brethren have upon the hymnody and worship practices of the denomination? How do we preserve our heritage as the denomination changes?

I have two modest proposals to bring before this group:

1) I was somewhat disheartened on Friday night to hear Brother Earle Fike call for less "theological navel-gazing," because I want to propose that what the Brethren need is, in fact, more theological reflection and conversation. I assume and hope that the critical word for him might be "navel-gazing," not "theological."

To anticipate possible misconstruals of this proposal, let me hasten to say that I am not calling for a creed or a card or even an identification of the range of what is theologically acceptable for any who call themselves "Brethren." Rather, I propose that we become more aware of what other Christians (and, beyond that, other religious folk) think. Not on issues, such as the peace witness, or even on practices, such as the Love Feast, but on theological matters. Who is God? What is the relation of God and the world? Are humans essentially good or essentially evil? Do we expect Christ to return, and, if we say "Yes," do we mean literally and physically or metaphorically and spiritually? I mean matters of theology, anthropology, and eschatology.

Let me also hasten to say that I am not suggesting that we replace the Bible with Thomas Aquinas or Martin Luther or Karl Barth. The Bible is the ground for all our discussions about beliefs and practices. But we must admit to ourselves that we bring something to the Bible—a way of interpreting it, a method of reconciling all its parts, a hermeneutic, if you will.

To show what I mean, let me apply this point to the two papers at hand. Is not the problem Durnbaugh addresses a problem of theological insensitivity? How do we preserve our German Pietist heritage? I don't think we do it simply by resurrecting as many of the hymns sung by Alexander Mack and company as we can find. We can, however, identify those theological themes that are Brethren and consciously select new hymns that reflect those themes and, correspondingly, reject hymns that embody theological views that are not Brethren. We can reevaluate our style of worship to determine if it expresses the Brethren belief in the importance of the community.

With regard to Brown's paper, I want to give an example from the classroom. I have been teaching a course at Elizabethtown College called "Biblical Perspectives on Peace and Justice." In January 1991 on the first day of the spring semester and at the time the Gulf War was getting under way, I asked students in that class to write a response to a letter that had been printed in the local newspaper. The author of the letter had expressed approval of the war and had quoted Scripture to show that God approves of war. I chose the letter because I expected students to comment on the writer's abuse of the Bible. Instead, to my horror, the first student to read her response expressed approval of both the writer's sentiment and his interpretation of Scripture. I sat there thinking, "This is going to be a long, hard semester."

What we learned in that class as the semester progressed was not simply that the Mennonites and Brethren in the class opposed the war as adamantly as the evangelical fundamentalists supported it. (The Presbyterians, Methodists, and Roman Catholics were somewhere in the middle.) We began to learn why we had different views, yet we all considered ourselves Christians.

That class brought into sharp relief for me the need to integrate our peace witness into our entire theological framework. Because, if you expect God will bring a worldwide war that will bring an end to this world, as the ardent supporter of the war in my classroom did, then it is not surprising that you view war differently than does someone who does not expect a literal return of Christ and a violent destruction of the present world. Our eschatology informs and influences our views on peacemaking; yet, how often do we Brethren discuss eschatological matters?

2) My second observation has to do with the mode of our thinking and discourse. Here I borrow from the pedagogical theory of William Perry, whose work has significantly influenced teaching at the college level.

Brethren discourse tends to be what Perry calls "dualistic." Everything is very clear cut—right or wrong, moral or immoral. "Nonviolence is right." "War is wrong." This form of discourse offers little documentation as support; rather, it appeals to authority. We say, "That is what Brethren believe. That is what Jesus taught." End of discussion.

This style may have its place. It can be rhetorically effective. It may wake up students in the classroom or Christians in the pews. But it does not effectively get individuals to think for themselves. It works only as long as they accept the "authority" and often operates best when individuals have little contact with those of differing opinions. In a sheltered community where people tend to agree on what is right and what is wrong, dualism tends to work.

What happens, however, when young people move out into the larger world and become acquainted with persons who hold differing views? As I reflect on what has happened within my own generation of Brethren, it seems to me that this sort of dualism has backfired. Young people went away to college, joined BVS, or left the farm for other jobs, and they began to understand that the world is more complex than they had been taught. This is why many who have viewed and now view the colleges and BVS as dangerous have, in fact, good reason to worry. As a result of these new experiences, many in my generation felt betrayed and misled. The dualistic mode of thinking had supplied them with answers, but not with the ability to explain "why."

Many people see as the only alternative to dualism a relativism that recognizes that problems can have many different solutions. Instead of turning to a so-called authority for an answer that fits all situations, one examines the context and considers how one might respond in a particular situation.

William Perry suggests, however, that there is a final stage of critical thinking that moves beyond both dualism and relativism. In this final stage of thinking, an individual makes conscious decisions to accept certain values and to reject certain solutions to a problem. While acknowledging the complexity of a situation, one willingly accepts responsibility for one's decision.

At our Friday evening session, Sister Dawn Ottoni-Wilhelm commented on how the Brethren fail to communicate. I attribute this failure to our dualistic mode of thinking. When we think dualistically, we cannot argue. If you disagree with me, it's not due to faulty logic or to lack of evidence. Rather, it's because you refuse to accept the truth. I can't convince you; I can only try to convert you.

To conclude—we cannot return to Schwarzenau or Germantown. I would not want to even if we could. But we can think more critically about our theological heritage and learn how to apply it to new situations. We can look to the past, learn from it, and chart our course for the future. The question for us is not, "How do we recreate the Schwarzenau Brethren?" The task for us is to determine, "What people do we want to become?"

PART VI

THE PAST AS PROLOGUE

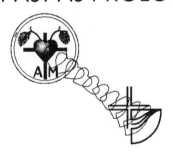

13

Now is The Time So Urgent:
Called Into God's Future

by Melanie A. May

Assuming a homiletic role and discarding the academic mode as untimely, Melanie A. May speaks to those in the church who, she believes, are seeking to pull us back into an older vision as a separatist, nonconformist body which wants to preserve its treasured unity by withdrawal from the world. In words reminiscent of the Old Testament prophets and of Brethren progressives from earlier in this century, she condemns this as both a betrayal of our calling and a denial of our heritage. The diversity within the contemporary church is a gift from God to be lovingly affirmed. To her, it represents a fuller image of God's world. While affirming the blessings of diversity, she confesses disappointment and sadness because this gift of God is not more fully affirmed. Those who seek to recover an older vision of the church are seen as backward-looking, prideful, self-pitying, duplicitous, scape-goating, blame-casting, finger-pointing, faithless, and confused. Brethren are called to witness to the God who dwells among all the people who inhabit the earth.

As I examine the life of the church today and where God has led us, it is with the sense that now is not the time for dispassionate scholarly discourse. Rather, I am called to assume a homiletical style. I also speak as someone who has been present at this conference primarily as an observer. My posture relates in part to my assignment, which was to listen and then to respond to the proceedings. More profoundly, my choice to observe—to watch and wait for signs of the Spirit moving in our midst—relates to my question about how it is possible for me to offer the gifts God has given me in service to the Church of the Brethren. I sense that my perceptions and my words may not be welcome to those who presently seek to set the terms for our life together. I am not alone. I stand before you to speak as a representative of a whole generation, many of whom have sensibilities and experiences that match my own. Many of them have already left the Church of the Brethren, hot on the heels of the greater part of the half-generation ahead of us.

I speak as someone whose life until now has been dedicated to ministry in the Church of the Brethren. My choice to commit my gifts to ministry in this church was nurtured in this Shenandoah District as I accompanied my mother on her laywomanly leadership rounds and later as I preached up and down this valley and all through these hills as supply preacher during summers home from college and divinity school. I do not recall these things of my past as "nostalgic representations of . . . a time irretrievably lost [or] . . . frozen in unchanging perfection," to borrow a phrase from Christopher Lasch's latest book, The True and Only Heaven.[1] Lasch makes a critical distinction between nostalgia and memory, a distinction I think can help us as we ask how to relate to the past. Making this distinction, Lasch speaks about nostalgic idealizations of the past that are prone to condemn the present, and memory which is "less concerned with loss than with our continuing indebtedness to a past the formative influence of which lives on in our patterns of speech, our gestures, our standards of honor, our expectations, our basic disposition toward the world around us."[2] The things of my past I recall at this moment are, in Lasch's sense, among the memories from which I draw hope. For these memories leave me with "the unshakable conviction, not that the past was better than the present, but that trust is never completely misplaced, even though it is never completely justified either and therefore destined inevitably to disappointments."[3]

I am disappointed, deeply so. I watch and wait for signs of the Spirit moving in our midst. I witness the ways our words and deeds testify instead to fear and to finger-pointing, finally pronounced as pride as we attempt to take God's future into our own hands. We have yielded to the temptation to worship as idols certain perceptions and conclusions created in our own end-of-the-twentieth-century image. For we, as surely as our eighteenth or nineteenth or earlier twentieth-century forebears in faith, are creatures of a particular time and place, however forgetful of our finitude we are. I *am* disappointed. But I do not despair. I do not despair because of my faith that God's future will become incarnate with or without the Church of the Brethren. God's work will be done upon this earth as in heaven whether or not we cooperate. My faith in God's promise of a new creation in Christ is founded in my Brethren heritage. My quandary and question, therefore, is not whether to leave the church, but whether the church has left itself.

"Now is the time so urgent." This is the time for decision not despair, the time for decision not definition. So the values and the vision that have formed me in faith, that have formed us in faith, may serve God's future, rather than be forfeited as we ask first and foremost about being separate rather than about being faithful. This is the time for decision, not despair or definition. So the life God has given us may be a blessing to all God's people. For thereby we may live and not die. For the sake of our life in God's future, I will speak about what I witness regarding our fear, our finger-pointing, and our pride.

As I listen during these days and during recent months and years within the Church of the Brethren, I feel our fear. I say I *feel* our fear since my sense is stirred not so much by what we say or even primarily by what we do. It is like the air we breathe, like an ethos that envelops us, eats at us. It diminishes our liveliness and dims our creativity. It hovers in the wings of unwritten rules: hold back, don't stick out, don't make waves, let the mind of the community hold sway. Subjugate your vision, vitality, and voice to keep the peace.

We cry, "Peace, peace!" when there is no peace. For we are at war within. It is true, however deep our denial, however much we heap a cover of concord on the conflict. Some of us are doing battle with the structures that dominate and deny a place to our diverse members. Some of us are doing battle with the so-called special interest groups growing up and grabbing at our cover of concord. All of us seem predisposed to regard one another from a human point of view rather than regarding one another in Christ as the apostle Paul teaches. This is to say, the particularities of culture, race, gender, age, and theological perspective are not recognized as the gifts of God and received as blessings brought by the many members to up build the body of Christ. "If the whole body were an eye, where would be the hearing? If the whole body were an ear, where would be the sense of smell? . . . As it is, there are many parts, yet one body" (I Cor. 12:17, 20). Particularities have on all sides become possessions to be preserved and protected. Self interests as surely as special issues are the shots we fire while we say, "Peace, peace."

Our loyalty to self interests as to special issues is fueled by our fear, by our sense that the things upon which we have come to count are changing, are out of our control. We have a sense that what was will no longer be. We fear we are perishing. Shrinking statistics seem a sure sign. And so we scramble to tinker with strategies and structures. Numbers of people and pieces of silver are our pursuit, our present preoccupation. Held in thrall by fear, we in our hearts, like the disciples, demand of Jesus: "Teacher, do you not care that we are perishing?" (Mark 4:38b). We with the disciples tend to think in terms of rescuing or resuscitating what has been. But brothers and sisters, let us wrestle with Jesus' words in response to the disciples' demand to be rescued from perishing: "Why are you afraid? Have you still no faith?" (Mark 4:40). Why are we afraid? Have we still no faith, faith being, in the words of the letter to the Hebrews, "the assurance of things hoped for, the conviction of things not seen. . . . By faith we understand that the worlds were prepared by the word of God, so that what is seen was made from things that are not visible" (Hebrews 11:1,3).

Why are we afraid? I offer these reflections in response. During the last year, as I have had to reckon the reality of my own life and death in dealing with a cancer diagnosis, I have begun to believe that deeper than our fear of death—of perishing—is our fear of life. We fear being fully alive, altogether alive in a death-dealing, drug-dealing world of divisions, in a world wherein moral and theological neutrality in tandem with spiritual numbness have come to count as humanity. We are afraid of life abundant, as the myth of scarcity has seeped into the very marrow of our bones.

Why are we afraid of life, of life abundant? We fear life for, first of all, it means facing and feeling our mere mortality, our frail finitude. We are flesh and blood creatures. Flesh is frail and failing. We bleed. Pain punctuates the passages of life. And all life passes away. "All people are grass, their constancy is like the flower of the field. The grass withers, the flower fades, when the breath of the Lord blows upon it; surely the people are grass," spoke the prophet Isaiah (Isaiah 40:6-7). Our comfort comes as the next passage from the prophet is pronounced: "The grass withers, the flower fades; but the word of our God will stand forever" (Isaiah 40:8). I am convinced that we will hear, really hear, the word of our God only when we reckon, really reckon, the reality of our mere mortality. Our lives are transitory. Life is transitory. Indeed, without transition there is no life. Death is stasis. Death is everlasting preservation. God is the living God, whose faithfulness may be the same yesterday, today, and tomorrow, but whose work of creation is unceasing. As long as we are preoccupied with the work of our hands lest it perish, as long as we are prepossessed by the work of our hands as intimation of our immortality, our hands will not be open to receive God's gift of new creation in Christ, a promise whose fulfillment we await.

We are flesh and blood creatures who bear God's image and so are called to be creators as well. But time and time again we confuse our work of creation with God's work of creation. Out of the whirlwind, God's words to Job—so sunken in self-pity by the passing away that accompanies all life—were:

> Where were you when I laid the foundation of the earth? Tell me, if you have understanding. Who determined its measurements—surely you know! Or who stretched the line upon it? On what were its bases sunk, or who laid its cornerstone when the morning stars sang together and all the heavenly beings shouted for joy? Or who shut in the sea with doors when it burst out from the womb?—when I made the clouds its garment, and thick darkness its swaddling band, and prescribed bounds for it, and set bars and doors, and said, "Thus far shall you come, and no farther, and here shall your proud waves be stopped?" (Job 38:4-11).

So to us, sunken in our own self-pity as statistics shrink or as our agenda is set aside or as the work of our hands appears to wither with the grass, God's words are heard again: "Here shall your proud waves be stopped." Anticipating the words of Jesus to the waves of which the disciples were afraid: "Peace! Be still!" (Mark 4:39). These words do not call us to cease our work. They do call us to clarity about what is in God's hands and what is in our hands. The new creation in Christ for which we watch and wait is God's gift, a gift we may receive and make manifest only as our hands are open, not preoccupied or prepossessed, not holding on in fear, rather hands held open ready to receive.

Our hands must be ready also to relinquish. For the theological context of relinquishment is creation, not cross. God's own act of creation was and is an overflowing from the fullness of God's life and love. The new comes to be only as the old has passed away. This passing away is not sacrifice or loss so much as self-offering for the sake of new life, a new creation in Christ.

This passing away is for the sake of the world God so loves. Love is the message at the heart of the Gospel, a message about loving our neighbors, those like us, those not like us, the unlikely, even our enemy. It is a message about loving the unlovely, about loving ourselves, our own unlikeliness, our own unloveliness. So we are not so prone to whip up our own "proud waves." For we are a generation of scape-goaters, prone to pointing our fingers at failures in those among us who do not follow the unwritten and written rules, at the faults in others out there in the world. We point our fingers to appease our fear that we are perishing. For it is easier to blame someone else than to be responsible for ourselves, easier to shift the blame—the game politicians play today—and avoid our own actions. For we would rather not reckon with the reality of our own lives, at once merely mortal and responsible as creatures who bear God's image.

Our persistent predisposition to point a finger at the world, from which we assume we are set apart, is particularly pernicious. First of all, it calls into question our self understanding as a biblical people. For the biblical term "world" is altogether ambiguous. There are times when "world" denotes the reign of powers and principalities that oppose God's reign. There are times when "world" designates the place in which we flesh and blood creatures live. There are times when "world" is that which God loves so much God sent Jesus Christ for its sake. In these latter senses, the world is not the object of blame, but the subject of salvation! One of the most tenacious tensions throughout Christian history has been the confusion between these senses of "world." Too often the translation of "being in the world but not of it" has led to a conflation of the meanings. The attempt to be a community of faith already living an alternative to present powers and principalities has been attended by accusations against the world in which we live, against the world God so loved.

Predictably the present resurgence of this world-denying and separatist spirit among us appears at a time when we are profoundly acculturated. This has been commented on by most of the speakers at this conference. I am concerned, and confounded, in so far as the way in which worldliness has been characterized is itself an indicator of our immersion into prevailing cultural perspectives. For example, as Warren Kissinger has pointed out, the very issues about which we are most exercised—such as sexual ethics—are the issues upon which contemporary culture is fixated. Accordingly, my concern is about the extent to which we have uncritically joined the elite and exclusive company of affluent, comfortable American citizens anxious to preserve our way of life. This was the rationale expressed by the president who led us to war in the Gulf and who continues to wage war against the poor and underprivileged in this society and around the globe.

This present confusion and conflation of what we mean by "world" and accommodation to the "world," often attended by condemnation of the "world" and those that dwell therein, threatens another aspect of our self understanding. Brethren have long taught that our heritage is discontinuous with the mainstream of the Christian tradition, this is to say, with Christendom in league with worldly powers. But our present propensity to pronounce a *contemptus mundi* outlook places us precisely and squarely in continuity with the stream of the Christian tradition over against which we say our identity is set.[4] The separatist spirit I hear increasingly invoked is not at all uniquely Brethren. It is not even genuinely Brethren. It is but one more indicator of our acculturation to the present end-of-the-century and end-of-an-era ethos, an ethos that slings accusations in order to save the appearances as old orders begin to break up and the new announces itself.

Today's separatist spirit is, in sum and in truth, the negative image of the triumphalist spirit we at one time abhorred. My disappointment in our present predisposition to sign on to triumphalism in the name of separatism is that we thereby forfeit a great gift we have to offer as a witness to the world. This great gift is our sensibility for the sacredness of all life, the traditional Brethren sense that there is no sacred sphere or space separate from the world of daily life. The sense that the commonplace is consecrated around a potluck meal or a shared cup of cold water has been the sinew of our peacemaking and our serving and our simple living. These disciplines of our common life were nurtured not by a world-denying, condemning separatist spirit so much as by an affirmation of the whole creation as the realm of God's work and reign. In these days of environmental danger, of wars and rumors of wars, and of economic crisis, our witness that all human beings are created to live as a community characterized by mutual receiving and giving in response to God's grace is more important than ever. To live life as sacred, as sacrament, is an act of resistance that reveals the reality of God's reign redeeming the whole creation that makes manifest an alternative to the ways in which present powers and principalities are determined to desecrate and destroy life. To live life as sacrament may lead to acts that set us apart from those around us, but sacred or sacramental living does not abide a separatist spirit. It does not seek to be separate *for its own sake*, for it is based on affirmation not accusation.

Our fear and its attendant finger-pointing tend to pronounce themselves as pridefulness. We partake of the American spirit and strategic assertion that states, in the words of Noam Chomsky, "We are Good, our intentions are Good. Period."[5] We forfeit our future insofar as we will not tell the truth, for we stand still more deeply in our own complicity in a culture of cover-up. Our cover-up attests to our acculturation as well. We perpetuate an identity as a persecuted and peculiar people, marginalized and misunderstood by those in power. But we do not speak about our own power and our abuse of it. We perpetuate an identity as a community of the redeemed. But we do not speak about the lack of integrity between what we say and what we do that drives people of integrity away from the church. The duo of deceit and duplicity paralyzes us. We lock ourselves into the past tense and retrospective reference. We lock ourselves out of God's future. We may walk into God's future only as truth-telling makes us free from the fear that grips us.

Here I recall a presentation by James Billington, scholar of Russian history, to the World Council of Churches Central Committee about the August 1991 events in the Soviet Union. He characterized these extraordinary events in terms of an enormous moral choice made by the Soviet people between the politics of fear and the politics of hope. They cast their choice for the politics of hope. Although Billington believes this politics of hope to be a fragile, new thing in human history, it flowers from roots that run deep in the Christian sensibility still suffusing Russian culture. Crucial to the ability to choose this new reality, this politics of hope, is repentance. People asked for forgiveness. People assumed responsibility, cutting the cycle of claim and counterclaim, putting an end to passing the buck that is the linchpin of every totalitarian terror as well as its repression.

The people of the Soviet Union, particularly the Christians who have borne faithful witness through darkest times, have pioneered a possible new politics for the twenty-first century. I hope the people of the United States, particularly Christians and among them members of the Church of the Brethren, will join Soviet Christians as faithful sisters and brothers. I hope we will repent of our half-truths and lies that are the linchpin of authority in our own land. We will be renewed with a courageous and creative spirit, a courageous and creative spirit able to bear witness to our own complicity, our own woundedness and well-won wisdom, thus engaging in an act of disarmament, disarming the powers and principalities whose deceit and duplicity depend on our own pretense.

Perhaps those elements which we fear are perishing, reminding us of Christ's words, "Teacher, do you not care if we perish?" are passing away in order that God's new creation in Christ can come to be more fully. My prayer is that in this time of transition we will not yield to the temptation to draw and defend boundaries, to perpetuate protectionism, to contribute to the cover-up. My prayer is that God may preserve us in the truth of the Gospel. For the Gospel's truth is not our possession to preserve or protect. My prayer is that, by God's grace, we may be set free to be faithful to our unique gifts as Brethren members of Christ's body, a body that offers its life as its Lord offered his life for the world God so loves. My prayer is that we may thereby be a witness to the living God who comes to dwell anew among all the people who inhabit this earth.

[1] Christopher Lasch, The True and Only Heaven: Progress and Its Critics (New York: W.W. Norton & Co., 1991), 83.

[2] Ibid.

[3] Ibid., 81.

[4] See Jean Delumeau, Sin and Fear: The Emergence of a Western Guilt Culture 13th-18th Centuries, trans. Eric Nicholson (New York: St. Martin's Press, 1990). Originally published as Le Peche et La Peur, by Librairie Artheme Fayard, 1983.

[5] Noam Chomsky, Deterring Democracy (London, New York: Verso, 1991), 172.

14

Closing The Circle:
Germantown And Philadelphia Revisited

by Donald F. Durnbaugh

In thoughtful response to the many viewpoints and varying assessments shared in the Brethren in Transition Conference, Durnbaugh suggests several important ideas and themes. Beginning with a review of the initial insights of the "urban village to urban society" presentation, he notes both gloomy and hopeful signs. He rightly observes that the Brethren have shown a tenacious persistence over time even under severe adversity. Despite numerical decline, significant signs of renewal are seen. In concluding, he draws on the title of Philip Jakob Spener's famous work, Pia desideria (1675), and offers pious desires for the Brethren as they approach the twenty-first century.

Stephen L. Longenecker began the conference by speaking of the experience of Brethren in the first place they inhabited in North America, Germantown, and then of its offshoot, the Philadelphia congregation.[1] I propose to complete the circle by ending the discussion with reference to the same sites. They can serve as useful paradigms to focus the concerns raised this meeting.

Longenecker refers to Stephanie Grauman Wolf's fine study of Germantown as an early urban village and the difficulty of sectarians such as the Mennonites and Brethren to succeed in that exposed and open setting.[2] He notes the decline of the congregation in the later nineteenth century and the comment by the aggressive pioneer missionary Wilbur Stover (1866-1930), briefly a pastor there, that, paradoxically, the cemetery was its most important reality. William McKinley Beahm (1896-1964), beloved seminary dean, liked to admonish Bethany students to welcome problems in the congregation, for that implied life. He pointed out that the easiest aspect of the congregation to manage was the cemetery.

Stephen Longenecker also correctly pointed out that the congregation in Philadelphia was perennially at odds with the church during the nineteenth century because of its innovations, including indoor baptisteries, instruments for worship services, and perhaps the first minister to receive regularly stated support.[3] His conclusion was that urban congregations, such as Germantown and Philadelphia, were left on the margins of Brethren life.

The points are well taken. However, some other realities of the Germantown and Philadelphia experience could also be cited that have equal relevance for our current situation of transition and uncertainty. Some will be briefly mentioned, followed by explanations why they are pertinent.

The first is that despite the troubles mentioned (and others unnamed), there is the simple but important fact that the two congregations mentioned still persist. Admittedly, the Germantown congregation disbanded in 1964 after a long decline; the change in racial composition of Germantown seems to have been the major cause. Nevertheless, the denomination kept a small but active program of community service going at Germantown. Ronald G. and Ila Lutz, fresh from similar work in the Washington (DC) City Church, mounted a multi-faceted program over a long period. Central to the work was a day care program. A mark of the respect in which the program was held by the economically and socially troubled neighborhood was the almost total absence of vandalism despite its exposed situation. The congregation voted to merge with the Philadelphia First Church which itself had moved in 1957 to the northern suburbs of the city in a similar pattern of white flight.[4]

More recently Germantown developed a low-key but faithful ministry to the homeless on the streets of Philadelphia. They were aided by area congregations of Brethren who volunteered to distribute food in subway stations and places where the homeless sought shelter from the cold.[5]

In 1980 the Atlantic Northeast district decided to begin work again in Germantown to develop an interracial congregation. This proved difficult and growth was slow until 1989. Currently Germantown is enjoying a remarkable renaissance under the leadership of a gifted pastor, Richard Kyerematen, a former Anglican from Ghana. His gentle but effective ministry was recently featured in <u>Messenger</u>. Beginning with but a handful of loyal members of several races, by spring 1991, Pastor Richard was leading lively worship services each Sunday with attendance numbering well over one hundred. For years the tiny congregation had used the small original meetinghouse as a place of worship but, since mid-1991, increased numbers dictated use of the larger worship area that had been added on to the meetinghouse in 1896-97. With the aid of the district, the larger space was completely remodeled and refurbished.[6]

This reminds us of another relevant part of the Germantown congregational story. That is that early in this century it leaped from its nineteenth-century lethargy and dwindling numbers to what its chronicler described as "phenomenal growth." Milton C. Swigart (1868-1939) found sixty members when he became pastor in 1905; by 1934 the membership numbered 463. The increase in numbers necessitated a second addition to the building in 1915; a Philadelphia newspaper headlined the story, "Famous Old Church Outgrows Its Home." Intense evangelistic efforts brought members from all over Philadelphia; the church profited from the work of visiting evangelists to the metropolitan area such as William A. "Billy" Sunday (1862-1935). Anna C. Swigart (1870-1923) developed a remarkable ministry through Christian education and work with women. The Swigarts' daughter, Esther, developed a strong youth program. The rapid increase of new members without strong Brethren rootage also probably permitted, in the last few years of Swigart's ministry after 1935, a significant loss as nearly 250 members shifted their allegiance to other, more conservative denominations. Both the rapid expansion and sudden decline of membership provide lessons for the current denomination.[7]

A key figure in the early nineteenth century of both Germantown and Philadelphia was Elder Peter Keyser, Jr. (1766-1849). His full life demonstrated that individual Brethren could function very well in urban settings. A self-made man of exceptional energy and ability, he memorized the entire New Testament and large sections of the Old. As he became blind in later life, this resource was very helpful for him; he continued to minister and preach using his memory to quote scripture. Originally a tanner, Keyser developed a prosperous lumber business in Philadelphia. He was civic-minded and highly respected. A longtime member and later a secretary of the city's Board of Health, he was Inspector and Treasurer of the prison, as well as being an active member of the Society for Alleviating the Miseries of the Public Prisons. He was a director and comptroller of the public schools when they were introduced in Philadelphia. Despite all of these voluntary civic activities, he maintained a regular ministry at Germantown as well as at Philadelphia, riding horseback or walking the distance to serve. It would be hard to find a record of urban activity to match this in later Brethren history, with the possible exception of another member of the Philadelphia First Church, Martin G. Brumbaugh (1862-1930); Brumbaugh was superintendent of public instruction in Philadelphia before becoming governor of the Commonwealth in 1914. It does indicate that Brethren have had significant involvement in service to urban areas.[8]

Although not directly flowing from the Philadelphian area story, a parallel instance can be cited from another early Brethren city church—Baltimore. In the 1870s an Irish immigrant named James T. Quinlan (1853-1943) became acquainted with Brethren in the New Windsor area and then became active in home missions in Baltimore. He distributed tracts and held bible schools for children. One of "Quinlan's boys," as they were called, was Charles Calvert Ellis (1874-1950), later well-known as C. C. Ellis, one of the greatest evangelists, preachers, and educators that Brethren history boasts. He was assisted by prosperous Hagerstown philanthropist Jacob F. Oller to attend Juniata College, where he later became a distinguished president, followed by his son, Calvert N. Ellis (b. 1904), as president.[9]

It was Keyser who opened the pulpit to pioneer woman preacher, Sarah Righter Major (1808-1884), an action accurately referred to by Stephen Longenecker as one of the many innovations of Philadelphia Brethren. In some

ways a more significant impact was made on Philadelphia-area Brethren by
Mary Schwenk Geiger (1828-1916) of the First Church of the Brethren. Her
benefactions were crucial in the home mission outreach in the city, leading to
the development of the Geiger Memorial, Calvary, and Bethany congregations,
as well as to mission efforts by the denomination in other countries. When she
died in 1916, Martin G. Brumbaugh traveled from the governor's mansion in
Harrisburg to preach the funeral sermon. Carl Bowman correctly pointed out
that the regnant twentieth-century interpretation of Brethren genius—which
posits great freedom and toleration—was largely crafted by Brumbaugh in his
path breaking and influential history. It is clear that Germantown and
Philadelphia have been important and continuing symbols of Brethren
transition.[10]

There is another point to be made about the Philadelphia congregation
that is often missed. Despite the steady stream of committees sent by the
Annual Meeting in the second half of the nineteenth century to bring the city
congregation back into the regular Brethren order, at no time was the entire
congregation disfellowshipped. There was certainly ample cause for such
drastic action. The congregation neither meekly accepted the Annual Meetings
dictates nor did it aggressively defy them. Members worked with the visiting
committees but did not markedly change their ways. Nor did the Philadelphia
Brethren depart the church in the 1880s when the Progressive Brethren began.
It speaks well both of the larger church and of the local congregation that
relationships held in spite of many years of tension and trouble. This is another
simple but significant truth.

Having added these additional parts of the story of Germantown and
Philadelphia to the depiction given earlier in the conference, it is necessary to
draw some conclusions from them.

1) The first is the plain fact of persistence. By all rights Germantown and
First Church, given the difficult, at times desperate, circumstances they have
experienced, should long ago have perished. Surprisingly, there have been
reawakenings, repositionings, and a critical mass of loyal members over the
decades sufficient to keep the congregations alive. Their story illustrates the
remarkable capacity for religious bodies to survive over long periods or to
experience reawakenings and revival.

2) The second is that the congregations have changed. They have
changed locations, or programs, or personnel to meet changing situations.
Change has been painful, often slow, and never easy. But change has occurred
and has been met with at least modest success.

3) Members of these congregations have ministered in at times
remarkable ways to the urban community. Peter Keyser's contribution to the
welfare of early nineteenth century Philadelphia was impressive. The
community outreach of Germantown won respectful attention. Feeding and
clothing the homeless is but the latest of the ministries.

4) The congregations have had a strong orientation toward evangelism and missions. Wilbur Stover was mentioned earlier as a pastor at Germantown before opening the first Brethren missions in India; to his name should be added H. Stover Kulp (1894-1964) and Ruth Royer Kulp (1896-1924). Stover Kulp was pastor at Philadelphia just before he and his wife left to begin Brethren mission activity in Nigeria. Hence, the Germantown and Philadelphia congregations are linked inextricably with pioneer and progressive mission outreach in India and Africa.

5) In the face of change and challenge, Brethren have maintained a mixture of social concern and evangelistic drive not always found in other denominations.

"For the glory of God and for my neighbor's good" was the early motto of the Sauer press in Germantown. In changing yet persistent ways this balance can be observed in these congregations. Recent converts at the Germantown congregation have testified to the appeal of this linkage.

Implications for the Broader Denomination

1) Signs of malaise and concern for identity are obvious among current members of the Church of the Brethren and have been eloquently described and analyzed in previous papers given at this conference. There are evident and real causes for concern. Some of these motivated the General Board last year to interrupt its regular meeting to issue a "Call for Spiritual Renewal."[11]

Despite this, there is no reason to believe the Church of the Brethren (or related Brethren movements) is caught in a process of inevitable decline. There is every reason to suggest that Brethren will persist in the twenty-first century. Students of church history are continually amazed by the longevity and persistence of religious movements long after outside observers have diagnosed terminal illness. (In late September the latest in a series of Lovefeasts was held in the Saal of the Ephrata Cloister conducted by remaining members of the German Seventh Day Baptist Church; they are the descendants of the "third order" or householders of the Ephrata Society, which disbanded as a monastic movement early in the nineteenth century. With scarcely more than 100 members the tiny body has maintained itself for many decades.)

2) Brethren will persist, but will need to change. Recent sociological and statistical evidence shows clearly that Church of the Brethren membership is predominantly aging and rural. The denomination faces the challenge of ministering to the baby-boomer cohort and their families. Mennonite social scientist Emerson Lesher has written that current church institutions—if they are to survive—will need to meet the values and criteria of the largely professional and well-educated age grouping. These values he identified as quality, uniqueness, participation, excellence, service, and diversity.[12]

Brethren are increasingly recognizing that the church needs to change in ethnic composition. Olden Mitchell, senior Brethren pastor, believes that minorities, who currently make up about one percent of the membership will increase to fully fifty percent of the membership by the year 2010, some twenty years from now. His reasoning is that the vitality he sees from the current one percent exceeds that of the remaining ninety-nine percent. And, he concludes, "the members with color are the ones with greater life, enthusiasm, and devotion to Brethren values and Way."[13] Henry Ford, it will be remembered, said that his customers could have any color they wanted in their new car as long as it was black. Brethren have allowed any ethnic composition desired as long as it was Germanic. This will change.

3) Brethren and the urban setting is more problematic. Although the church has been challenged for well over a by the needs of the city, the record, with some exceptions, has not been good. There are indeed some grand stories of home missions in places like Brooklyn (with Italian and now Hispanic residents) and Chicago (with the Chinese community) and supportive but small city congregations. Yet, Brethren impact on large cities has been minimal as compared to the energies and contributions in small towns and rural areas. New strategies will need to be developed if dramatic change is to come here.[14]

Part of the answer lies no doubt in the development of minority congregations which are primarily urban. Thus, for example, there are Haitians in Miami, Hispanics in Lancaster, and Koreans in Los Angeles forming new Brethren congregations.[15] Another model is suggested by the Reba Place Fellowship in Evanston, Illinois, which maintains both Mennonite and Brethren denominational links. Partly communal and partly familial in structure, it provides richly spiritual worship and a wide number of effective ministries to a multi-cultural and urban setting.[16]

And just perhaps technology will come to the aid of the Brethren as more and more people find it unnecessary to locate in large metropolitan areas to carry on highly technical work. Computers and modems make location optional. As the quality of life in the cities continues to decline, it is arguable that the long trend towards urbanization will in fact shift again. This does not mean that Brethren do not need to be concerned with the cities. Possibly it is the new frontier for a massive Brethren Service-type program.

4) The long-standing struggle within the denomination about appropriate theologies of mission, as evidenced in a series of Annual Conference issues over the past years, seems to have achieved a certain resolution. At least the extreme positions seem to have become more tempered. The future health of the denomination will not allow this issue to drag on without full clarification. The debate has unfortunately tended to direct energies inward rather than toward the task.[17]

5) Brethren have a winning formula in the combination of service outreach and evangelistic concern. At times, however, one emphasis has predominated over the other. Although overgeneralized, it could be stated that foreign

missions was considered to be the "great first work of the church" in the beginning decades of the twentieth century, and that Brethren Service captured the imagination, personnel, and resources of the church in the mid-twentieth century. There followed a time of comparative inner-directedness when many congregations built massive church edifices and retirement homes burgeoned. Denominational structures were rationalized following the latest theories of business management, and district programs were greatly enlarged. For a time it seemed as if the next major emphasis would be ecumenical as Brethren leaders played down the particular heritage of the Brethren (who had once been known as a "peculiar people") and nudged the denomination toward merger with mainline communions. The debate on the Consultation on Church Union in 1966 put an end to that initiative, as an awkward and temporary alliance of theological conservatives, Anabaptist-leaning radicals, and stand-pat Brethren defeated the liberal-oriented leadership. This left the 1970s and 1980s marked by the sharp transitions on which this conference has been focused.[18]

There are clear signs that momentum in the denomination is shifting to a renewed emphasis upon evangelism. It has become institutionalized in the Evangel 21 movement and revealed by the appeal at the 1991 Annual Conference in Portland, Oregon, for a confessional statement. The current move toward new and evangelical centers of theological training is another sign. Increasing numbers of Brethren believe that the emphasis of the church has been too heavily weighted on the service side, leaving the evangelistic thrust under-represented. They contend that the current swing toward evangelistic concerns will provide a necessary corrective, while still maintaining traditional Brethren passion for peace and justice issues.[19]

It could well be that the last decade of the twentieth century and the first decades of the twenty-first century will be identified by future historians as the era when Brethren caught fire with evangelism, at the same time maintaining their longstanding concern for the near and far neighbor. Time will tell if this anticipation is accurate.

Conclusion

There follow some *Pia desideria* (pious desires)—to borrow a phrasing from one of the constituent and formative strands of the Brethren heritage. These are desired outcomes and emphases for the Brethren for the next years. Some are modest and eminently realizable; others more ambitious but not impossible.

1) It is to be hoped that reflection and analysis such as has been experienced here could shape decisions on practical issues coming before the denomination. The dissection performed by Carl Bowman, for example, of the later misinterpretations of the early Brethren position on non-creedalism could have been of great help in deciding the queries at the 1991 Annual Conference

on the issue. The denomination needs the best scholarship it can get and needs to heed those findings.

2) It is to be hoped that Brethren can live with some ambiguity and diversity because that is the human condition. Careful investigation of Brethren heritage reveals that there was never a time when all issues were clear-cut and neatly decided. There have always been issues of great complexity, argued with great intensity.

Nevertheless, Brethren can aspire to the spirit expressed by Alexander Mack, Jr., when the colonial church was exercised about the correct procedure for holding the Lord's Supper. He stated in reference to other members that he would "lay his views before them according to the Scripture, and wait, in love, and have patience with them, until they could see it so, likewise." The principle to be followed, said Mack was: "Scripture must be understood and looked upon with a spiritual eye of love and calmness." For, Mack concluded,

> the Scriptures require spiritual eyes, mind and understanding; otherwise by the letter we would be having nothing but trouble and division, if without true illumination one would think to hold fast to the letter in one place, but would act contrary to it in another place. . . . Therefore, dear brethren, let us watch and be careful. Above all preserve love for then we will preserve light.[20]

3) It is to be hoped that greater emphasis will be placed upon preparation for membership. It is not surprising that Brethren find themselves with tremendous diversity because preparation for prospective members is such a cursory procedure in too many congregations. Brethren in the USA could learn from the Nigerian brothers and sisters. Although growing at a rapid pace, they require substantial periods of training and testing before they admit new members.

4) It is to be hoped that the Church of the Brethren will continue to move toward greater fellowship and association with those Brethren groups of common heritage. Some form of structured relationship is not yet on the horizon, but increasing experiences of shared ministries and fellowship might bring that in God's good time.

Perhaps the way forward is to join with other Brethren groups in a broader connection of "like precious faith." The Mennonite Church and the General Conference Mennonites are exploring union. Could it be that several Brethren bodies could join with them in a great Anabaptist/Pietist body? Ludwig Keller, the German scholar of Anabaptism, had this vision more than 100 years ago. He suggested in 1887 that the "Mennonites of several branches could join with the Quakers, Schwenkfelders, . . . Dunkers, several branches of the General Baptists, . . . , in brief all the parties that grew out of old Anabaptism, in an 'Old Evangelical Alliance.'" If that is too ambitious, it could be recalled that Count Zinzendorf's Pennsylvania Synods concluded in 1742 that the Mennonites and Dunkers should agree on baptism and then unite. The synod held that this was the only serious point of difference between them. If they were linked that would mean "at least one less sect in the country."[21]

5) It is to be hoped that Brethren polity could be restructured to provide longer tenures and greater possibility for training and growth of the leadership. While short tenures and quotas of several kinds have brought greater involvement of several segments of the membership, such as youth and women, this improvement has had a downside as well. Several papers at the conference have noted the shift in denominational leadership patterns over the years, particularly the lack of "weighty Brethren" so noticeable in the past. This shift no doubt reflects as well changes in cultural patterns which encourage democracy and discourage authority. Nevertheless, the church will need to be proactive in providing ways for outstanding leaders to be identified, and allowed to mature and develop.

6) It is to be hoped that Brethren educational institutions, particularly the colleges, could intensify their efforts at communicating core values of the heritage. These schools have been identified as massive change agents in the transitions documented at this conference, often seen negatively. It must be recalled that they have also stimulated and indoctrinated large numbers of their students in basic Brethren values. It is no accident that most of the Brethren-related colleges have curricular emphases in conflict resolution and peace, to take one example, and others could be named. This success should not be romanticized unduly, but neither should it be ignored.[22]

7) It is to be hoped that the Brethren peace witness can be perpetuated and even strengthened. It is one thing, and that is good, to have the Brethren recognized as an Historic Peace Church. It is another and better thing for the Brethren to be recognized as a Living Peace Church.

8) Finally, as Brethren engage in the search for greater numbers and new congregations, it should be recalled that the New Testament nowhere demands or commands that the Christians be successful. Followers of Jesus Christ are not necessarily called to be successful; they *are* called to be faithful. In the irony of history, it could be that honest concern for faithfulness to Jesus Christ in this time, as interpreted by the best in the heritage, might result in a witness so appealing and winsome that others might be drawn to the Brethren. Several of the papers at this conference reflect this hope.

In closing, the ruminations of a great leader, one native to the Shenandoah Valley and possibly the best-loved personality among the Brethren, may be recalled. Elder John Kline (1797-1864) meditated in 1854 after visiting a fashionable Methodist Church in Washington, DC, that if plain John Wesley were to appear, he might disown his followers and they, in turn, might not accept Methodism's founder in his "plain dress and old-fashioned ways." And then a thought came to Kline: "What if the next hundred years bring on as great a change in our Brotherhood as the past seventy-five years have unfolded in the Methodist society? But there I let the curtain fall upon my thoughts, to hide them from my sight, for I cannot endure the prospects of such a change."[23]

Obviously that change has taken place and that more thoroughly than Elder Kline could have imagined. Yet, his memory remains green as generation after generation have taken heart at his sacrificial life and martyr's death. The church he loved continues, although its outward form is vastly different than he would recognize or appreciate. He was the hero of M. R. Zigler, born in a neighboring house in Broadway, who in his own long lifetime himself saw, and brought about tremendous change. Who can claim with certainty that this chain of persistence through change must inevitably be broken?[24]

Christians have their treasure in earthen vessels and clearly some of the vessels are more earthen than others. But the treasure itself does not change. The mystery and glory of Christian history is that God's message has always been expressed in saving ways despite the weaknesses of the messengers. This provides real hope for Brethren as they experience painful transition.

[1] Stephen L. Longenecker, "From Urban Village to Urban Society: The Church of the Brethren and Modern America," paper presented at the conference "Brethren in Transition: Trends and Implications," Bridgewater College, Bridgewater, VA, October 4-5, 1991.

[2] Stephanie Grauman Wolf, Urban Village: Population, Community, and Family Structure in Germantown, Pennsylvania, 1683-1800 (Princeton, NJ: Princeton University Press, 1976), 327-337.

[3] Documentation can be found in Annual Meeting minutes and conveniently in Roland L. Howe, The History of a Church (Dunker) with Comments Featuring the First Church of the Brethren of Philadelphia, Pa., 1813-1943 (Philadelphia: author, 1943), the largest history ever published of an individual Brethren congregation (itself perhaps a sign of modernity); see also Elmer Q. Gleim, From These Roots: A History of the North Atlantic District [of the] Church of the Brethren (Lancaster, PA: Atlantic Northeast District Historical Committee, 1975), 164-192.

[4] Gleim, From These Roots, 125-126. See also "Germantown: In Search of New Patterns," Messenger (June 24, 1965), 13-14; Kenneth I. Morse, "New Opportunities for an Historic Church: A Report on the Germantown Ministry," Messenger (September 11, 1969), 2-5; "Encounter at Germantown," Messenger (June 4, 1970), 18-19.

[5] William J. Speers, "The Homeless in Philadelphia," Philadelphia Inquirer (June 4, 1989).

[6] Ronald G. Lutz, "Philadelphia, PA, Germantown Church of the Brethren," The Brethren Encyclopedia (1983-1984), 1016; "Germantown Church Gets Another Start," Messenger (October, 1985), 6; Don Fitzkee, "New Life in Germantown," Messenger (December, 1987), 17-21; Don Fitzkee, "From Ghana to Germantown: An African Missionary in America," Messenger (May, 1991), cover, 38-39.

[7] "Famous Old Church Outgrows Its Home," The Philadelphia Record (July 12, 1915); Gleim, From These Roots, 115-121; Dennis D. Martin/Elgin S. Moyer, "Swigart, Milton Clarke," The Brethren Encyclopedia (1983-1984), 1245.

[8] D. F. Durnbaugh and Elgin S. Moyer, "Keyser, Peter," The Brethren Encyclopedia (1983-1984), 691-692; Dennis L. Slabaugh, "Brumbaugh, Martin Grove," The Brethren Encyclopedia (1983-1984), 222-223. Additional sources are found in the bibliographies of both articles.

[9] Kenneth I. Morse, "Quinlan, James T.," The Brethren Encyclopedia (1983-1984), 1076; Elizabeth Ellis Cherry, "Ellis, Calvert N.," and "Ellis, Charles Calvert," The Brethren Encyclopedia (1983-1984), 441-442.

[10] Gleim, From These Roots, 167, 171-172, 173-175, 179-180; Carl Bowman, "The Therapeutic Transformation of Brethren Tradition," paper given at the conference, "Brethren in Transition: Trends and Implications," Bridgewater College, Bridgewater, VA, October 4-5, 1991.

[11] Cheryl Cayford, "General Board Receives Call to Spiritual Renewal," Messenger (December, 1990), 6; George Keeler, "Portland: A Report of the 1991 Annual Conference," Messenger (August/September, 1991), 16.

[12] Emerson L. Lesher, "Which Mennonite Organizations and Institutions Will Survive?" Festival Quarterly 17 (Winter, 1991), 25.

[13] Olden Mitchell, "New Day Coming to Brethren," Brethren Peace Fellowship [Newsletter] 25 (October, 1991), 3.

[14] Thomas D. Wilson and David M. Bibbee, "Urban Ministry," The Brethren Encyclopedia (1983-1984), 1295-1298; special issue on Urban Ministry, Messenger (June, 1990), 10-19, especially Beth Holmes Nonemaker, "Which Way to Nineveh?" 12-13.

[15] See the feature "Planting New Churches" incorporating several articles in Messenger (May, 1991), 28-41. For a more general account, see James Lehman, Thank God for New Churches! (Elgin, IL: Brethren Press, 1983).

[16] The best account of the Reba Place Fellowship is Dave and Neta Jackson, <u>Glimpses of Glory: Thirty Years of Community</u> (Elgin, IL: Brethren Press, 1987).

[17] A significant turn occurred at the 1990 Annual Conference: see Wendy Chamberlain and Cheryl Cayford, "Delegates Endorse Overseas Church-Planting," <u>Messenger</u> (August/September, 1990): 15.

[18] This history is discussed in Donald F. Durnbaugh, ed., <u>Church of the Brethren: Yesterday and Today</u> (Elgin, IL: Brethren Press, 1986).

[19] Don Fitzkee, "A Full Menu," <u>Messenger</u> (August/September, 1991), 22.

[20] "Appendix by the younger Alexander Mack," in Alexander Mack, Sr., <u>Rights and Ordinances . . .</u>, eds. Henry Kurtz and James Quinter (Columbiana, OH, 1860), 143-144.

[21] Elizabeth Horsch Bender, ed., "The Letters of Ludwig Keller to John Horsch," <u>Mennonite Quarterly Review</u> 21 (1947), 202. Keller developed his thesis of connection between "Old Evangelical Brotherhoods" in <u>Die Reformation und die älteren Reformpartein</u> (Leipzig: S. Hirzel, 1885) and <u>Zur Geschichte der altevangelischen Gemeiden</u> (Berlin: Ernst Siegried Mittler und Sohn, 1887).

[22] See the articles in <u>Messenger</u> (July, 1991), 17-23 and the <u>Bulletin of the [Manchester College] Peace Studies Institute</u>.

[23] Benjamin Funk, ed., <u>The Life and Labors of Elder John Kline</u> (Elgin, IL: Brethren Publishing House, 1900), 346-347; this is quoted in Donald F. Durnbaugh, "Will the Brethren Prevail?" <u>Brethren Life and Thought</u> 10 (Winter, 1965), 54-62.

[24] Donald F. Durnbaugh, <u>Pragmatic Prophet: The Life of Michael Robert Zigler</u> (Elgin, IL: Brethren Press, 1989), 313.

15
Reflections Along The Way. . .

by David G. Metzler

The Occasion for the Brethren in Transition Conference

The journey of faith begun at the Eder River in 1708 by our Brethren forebears, like that of all spiritual descendants of Abraham, was a going forth whither they knew not, dwelling in tents, and was a calling by God to be a blessing in the world. Nearly three hundred years have now passed during which we heirs of the Schwarzenau beginnings, though sometimes tempted to turn our tents into permanent settlements, have been swept along in the tides of history. (Has God been using those tides to disrupt our settlements and keep us moving on the way of faith?) Thus, changes have come. Today's children of Schwarzenau live in tents of a different style, in lands far removed in time, space, and culture from the Schwarzenau of 1708. The currents carrying us along swirl into cross-currents threatening, we sometimes fear, to capsize our ship of faith, the Church of the Brethren. Since changes of place, time, and style have come upon us, the question arises, "Are we still spiritual heirs of our Schwarzenau forebears?" Alexander Mack's reflection relative to the prospects of the Brethren comes to mind, "As their faith, so shall their future be."

Thus, the reflections contained in the essays in this volume need to be seen as taking stock of the Church of the Brethren at this critical point in its history—even as Mack and his companions sought to be faithful in their particular moment of history. Because God, the Lord of History, is living and dynamic, we should not be surprised that history is the story of living peoples in powerful social movements interacting with the loving God who guides and leads onward. It is a given that any particular movement will not be static or immune to change. *The task is to determine the forms in which the authentic faith may live in each new age.*

Contributions to Knowledge Generated by the Conference

All of the papers by Church of the Brethren scholars, beginning with Longenecker's setting of the theme in "From Urban Church to Urban Society" through Brown's "What Happened to Our Peace Witness?" clarify patterns in which the early Schwarzenau faith was lived out and the degree to which those patterns had been altered by the late twentieth century. Bowman in his "Therapeutic Transformation of Brethren Tradition" identifies fundamental Brethren values at stake: *Childlike Faith, Obedience, Christian Unity,* and *Separation.* He concludes that contemporary patterns in which Church of the Brethren faith is lived today demonstrate that these commitments have been radically reconceived. Benedict, Stoffer, Juhnke, and Hamm similarly analyze the transformation of life patterns over time among the Old Order Brethren, the Brethren, the Mennonites, and the Quakers. Respondents, Kissinger, Kraybill, Miller, and Bucher, sharpen and sometimes adjust the focus of the issues raised. Contributions of the panel of pastors illustrate that there are present among the Brethren diverse and passionately held perceptions of how our heritage may be authentically and appropriately expressed in our times.

Although the papers describe well the progressive transformation of the ways the Brethren have expressed their life and faith, the question remains which the Lord of History kept before His people at Schwarzenau in 1708 and continues to keep before them today. How will the Brethren today live in faithfulness to the covenant passed down through their Schwarzenau heritage? The reflections presented in this volume provide materials essential in constructing the scaffolding from which the Brethren can examine this question with a faith vision informed by our heritage. Donald F. Durnbaugh in his "Closing the Circle: Germantown and Philadelphia Revisited" has begun to trace the design by drawing together valuable insights shared in the conference.

Contexts for Future Reflections

It would be a truism to observe that the eighteenth century was not the first time God (as Creator, Sustainer, and Lord of History; Redeemer; Reconciler; and Energizing Presence) has called forth a people to be faithful. It is equally true that God did not create at a single time one universal people of God. Rather, the people of God are united through all time and in every place in their authentic response to God's call to covenant. And, paradoxically, those people of God are embodied in particular communities, conditioned by time, culture, and place, each being specially gifted in the unique patterns in which the Holy Spirit becomes incarnate in them. Just so, God became incarnate in

Christ, identifying with his world and initiating redemption in a particular time and place. Similarly, the church as the Body of Christ lives in particular cultural, historical, and temporal embodiments so that God's redemptive life may call people *where they are* into reconciliation. The church is a redemptive paradox; it is at once one authentic body of Christ transcending all time, culture and place. At the same time it is local and unique. It is the flower garden of God, beautiful because each unique blossom in its own perfection is part of that whole. The Church of the Brethren is one of the unique blossoms in that garden. The wholeness of the church is completed through the uniting of the special diverse gifts that each unit within it brings.

Thus, consideration of how we Brethren shall be faithful today needs to occur within a tension between the *inclusive sphere of the ecumenical church*, with its rich deposit of experience, and the *particular Schwarzenau heritage* that has been entrusted to us. Living in that tension will enrich both the world church and the Brethren.

Brethren and Anabaptist Studies

As Brethren search for Divine leading, they will seek to identify and cherish the unique gifts which God has given the world through us. The study of our history is essential in this search. Both May and Bowman note that our heritage shapes how we move into the future. How that heritage will shape our venturing forth depends upon *how* we choose to treasure it. Will we share it with the world or will we possess it "under a bushel?" Referring to the imagery of Lasch, both Bowman and May note that in considering our past we may be moved by nostalgia or allow it to become for us a living and powerful memory. Nostalgia can lead us to worship the past, binding us to it. Thus we become unable to follow the Holy Spirit which in every age calls us forth into new expressions. Or, we may be moved by "memory," cherishing the spirit of that host of heavenly witnesses who went before us and were faithful. Thus, rather than duplicating patterns of faithfulness relevant only to an earlier age, our Anabaptist vision will seek to share in the living *spirit* that moved our forebears. We will cherish their authentic insights into the life of God's people, and we will embody that spirit in fresh patterns of faith and life which are relevant to this day.

The Ecumenical Church

The early Brethren founded our particular heritage in relation to the world church. They were familiar with the received doctrine of the historic church through their origins in the Reformed tradition. They accepted the basic doctrines of the historic church, cherishing the scriptures, especially the New Testament witness to the life and teachings of Jesus. Finding some patterns in the established church to be in contradiction to the teachings of the New Testament, they left the established church, being led by other voices. They learned from the Pietists and from their Mennonite neighbors. Then in their particular place and time they sought the leading of God's Spirit. The Brethren heritage with its rich history was begun.

The ecumenical landscape on which we live is very different than the Schwarzenau context of 1708. Convictions which the Pietist, Anabaptist, and Brethren heritages treasured have come to enrich many of the formerly established church traditions in various ways. Many believers in all Christian traditions now call for biblical obedience. The ecumenical conversation within the whole people of God is much larger than it was in 1708. We still have much to share, and we can also learn. That greater ecumenical church opens to us perspectives on the larger, historic deposit of faith which were not seen by Mack and his friends. Within the ecumenical context we may learn much about the Trinitarian working of God in the world. We may gain new insight in considering marks which Bowman identifies as distinctive to the Brethren—unity, discipline, faithfulness, and obedience—when considered alongside the ancient understanding of the authentic marks of the universal church—unity, holiness, catholicity, and apostolicity.

Historical Context

Alexander Mack and his fellow believers lived in a corner of western Germany tired from the wars of religion which had racked reformation Europe. The concept of a believers' church had not dislodged the prevailing idea of the established religion. Those who set themselves outside the establishment suffered persecution. The Enlightenment, in its early stages, would bring in its train industrialization, colonialism, continued political flux, migration, and more war. Our forebears sought the leading of the Holy Spirit on that particular stage of history. So it has always been. God is always doing a new thing. In the light of this, the church is called to embody the redeeming life of the Spirit.

Most of the papers presented in this book identify challenges of the times in which we live. It would not be surprising if, moved by the same reconciling spirit as moved our forebears, we will live out our faithfulness in patterns that differ from theirs. Living today out of memory, not out of nostalgia, the question we must answer becomes, *is it the same spirit that leads us today?* In our contemporary setting do we hear the same voice that called forth Abraham and the Schwarzenau eight?

The Brethren, having journeyed nearly three hundred years, still move into an uncharted future. In discerning the way in which God would lead us, we will remember what God has done in our particular past. In our journey, we will learn from companions of other traditions who also have memories of

God's leading. We will respond to the needs of the times, to the pain, the per-plexity, the anguish, and the opportunity, yet remaining sensitive to the lead-ing of the Spirit.

DATE DUE

11-24-94			
GAYLORD			PRINTED IN U.S.A.